COME ABOARD

Frontispiece. With faded sails at the end of the voyage, *Wanderer IV* has her small jib set as she sails in the Bay of Islands. (*Photograph by courtesy of Victoria Carkhuff.*)

COME ABOARD

ERIC C. HISCOCK

Author of
Wandering Under Sail
Cruising Under Sail
Around the World in Wanderer III
Voyaging Under Sail
Beyond the West Horizon
Atlantic Cruise in Wanderer III
Sou'West in Wanderer IV

ADLARD COLES LIMITED
8 Grafton Street, London W1

Adlard Coles Ltd
William Collins Sons & Co. Ltd
8 Grafton Street, London W1X 3LA

First published in Great Britain
in hardback by Oxford University Press 1978
Published in paperback by Adlard Coles Ltd 1986

British Library Cataloguing in Publication Data

Hiscock, Eric C.
Come aboard.
1. Voyages around the world—1951– 2. Yachts and yachting
I. Title
910.4′1 G419

ISBN 0–229–11768–6

Printed and bound in Great Britain by
Mackays of Chatham Ltd, Kent

For
SUSAN
seaman–navigator–wife

PREFACE

When sharing an anchorage with a handsome yacht which we know has found her way across the oceans to faraway places, Susan (my wife) and I usually row over to have a closer look, and if there happens to be someone on deck we probably make a complimentary remark. How pleased we then are if he proves to be the owner and says 'Come aboard', for such an invitation will give us the opportunity not only to examine the details on deck and aloft and the general arrangement below, but perhaps a chance to hear the ideas, impressions, practices and experiences of another voyager: the methods of navigation he uses; his procedure in heavy weather; how he makes a living as he goes; what his thoughts are on compasses, flags, other people's children, writing letters, port officials, yacht clubs, self-steering gears, the environment, the Panama Canal . . . There is a lot that we would like to know, and his answers may give us much to think and talk about, and perhaps even incorporate, when we return to our own vessel.

Voyages round the world are commonplace today, and many books have been written about them. This book is yet another, because it gives some account of the third circumnavigation which Susan and I completed in 1976. I have, however, tried to make it something more than that, for as I reread my journals and the story unfolded, I was reminded of matters technical and non-technical about which our many visitors over the years had frequently asked our views and advice, so here and there I have digressed to write about such things, hoping that by so doing the book may prove to be of more general interest and use to the reader than perhaps might be a plain account of the voyage itself, and that the index on pages 233–37, may assist him to find the matters in which he is most interested.

ECH

Yacht Wanderer IV
Bay of Islands, N.Z.
July 1977

CONTENTS

ILLUSTRATIONS

CHARTS

ACKNOWLEDGMENT

The acknowledgments of the author are due to the editors of *Cruising World, Sail, Yachting Monthly* and *Yachting World*, in which magazines some parts of this book were first published.

PART I

NEW ZEALAND TO DURBAN

WITH SOME THOUGHTS ON

Planning a voyage—The compass—Flags—Ventilation—Wind-vane gears—Children and other visitors—The dinghy—Meeting big ships—Navigation lights—Radar reflectors—Too many yachts—Clubs—Lectures and films—Making a living

All day the wind had been freshening from the south, and by nightfall we were running fast under the close-reefed mainsail only somewhere off New Zealand's North Cape. When I went on deck at 2 a.m. to relieve Susan, I found that the wind had increased still more, and with it the shrilling in the rigging and the roar of the bow-wave. I had closed the companionway door but had not yet drawn over the sliding hatch, and I had not fully got my night vision when I was startled by a crash from forward, loud and clear above the noises of the night. I was starting to go to investigate when Susan shouted the astonishing information that the hinged forehatch, which had been closed but not secured, had blown fully open. Apparently, the gale had entered through the open sliding hatch, and rushed through the saloon with such force that it lifted the heavy teak forehatch sufficiently for the wind on deck to catch its underside and lift it right up and over the vertical so that it fell flat on its back. Fortunately, no serious damage was done, and Susan was able to close the hatch from inside and lash it down while I belatedly drew shut the sliding hatch.

Wanderer IV, our 49-foot (15-metre) steel ketch then six years old (Frontispiece and Appendix 1), seemed to be doing well enough, tipping her bowsprit towards the back of each foam-streaked retreating sea as her stern lifted buoyantly up the steep advancing face of the next one, and a great froth of phosphorescent bow-wave spread out each side to mingle with the wake. The compass showed that the wind-vane steering gear, though it could not prevent her yawing, was holding the ship more or less on course for Aneityum, the nearest island of the New Hebrides group about 1000 miles away. There was plenty of water on deck as we rolled our bulwarks under, and spray was flying, but I settled myself in the leeward after corner of the cockpit, which was the most sheltered place, and from where, by standing up every few minutes, I could keep a lookout for other vessels, which was my only reason for being out there in the wet.

I thought a bit about the voyage on which we had only that morning embarked at Whangaroa, where bad weather had held us for a few days. That lovely landlocked harbour had given us perfect shelter, and then with its light airs had seemed as reluctant to let us go as we had been reluctant to leave it; but this time we did not look back with the sadness of earlier departures when we had thought we would never see it again, for now we had every intention of returning to New Zealand at the end of this voyage.

Our plan was to sail by way of Torres Strait and the Cape to England to see our friends and take a look at the modern yachting scene, then to return to New Zealand by way of Panama; if all went properly the trip would develop into yet another circumnavigation, with all the worry, excitement, frustration, delight and satisfaction our earlier two-and-a-half times round had shown us such a voyage entails. Inevitably much of the trip would be repetitive, for on a trade wind circumnavigation there are certain staging points that can scarcely be avoided, but we had friends in most of them who we would much like to meet again, and no matter how often a stretch of ocean may be traversed, conditions on it are never quite the same, so a sense of adventure is retained and realized.

We had planned the voyage in broad outline with the help of *Ocean Passages for the World*, and the American pilot charts which we preferred to the more detailed but not so easily read British routeing charts. On these the oceans are divided into rectangles of five degrees of latitude and five degrees of longitude, and the direction, proportion and strength of winds (which observations made from ships over many years have found there) are shown diagrammatically in each square. Also shown are the directions and rates of currents, percentage of calms and gales, and a wealth of other interesting and useful information, such as magnetic variation, average barometric pressure, sea temperature, percentage of fog, tracks and dates of great storms, and shipping routes. Assuming that our average progress would be not less than 100 miles a day, and allowing ourselves ample time in port, our basic dates were to leave New Zealand early in May, Torres Strait in

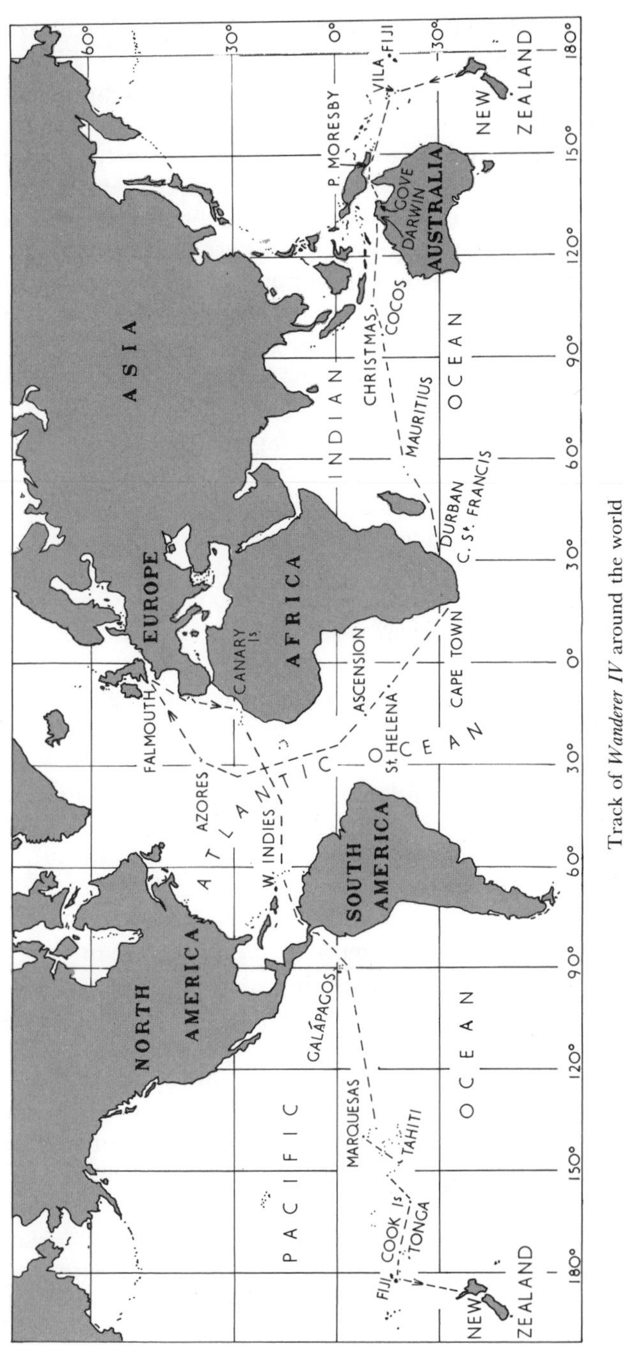

Track of *Wanderer IV* around the world

mid-July, and Mauritius in mid-October, thus getting clear of the Indian Ocean before the cyclone season was due to start in November. Rounding the Cape early in the new year and leaving South Africa in March, we ought to reach England in May, spend the summer there and depart at the end of August, thus avoiding the autumnal gales which, in the western approaches, have badly delayed many a late starter and have quite defeated some others. Stops made in Spain and the Atlantic islands could then be so adjusted that we would not leave on the crossing so early as to arrive in the Caribbean before the hurricane season was over. We like to depart from Panama on a westward crossing of the Pacific in January or February, because the wind is then more likely to be favourable for getting out of the Gulf of Panama and down to the equator than it is later in the year, and this would give us at least six months to dawdle (if we chose) by way of islands across the South Pacific to Fiji, and from there we would sail the final leg to New Zealand in September or October, thus arriving in the higher latitudes in spring, and avoiding the western Pacific cyclone season, which can be expected to start in November. The round voyage would, therefore, take about two-and-a-quarter years.

I suppose the chance of a yacht encountering a hurricane, cyclone, typhoon or willy-willy (all much the same thing, that is, a tropical revolving storm, the name depending on the locality) is small, yet it seems sensible to me to avoid, if possible, sailing through the danger areas during the dangerous months, though if good hurricane holes are readily available, as they are, for example, in the West Indies, pleasant cruising can often be had in the hurricane season. I recall that when Susan and I had a house in England, an Australian telephoned one evening in October to ask my advice as to the latest he could reasonably sail from England bound south and west. I said that it was already late and advised him to go, if he must go, immediately.

'Oh, I can't possibly leave before December,' he replied.

'In that case,' I said, perhaps rather crossly, for I do not like being asked for advice by someone who has no intention of taking it unless it agrees with what he has already decided to do, 'I suggest you postpone your voyage until next spring or summer.'

But he did not. He and his brave wife left late in the year, met very bad weather off the Portuguese coast, the steering gear of their ketch broke down, they became exhausted, and eventually were towed into Casablanca where the following autumn we met them, their repairs and refit just completed, and they crossed to the West Indies at about the same time as we did, ten months behind their schedule. I have mentioned this not unusual incident not with the wish to show how right I was (in similar situations I have often been proved wrong) but to emphasize the principle to which we attempt to adhere: it is no bad thing to heed the accumulated information and lore of past seamen, for a brush in a small vessel with violent weather is something to avoid if at all possible, especially at the beginning of a voyage when ship and crew are still untried.

By dawn the wind had started to take off; by noon we had made a day's run of 133 nautical miles [in this book all sea distances are given in nautical miles of 6080 feet (1853 metres)], the sun was shining, and as the sea no longer ran quite so high or steep we made more sail; the temperature began to rise, the barometer to make diurnal movements, and we peeled off some of the layers of clothes that had accumulated during the past thirty hours; we ate thick slices of a splendid cake made by a friend and iced with the words 'Good luck Wanderer' flowing boldly on its broad white top, and we opened an envelope sealed by another friend and read:

> Spread your wings *Wanderer IV*,
> Stir the dreams of those
> Left earth-bound on a distant shore
> Bereft
>   to see you go, proud to call you friend.
> Sail
>   on for ever, a living legend.

Dear little Eve Wright had written that, and we wondered what Keith, her no-nonsense, barge-, tug- and plane-owning husband, thought of such fulsome sentiments.

Our passage then continued pleasantly and uneventfully, and the wind hauled more into the east as we approached the trade wind belt, but each day, when working out the noon position, we found ourselves a long way west of where we ought to have been with regard to the course steered by compass. Although we were by then in the west-running current, it seemed unlikely that it could have a rate of one-and-a-half to two knots, and we suspected the compass, though with no good reason, for we had swung and checked it only a few weeks before and had found very little deviation on any heading.

In a steel vessel, or one built of ferrocement, the magnetic compass can be badly upset by the ferrous metal surrounding it, and magnets then have to be placed in positions found by trial and error to offset the effect; even in a yacht built of wood or glass-reinforced plastics (GRP) such adjustment may be, and often is, needed to overcome the magnetic influence of an engine or other steel or iron gear or fittings, but once done that is usually the end of the matter. A steel vessel, however, particularly when she is new, may change her magnetism considerably, as we had found, and there may be other things not easy to trace that upset that seemingly simple, but delicate navigational instrument. Originally, *Wanderer*, built in Holland, had a Dutch steering wheel, the iron boss of which caused interference with the compass which was mounted close to it during her maiden trip to England, so we changed the wheel for one with a non-magnetic boss; but even so, and all the way to California, we had a strange compass error until we discovered that in the upper bevel-box of the steering gear, on which the compass was mounted, was a magnetic key on one of the shafts; small though this was, it upset the compass to the extent that half a turn of the wheel moved the compass card ten degrees. An American friend had made for us a lock-box in which, presumably, the ship's money was intended to be kept; it was a lovely thing of mahogany and brass. We found by experiment that if we placed this on top of the bevel-box, and mounted the compass on its top, the influence of the magnetic key was outdistanced. Mounting the compass thus, five inches (thirteen centimetres) higher than in its original position, had the added advantage that it now had an all-round view; so, after I had made a sight ring to fit on it, we could take bearings direct, the point being that, in a steel vessel, a hand bearing-compass is useless as its card is deflected to an unknown degree by the metal all around. Nevertheless we were not out of the wood yet, because on a voyage south and west from San Francisco, during which we crossed the magnetic equator, the compass developed twenty degrees of deviation. Experts agreed that this must have been due to the ship changing her magnetism as she sailed diagonally across the Pacific. Once again, we swung and adjusted the compass in New Zealand but, while in those waters, we became very aware of dip. As the north or the south pole is approached, the card of the compass is tilted down towards it, and because of friction then created within the bowl this makes the compass sluggish. This was particularly noticeable when we visited Stewart Island in latitude forty-seven degrees south, where the angle of dip, originally measured by Cook, is about seventy degrees. Our compass was of the grid type by which the course is steered by keeping the north–south line on the card parallel to two lines on top of the bowl; a tilted card in such a compass causes parallax unless the helmsman's eye is directly over the centre of it. Some firms in the northern hemisphere which make compasses for yachts, place a counterweight on the south-seeking part of the magnetic assembly in an attempt to overcome dip but, when such a compass is used in the southern hemisphere, the counterweight aggravates the dip. Recently, when examining in an Auckland chandlery a display of Japanese compasses, I saw that all of them were badly affected by dip. When I mentioned the matter to the makers of our compass (Henry Browne Ltd) they sent me a new magnetic assembly counterbalanced for the southern hemisphere, which much improved the behaviour of the compass there; on recrossing the magnetic equator we ought to have changed back to the old assembly but, as this involved a rather delicate operation and called for emptying the damping fluid from the bowl and refilling, we did not do so. I think it might be best if no attempt were made to counterbalance the assembly of a compass intended for worldwide voyaging, so that it would be equally satisactory (or unsatisfactory) in any part of the globe.

Heeling error, the effect on a compass of ferrous metal moving from side to side beneath it as the vessel rolls, also needs consideration. It can be reduced or perhaps eradicated by placing a magnet vertically above or below the centre of the compass. Theoretically, this magnet should be reversed when crossing the magnetic equator; we did so but failed to observe any change in behaviour, and the last time a professional (in England) adjusted our compass he removed the heeling-error magnet which he considered to be unnecessary and undesirable.

It may be of interest to add that the grid of our compass was luminous so that no light was needed by night. The north–south line on the card consisted of a thin glass tube filled with luminous powder and, being sealed from the air, had a very long life, but the two grid wires on top of the bowl were exposed, and on them the paint had grown dim, and I asked the makers to send me a tiny quantity of luminous paint to give them a new lease of life. The reply was that, because of government restrictions, they were no longer permitted to use such paint in their factory, and it was an offence to send it through the mail. I bought paint in New Zealand and South Africa, but neither was of any use because, although it glowed after a light had been shone on it, the effect quickly faded away. Presumably this problem could be solved by using sealed tubes like the one within the bowl, alternatively the now widely used Betalight could be employed.

Unless a compass is provided with an azimuth mirror which, in those made for yachts, is rare, it cannot be used for taking bearings of celestial bodies unless they are close to the horizon. This is unfortunate because, if bearings could be taken at any altitude, it would be possible to check the compass every time the sun was observed for navigational purposes, because the tables used for working sights give the body's true bearing at the moment of observation. Therefore, at sea, even those of us who are fortunate enough to have the compass so placed that it has a clear all-round view are limited, for the purpose of checking the compass, to taking amplitudes, that is, bearings of the sun at rising or setting. A table in *Reed's Nautical Almanac*, and in some other publications, when entered with the sun's declination and the ship's latitude to the nearest whole degree, gives the sun's true bearing at rising and setting; so, having taken an amplitude and converted it from magnetic to true by applying the local variation for that part of the ocean in which one is sailing, it is only necessary to compare the result with the figure given in the table, and any difference will be the compass error (or deviation) on the course being steered. Susan and I have used this simple and effective method (when the sun chose to show at rising or setting) repeatedly; we did so again on this occasion (Plate 4 B), and discovered that, on the north-west course that we were steering, the compass had twelve degrees of westerly deviation; we could not account for this unless it was due to a small welding job done on the hull shortly before we left, but at least we could now allow for it, and from then on we sailed in the right direction.

It was not until after dark on our eighth day at sea that we drew near to Aneityum. A year before we had found this to be a pleasant island with 300 shy and unspoilt inhabitants; only one of them was white, an Australian known as Artie Kraft(y) who had hospitably plied us with beer every time we landed and who, in his spare time, felled and milled a little timber. Its reef-protected harbour at the south-west corner was no place to attempt in the dark, and as we did not wish to spend the night standing off and on, we passed it by and went on towards Tana, the next island to the north, and sighted it at dawn. Apparently Tana is a sophisticated island with a school, a hospital and an active volcano; but its north coast is reported to lie four miles north-west of its charted position—such things are not uncommon in that part of the Pacific—and naturally we wondered what had happened to its west coast where we were thinking of putting in at Lenakel. But we failed to find the anchorage there, not because it had shifted but because a heavy swell was breaking all along that coast in the early morning when we came to it, and in the *contra jour* light we could identify nothing through the spume from the breakers which hung in the air like mist. It did not seem wise to attempt to close further with that coast in so heavy a swell, so we continued to Dillon Bay in Eromanga, the next island, where a neat little village of bamboo and thatch stood beside a stream. Much of the charm of the smaller New Hebridean islands lay in the fact that they were rarely visited by anyone except such as might come by the interisland ship, *Konanda*, a busy little vessel smelling strongly of copra; she usually had her derrick rigged and her motorboat and barges launched and loading by the time she got her anchor down. During our visit the previous year to Aneityum, however, to which island an occasional small plane flew from Vila, Artie had been a little put out at having to act as host to an elderly woman who had, as it were, dropped in on him out of the sky with the intention of converting the islanders to the Bahai faith, though apparently with little success.

The New Hebrides, under the joint control of France and Britain (France seemed to have the upper hand), consist of about forty mountainous islands in a chain nearly 400 miles long in a north-west/south-east direction. Vila, capital and port of entry, is on the island of Efate (pronounced 'Farty') in the middle of the chain, and that was our next stop. Although we flew international code flag 'Q', the port officials did not come off to enter us until late the next day, but things tended to move slowly in the condominium where two officials, French and British, occupied every government post. We then were free to move into the inner harbour and take up our old berth on the windward side of Iririki Island (Plate 1 *top*), where stood the British Residency and hospital, and, having let go our anchor, we took a stern-line to a tree. There we were well away from the noise, dust and flies of the town, and got the benefit of what little wind there was; but it was a half-mile journey by dinghy to reach the town, which was in a state of chaos, for most of it had been torn down and was being rebuilt in modern style, a fate that has overtaken many a characterful south-sea island town, where the prevailing sound is no longer the mournful note of the conch shell announcing that someone has fish for sale, or the joyful beat of guitar and drum, but the roar of diesel-driven earth-moving machines. Vila still had its attractive market (Plate 1 *bottom*), however, excellent crisp French bread and good wine, and the inhabitants were generous with their hospitality.

For people like us who live aboard, shore hospitality sometimes presents difficulties and worries, such as the business of getting ashore in a small dinghy and landing on a beach or climbing a greasy ladder without spoiling our best clothes or filling our shoes with sand, and the apprehension about what may be happening to our uninsured floating home during our absence. Mr Justice Ren Davies, judge for the Western Pacific, kindly invited us to his Vila home for dinner. So as not to arrive in a sweat, we used the outboard engine on the dinghy, and the steamy night had a sinister air as we made our way across the harbour's black, mirror-like surface under a low and threatening sky. We were in the middle of dinner when there was a sudden crashing of doors slamming, and the curtains streamed horizontally as a violent gust of wind rushed in through the open windows along with a deluge of rain. We wondered if *Wanderer* was all right on the windward side of Iririki, with her anchor on coral in twelve fathoms off the steeply-shelving shore and with only a few inches under her keel; when the windows had been closed the conversation continued as though it had never been interrupted, but in louder tones against the drumming of rain on the roof. The sudden short-lived storm was over, and the harbour as black and calm as it had been before, as we emptied the rainwater out of the dinghy, persuaded the reluctant outboard to start, and made our way across to find *Wanderer*'s familiar shape looming unperturbed just as we had left her.

In small return we invited the judge aboard for drinks. We had arranged to pick him up by dinghy at the beach where the local sailing club used to stand before it was removed to a remote part of the harbour. Unknown to any of us, the beach had been taken over by a French company, and had that day been railed off from the road by a wire fence and padlocked gate. The judge arrived by car to discover the barricade. He told us later that in his position he did not like to climb the gate, but thought it might be all right to get over the fence, which he did. The second time he came to see us, however, he was caught in the fence-climbing act by a couple of gendarmes, but as we left the next day we did not learn the outcome.

One afternoon a New Zealand couple drove us to a delightful home overlooking the harbour, where the English owner entertained us to coffee and 'rusty nails' (equal parts of whisky and Drambuie). We got to talk about the weather, and I hazarded the opinion that with all their modern aids, such as computers, satellites and balloons, the meteorologists seemed to be no better at forecasting than they had been in less sophisticated days. A curious hush followed this remark and, as we were being driven back to the landing-place, I asked what our host did on the island. I was told that he was the chief meteorologist for the condominium.

I like to see correct flags properly flown and was, therefore, surprised to find that government vessels, such as the harbour tug, wore on twin gaffs of identical length the union flag and the tricolour. In the condominium this was always done ashore, but it was the first time I had seen the union flag worn by any vessel except the royal yacht and men-of-war. I thought the red ensign would have been correct, but was assured that in the New Hebrides the union flag was the right one to fly, but by New Hebridean vessels only, not by visitors which, if British, should fly as a courtesy ensign the tricolour, if French, the red ensign, and if of other nationality, both tricolour and red ensign.

I feel it is a pity that so many people who voyage in yachts are so lax about flags; often we have seen an overseas yacht wearing nothing but the courtesy ensign of the country she was in; frequently this was hoisted to a sort of half-mast position instead of being close up against the starboard crosstree, and sometimes was so dirty or tattered that it was hardly recognizable; there was no clue to her nationality, and she gave the impression of being ashamed of her own country. There is also sometimes a lack of understanding about courtesy ensigns, and it is not always realized that it is the merchant ensign that should be worn, not the national flag where this differs from it. For example, a foreign vessel in a British port should not wear the union flag but the red ensign; in New Zealand she should not wear the blue New Zealand flag but the red New Zealand merchant ensign; in Norway, Sweden and Denmark the merchant ensign is rectangular, that is, it does not have the swallow-tail of the national flag, while in some other countries, such as Spain, Haiti and Venezuela, the ensign is without the coat-of-arms; this also applies to Mexico and Italy, and has the unique result that the merchant ensigns of both those countries are identical. Although there was and still is a wide choice of unused arrangements of red, blue, yellow, green, black and white, some of those who designed or chose flags showed little imagination; the flags of Holland and Luxembourg are similar except for a slight difference in the tone of blue, and the merchant ensign of Ecuador is the same as the national flag of Colombia; some of the newer countries' flags, such as those of West Indian islands when they became independent, are so difficult to copy that even professional flagmakers sometimes do not get them right. It may be argued that there is no compulsion for a yacht to wear a courtesy ensign when in a foreign port (the Royal Navy never does), but some port officials may impose a fine on a yacht without one and/or make her owner buy one at high cost; I doubt if this is legal but can guess where the money goes.

Certainly, flags and their correct use can be confusing, and to a foreigner surely our own bunch of British flags must be the most puzzling of all: union flag, white, blue and red ensigns, and many of the blue and red ones defaced with all sorts of designs and emblems of yacht clubs. Sometimes I feel that British yachts abroad might do better to wear the plain red ensign, for that at least is understood worldwide, and no longer is the yacht wearing the blue treated with the courtesy and priority which in some places attended her arrival in the past. There may even be disadvantages in wearing the blue, as we discovered on a visit to New Caledonia, where none of the French inhabitants, except a few shopkeepers, spoke to us. We believed this was because we were wearing the plain blue ensign (a club to which we belonged gave us this privilege, and we held a warrant) and may, therefore, have been mistaken for New Zealanders, as some yachts from that country, notably those whose owners were members of the Royal New Zealand Yacht Squadron, also wore the plain blue; and New Zealand had only a short time before made loud and telling protests about the French nuclear tests in the Pacific, with the result that New Caledonia lost some of her tourist trade.

As most flags mean something, they should, even in the smallest of yachts, be of a size that can be seen, and obviously should be flown in positions where they are visible. In this respect the modern merchant ship is often at fault for, in an attempt to make her look modern and perhaps reduce wind resistance a trifle, her designers and builders provided her with only a short stump of a mast bearing one small yard; on this, poor thing, she has to display, all at the same time, her house flag, her signal letters, a courtesy ensign, and probably the pilot flag or the blue peter to indicate that she has a pilot on board or is preparing to sail that day; if she is a tanker, room has also to be found for international flag 'B' to indicate she carries a dangerous cargo. Her own country's ensign will probably be on the staff right aft, but if she is under way it will more likely be on a short gaff on that same stump of a mast. Because they are bunched so close together, rarely can more than one or two of the flags be seen at a time, and often they are black with soot from the funnel. It should be mandatory for naval architects to take a look at the royal yacht, and it need not be a close look, for clearly separated on each of her masts and on the staffs fore and aft her big and splendid flags can be seen from far away.

Some people have the curious idea that it is snobbish to fly flags, or to take the ensigns in at sunset and put them up again at 8 a.m.; whether this is so or not, it is certain that a flag taken in for the night will outlast one kept flying all the time. To my old-fashioned eye there is something very satisfying in seeing all the ensigns in an anchorage come fluttering down or go up together, and even more so if that happens at the boom of a gun fired from a naval ship or by the senior flag officer—but the evening flag etiquette does pose a problem if one has been invited ashore before flag time. Whether or not the burgee should also be taken down is debatable. Some people, and I am one of them, regard it as a commissioning pennant and leave it up; others, although they may think it wrong, leave it up because their mastheads are so cluttered with wind-speed-and-direction sensors and radio aerials that it is almost impossible to get a burgee on its stick up or down among them. We do not use ours at sea, but hoist in its place a windsock of thin scarlet nylon sewn to a light wire ring which is free to pivot on the burgee stick; this remains steadier than a burgee, gives a better indication of wind direction, costs little and has a very long life.

On leaving Vila we spent three weeks cruising among the islands north of Efate, and much the best harbour that we found was Port Sandwich, which is landlocked and has good mud holding ground instead of the more usual coral on which we were always reluctant to drop our anchor for fear we might not be able to recover it. This was on the island of Malekula where, deep in the jungle of the interior, the Big Nambus tribes lived (nambus is a penis sheath) and now and then raided the villages of the peaceable saltwater men of the coast. Much had yet to be learned of the ways of those people who practised cannibalism not very long ago, and it was still considered unwise to go inland except in a party with a bodyguard. At Port Sandwich we found a French settlement with mission, hospital, airstrip, store, enormous banyan tree and a lighthouse. There are only eight lights in the entire New Hebrides group, and of this one the sailing directions said: '. . . should not be confused with a much brighter light in a house nearby'.

Having seen the French settlement, we naturally wished to have a look at that of the British at Port Stanley further up the coast, but we thought so little of the anchorage there, which everywhere within the twelve-fathom line appeared to be on coral, that we brought up instead in Norsup Bay in the evening intending to go ashore next day. But during the night the wind came onshore and we had to clear out.

It was unfortunate that the south-east trade wind, which had brought us so swiftly and pleasantly to the islands, died away soon after our arrival; while we were cruising there we had calms and occasional winds from unexpected directions, and Norsup Bay was not the only anchorage we had to leave in a hurry when it became a lee shore. With so little wind to temper the heat it was oppressive, and our discomfort was increased because we had screened the accommodation against flies by day and mosquitoes, which here carry malaria, by night; it was not that we were much worried at the risk of getting malaria, for we had started a course of antimalaria pills two weeks before our arrival, but because a single whining mosquito on a hot and humid night can spoil one's sleep. We had screens for all hatches, skylights and doors, as well as for each of the thirteen opening ports in the coachroof coamings, and they could be shipped or unshipped in a few moments;

but with them in position in that kind of weather they reduced the already too feeble circulation of air, and even the windsail failed to produce a draught. No doubt we should have provided ourselves with a large, silent electric fan, for the only fan we had on board made too much noise and so was used only when work had to be done in the darkroom or in the engine-room. All the skylights had removable pins and two sets of hinges so that they could be turned round on their side flaps either to suck or blow, and in normal weather our screening and ventilation worked very well. We have often been asked if our steel hull was not too hot or noisy, but as the deck, coachroof and topsides were lined with insulating material sealed in with plywood, the hull was cooler and just as quiet as were the wooden hulls of our earlier yachts, and there was no condensation.

I have no doubt that most voyaging people know about and make use of the United States radio stations WWV and WWVH which, broadcasting on 5, 10 and 15 megahertz give Greenwich mean time (they now call this 'universal consolidated time') once every minute throughout the twenty-four hours; this is the best means of checking our watches or chronometers for the purpose of navigation. But perhaps it is not so well known that once in every hour (at last listening this was at eight minutes past the hour but is liable to change) these stations provide brief weather information for the Atlantic and Pacific and, if there is anything unusual or of particular interest, such as a hurricane brewing, give its position. It was from this source that we learned that the long-lasting calm we were experiencing was due to a huge bank of thunderstorms, 400 miles wide and extending from the Solomons to Norfolk Island, a distance of some 1600 miles. Apparently the trade wind with all its mighty power could not penetrate that belt.

At about that time there was talk, promulgated frequently, that the two time stations might be going on to half power because of the fuel crisis, and I believe that they may have done so, because we had difficulty in receiving either of them throughout the Indian Ocean crossing. But as users of the service were asked to comment, it is likely that the resulting outcry persuaded the service to resume full power; certainly on subsequent crossings of the Atlantic and Pacific we were always able to receive one or other of them.

Our final stop among the New Hebrides was at Santo on the

island of Espiritu Santo, the only town in the group besides Vila; but anyone with British charts and no local knowledge might be hard put to it to find this place because, although the harbour is shown on the chart, where it is called Second Channel, the name Santo does not appear either there or in the sailing directions, yet in the last war it was of considerable importance, and, when the Americans left, they dumped millions of dollars-worth of equipment into the sea there. We had the latest chart, but it was curiously out-of-date: leading and anchoring marks shown on it did not exist, wharves on it had vanished, while others marked 'destroyed by earthquake' had been rebuilt and had ships lying at them.

* * *

The 1260-mile passage to Port Moresby in Papua/New Guinea proved to be one of the easiest and most enjoyable open-water trips we had ever made. At last the bank of thundery weather had moved away bodily to the east, and the trade wind was resuming business but, instead of blowing from east or south-east, it blew from the south, so it was on our beam, and there is nothing the ketch likes more than that, for all the sails, even the much-talked-of but rarely used mizzen-staysail, can be made to draw without in any way interfering with one another. There was very little swell or sea, the flies abandoned ship as they always do when one leaves the land, we stowed the screens away, and it was cool and pleasant down below where we spent the greater part of our time, for all the steering was done by the vane gear.

Originally we had provided our ship with an electric autopilot because we thought she was too big and heavy to be steered satisfactorily by a wind-vane gear. It had worked fairly well but, because we had been unable to eradicate the heeling error which affected its magnetic heading unit, it worked too hard, switching on and turning the wheel each time the ship rolled; this was bad for its motor, and too much electricity was used. While we were in New Zealand, however, where we had made some alterations to the rudder which much improved the steering, Susan, with feminine intuition, suggested that we try one of the Aries vane gears (Plate 4C) of which some other voyaging people with large yachts had spoken highly. I did not agree with her, but I did write to Mr Franklin who made the Aries gears at Cowes on the Isle of Wight, and he replied that he thought the gear would at least steer our big ship some of the time, so I asked him to send one out. When it arrived and I saw its tiny vane [only 3 feet by 8 inches (0·9 metre by 20 centimetres)] and its small servo-blade, I felt we were wasting our time and our money. We fitted it, however, and had an auxiliary tiller 30 inches (76 centimetres) long made to ship on the head of the rudder stock where that came to the deck, for the gear to work instead of taking the lines to the wheel in the centre cockpit. As it was not possible quickly to disconnect or reconnect the Mathway steering gear (a sophisticated train of torsion tubes, universal joints, ball-races and bevel-boxes) the Aries would have to drive all that as well as turn the big rudder. We had no opportunity to try it out before we sailed away on a trip to the Fijis and other islands, when to our enormous delight we found that it worked very well. There was plenty of wind on the trip north to Suva, twenty to thirty knots, and more in squalls, and the sea was rough, but the gear steered all the way, its little varnished vane flip-flopping busily, its small white servo-blade hurrying from side to side like a porpoise. It seemed to be agitated, yet it kept a near-perfect course though it rarely moved the wheel more than a spoke (one sixth of a turn); even when running dead before the wind we soon learned to have complete confidence in it, and it was pleasant to relax and enjoy the swift progress of our fine vessel as she thundered along over the vivid, white-capped sea. I remember Ernest Harston once referring to *Amokura* as his 'flying armchair'; I felt the same about *Wanderer* just then. Since that first trial, we rarely steered by hand when out of sight of land and away from other vessels, and that made a great difference to our way of life when at sea, for we now had plenty of time to sleep, cook, eat, navigate and read without the feeling that one must hurry because there was the man at the wheel to be relieved, and no longer did we reach our destinations exhausted.

Ever since people started making long voyages running in the trades in small yachts with small crews, attempts had been made to perfect some form of self-steering, and the most common method was the twin rig in which two sails of equal area were set one each side on a boom of its own forward of the mast; the sheets (or braces) controlling the outboard ends of the booms were usually taken aft, led through blocks at each quarter, and were attached to the tiller or to a drum on the wheel. Probably this rig was first used successfully aboard *Imogen* in 1930, but the rig had several drawbacks: it was only effective within narrow limits down wind, and on any other point of sailing the twins had to be changed for normal sails and some other forms of self-steering arrangement rigged; avoiding action could not be taken quickly on meeting another vessel; if the twin sails were to be used in strong winds they were not large enough to give good speed in light breezes, and with no fore-and-aft sails to steady her the yacht rolled heavily.

Clearly something better than this was needed for use in the single-handed Atlantic race and, although some earlier attempts had been made to get a wind-vane to steer a yacht, it was not until Colonel H G (Blondie) Hasler gave his brilliant and inventive mind to it that vane gears became effective, and today there are several commercially made gears that can be bought as complete units, and which call for little or no alteration to the yacht or her rudder. The principle of the kind we used is this: a small plywood vane is mounted in such a way that it can be turned in any direction and locked to the gear so that when the yacht is on the desired course it is head to wind and upright; the vane is mechanically connected to a servo-blade in the water. If the yacht should go off course the wind will strike one side or the other of the vane and force it to heel over (it is pivoted in a horizontal manner, which has been found to be more sensitive than one vertically pivoted), and through the linkage the vane turns the servo-blade out of the fore-and-aft line. As the water of the yacht's passage is flowing past the servo-blade, the latter is forced to swing pendulum fashion upwards one side or the other out of the vertical; it is this powerful force, transmitted through a pair of lines led to the tiller or wheel, which steers the yacht by way of her own rudder. An alteration to the course being steered is made by pulling one of a pair of lines, which through spring-loaded pawls move the vane in relation to the servo-blade and relatch it, each single pull on a line resulting in a six-degree alteration of course. The theory is simple, the mechanical problems quite considerable, but so far as the Hasler and the Aries gears are concerned these have been satisfactorily solved. By the end of the voyage ours had steered for about 40 000 miles, and all it had asked for were new steering lines every 5000 miles and a new nylon washer to replace a worn one; but it did suffer some damage in a gale off South Africa to which I will refer later. After installing the Aries the autopilot was used only when we were under power and the engine was putting back into the batteries the electricity used, or sometimes when we were both forward making a change of sails which while being done might temporarily have upset the Aries.

So, pleasantly and uneventfully we came by night to Basilisk Pass and, on the excellent leading lights, made our way in to a temporary anchorage, for we do not care to enter commercial ports during the hours of darkness because of the unlit obstructions and dazzling lights with which most are lavishly provided. After breakfast we moved to the anchorage off the yacht club, where we were exposed to the 'bullets', as the short but violent squalls that roar across the harbour are called; there was no other voyager in port, but all the moorings were occupied by new yachts locally built.

As all the government and commercial vessels in port were wearing the new Papuan flag, though independence was not due for several months, we thought we should wear one and asked the harbourmaster where we could buy one, and he kindly presented us with the smallest he had which was four feet (1·2 metres) square. The flag is divided diagonally, one half being black with the Southern Cross in white upon it, the other is scarlet and bears a golden bird of paradise; at our crosstree this splendid flag looked more like a royal standard than a courtesy ensign. The town was bursting at the seams, there was much unemployment and the crime rate was soaring.

A highlight of our visit was when we were invited by the Speaker to attend the House of Representatives for the debate on the date for independence. The Speaker ruled the House, and the television cameras that had invaded it for the occasion, firmly and justly, but we did wonder if such a mixed body would ever succeed in governing the vast and, in parts, still little known country where no fewer than fifty different languages are spoken.

There are, on most voyages, certain stages to which one looks forward with apprehension, and one of these now lay ahead of us. To reach the Indian Ocean from Port Moresby we would need to pass through Torres Strait, and to get there would have to go by way of the Great North-east Channel, which threads its way for 130 miles through a complex of reefs and islets. There is no great difficulty about this, but the channel begins at Bramble Cay, and the problem is to find that tiny speck of land which is only ten feet (three metres) high and 300 yards (275 metres) in diameter; one could not steer directly for it from Port Moresby because Goldie Reef, which was said to be awash at low water, lay in the way. Far better navigators than I had failed at the first attempt to find the cay round which the currents are strong and unpredictable, and by overstanding too far to the west became involved with the shoals and waterlogged lumber at the murky mouth of the Fly River. There is a light on the cay with a listed range of fourteen miles, but I think it must be of low power because on an earlier occasion we failed to sight it although we were quite close. On this trip there was a strong wind when we had drawn clear of the mountains, and we had to reduce sail to keep our speed down, for we wished to pass Goldie Reef while the sun was high but not to sight the light seventy-five miles beyond until shortly before dawn. We did not sight Goldie, indeed, we did not expect to for we had been steering to pass a safe ten miles north of that mysterious danger which, although shown on the chart, was not mentioned in the sailing directions; but some time during the night we may have passed over an uncharted shoal, for suddenly the sea around us became steep and confused, and one heavy crest built up so high it lost its balance and fell into the cockpit from which it poured through the open companionways into the sleeping cabin and the chart space. We did not pick up the flash of the light when we expected to, and so became anxious; but at dawn we got a poor fix from observations of the moon and a planet taken through low, fast-moving cloud; this placed us only six miles east of the cay, and not long after, Susan's wonderful eyes sighted, faint against the sky, the thin latticework structure of the light tower. That was a wonderful moment of relief, and with light hearts we turned south-west, made full sail to the twenty-five-knot beam wind, and hurried on our way, brilliant little islands with leaning palms and gleaming beaches popping up over the horizon ahead, sweeping past at seven knots, and quickly dropping into the sea astern; all were in a setting of vivid green, for the water in that area is not clear but contains some substance in suspension which gives it that remarkable colour, and the occasional brown or yellow sea-snake writhing on the surface stands clearly out against it. Towards evening we brought up on a sandy spit in the lee of uninhabited Rennel Islet (Plate 2 *top*), a beautiful thing

---

1 *Top* Vila Harbour with Iririki Island, on which stands the British Residency, in the middle. *Bottom* Vila market.

bedecked with palms and casuarinas; we found nautilus shells on the untrodden beach while angry terns protested overhead. The next night was spent in the lee of Cocoanut Island, but that was not so good, for the mission ship was lying near with her loud-voiced generator running all the time, and drumming, whistling and screaming went on well into the early hours.

We entered Australia officially at the fine old colonial-style custom-house on Thursday Island, which is generally known as 'TI', and, although that island is less than two miles long, 3000 people were living on it; there was little for them to do because the pearl-shell industry was almost dead, and most subsisted on unemployment benefit; this was paid out on Friday when much beer was consumed and brawls were common, and the landing beach consisted largely of broken bottles. There were still a few luggers with cut-down rigs and big engines engaged in the culture pearl business, but unfortunately a tanker had recently struck a rock in the strait, and the oil she spewed was treated with detergent which killed the oysters in the farms. The pilots were busy enough, however, with an average of fourteen ships a day passing through. Ashore we found no fresh provisions available because the refrigerator ship, *Safari*, bringing them north from Cairns, had burst into flames and become a total loss. As TI was so overcrowded and its anchorage in the tideway off a lee shore so uneasy, we spent most of our time in the area across at Horn Island, where we found perfect shelter out of the tide and a small store to provide our simpler needs.

Tides in the area are peculiar, and during one five-day period we witnessed only one high water in each twenty-four hours instead of the usual two, and this occurred at the same time each day instead of the usual forty minutes later; also there were occasions when the east-going tidal stream was defeated by the stronger west-running current and failed to run at all, and so it was the day we sailed away to take our departure from Booby Island, western outrider of Torres Strait. That evening as the crisp flash of Booby Island light dropped astern I felt I had a tenuous connection with it, because a few days before, Len Foxcroft, an old friend in those waters and now skipper of the light-tender, *Wallach*, had taken me with him on a relief trip. We had anchored

---

2 *Top* Uninhabited Rennel Islet in the Great North-east Channel. *Bottom* For sixteen miles from mine to plant the Gove bauxite travels by conveyor.

in the lee of the island and landed from the longboat, and up in the tower I had in typical tripper fashion, with gentle pressure from one finger, revolved the three-and-a-half-tonne lantern-lens floating in its trough of mercury. Manned lighthouses are becoming so rare that it might be a good idea if charts indicated them with an (M) or (W) like they used to mark unwatched lights with a (U). As automatic lights increasingly take over, most small-boat people have a feeling of loss, for though we may need no assistance and perhaps would not ask for it if we did, there is something comforting in knowing that one's presence has been observed by a pair of human eyes. Also we in our isolation have a fellow feeling for the keepers of 'rock' lighthouses; but, as Booby Island was only eighteen miles from TI, the keepers had their wives and families living with them, and I was entertained to tea and cakes while the routine of relief was being attended to. Incidentally, Len gave me the interesting information that Goldie Reef, the vigia which had been such a worry to navigators seeking Bramble Cay from the east, was believed not to exist and had been deleted from the latest chart.

To make a deviation from the usual track to Darwin, we headed for Gove, which lay 360 miles away at the western side of the Gulf of Carpentaria—the huge bight in the northern coast of Australia. We knew very little about that place set in the low, sparsely populated wilderness of Arnhemland, except that a bauxite-mining complex had recently been established there, and the chart suggested that we would find good anchorage in Melville Bay on the shore of which Gove lay. Thus, we could split into two the passage from TI to Darwin, and perhaps see something of unusual interest on the way.

The wind blew hard from south-east and the sea was steep and short—typical Carpentaria conditions, for nowhere there is the depth greater than fifty fathoms. Big areas of the gulf had not yet been surveyed, and much of it still had an air of mysterious menace; its east and west coasts, which are largely a confusion of river mouths, estuaries, and mangrove swamps where crocodiles and sharks roam, were now believed to lie five and nine miles respectively from their charted positions, and it was likely that many unreported shoals existed. I suddenly had occasion to wonder about all this when one afternoon I went on deck to have a look round, and saw ahead and on both bows a large area of grey and light-brown discoloured water. This had every appearance of an

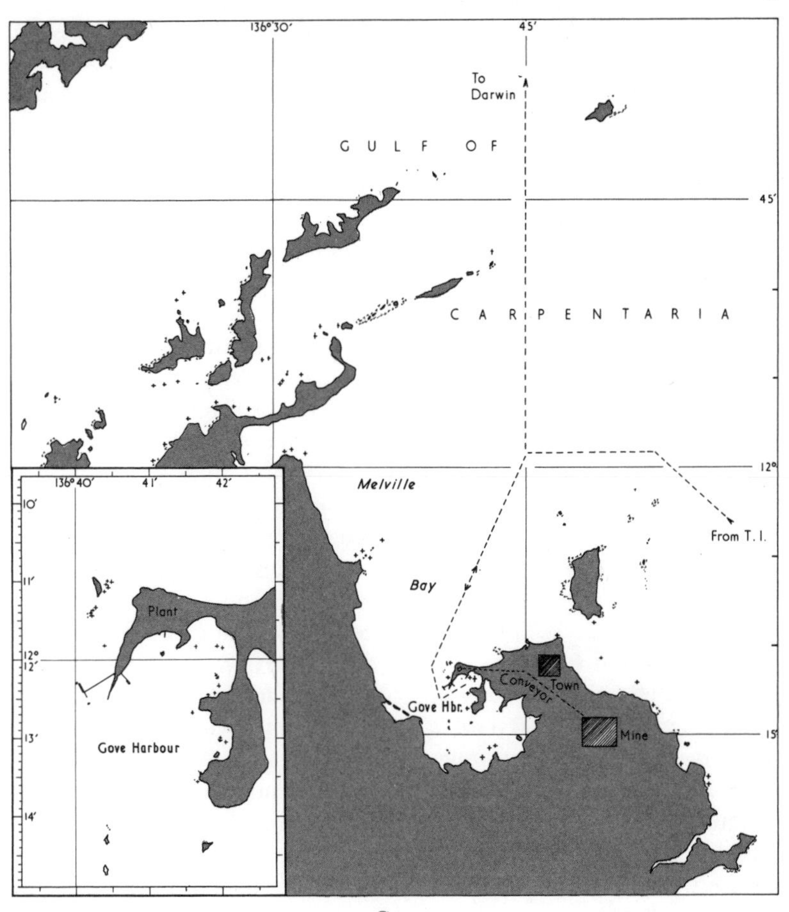

Gove

extensive shoal, but as the staysail was boomed out as a running sail it was not possible to alter course and come on the wind quickly. Fearfully, I switched on the echo sounder as we plunged into the discoloration and was much relieved to see it register twenty-five fathoms. Later we learned something about this phenomenon. It seems these discoloured patches, which can cover as many as ten square miles, and are known as 'coral spawn' or 'sea sawdust', have proved under microscopic examination to be a seasonal form of marine alga, which is a vital part of the pasturage of the drifting life of those tropical and highly populated waters.

We knew our landfall would be an awkward one, for in the

vicinity of Melville Bay three fingers of land project in a north-east direction, each with a bunch of small islands off its tip; all of the land and the islands are low and featureless, and there is no beacon, buoy or other navigational aid. Of course, it was vital that we should make our entry between the correct pair of fingers, but the sky had clouded over so we were not sure of our position. Therefore, when the outline of land appeared ahead faintly through the haze, which a strong sou'easter usually produces on that coast, we could not be certain which piece of land we were looking at; so we hove-to and waited until noon, when the sun obligingly let us get a latitude sight which gave us the answer. We let draw then and ran on in, rounding a bunch of rocks and islets (a recent correction to the chart, an Australian one we had bought with Gove in mind, showed that an extra rock three feet (0·9 metre) high had been discovered), and then steered south close-hauled for twenty miles towards our destination. As we came swiftly nearer to it a huge mass of buildings, including silos and tanks, of which there was no indication on our new chart, materialized through the haze, and then a bulk-loading jetty half a mile in length appeared. This we rounded and found an anchorage partly sheltered by a small island and close to a pumping station; but although we were obviously in the heart of the giant enterprise there was no sign of a dwelling, and we saw only three people, none of whom showed any interest in us. Within a short time our galvanized anchor cable had turned black due to some impurity in the water, and we began to fuss about what might happen to our steel hull if we remained there; so we left that berth and found a good though lonely anchorage in a bay two miles to the south, and spent the night there.

We felt sure there must be a town or settlement somewhere near, for so large a concern would employ a lot of people; we landed to look for it, and made our way along a track where cloven hoofprints showed in the dust; on either hand giant anthills six feet (1·8 metres) high stood among the grey, dried-up bush which gave little shelter from the sun. We had walked some distance and were beginning to wilt when a car came lurching towards us, braked in a cloud of dust, and the bearded young driver jumped out to shake us vigorously by the hand.

'I thought that was *Wanderer IV* I saw at anchor off the plant yesterday,' he said, 'so you must be Eric and Susan.'

Bob Cooper and his friend Cole Anderson, with whom he

shared a house, had arrived a year before in the steel sloop, *Patience III*; they were working at the plant and rebuilding the yacht in their spare time. These two friendly young men looked after us remarkably well; they drove us several times to the town eight miles away to do our shopping, while our dirty laundry revolved in their washing machine under the supervision of a jet-black great dane and an equally black cat; they took us to the mine and the mission, fed us again and again, and arranged for us to be shown round the alumina plant off which we had temporarily anchored on arrival, and they introduced us to many kind and hospitable people.

Gove had been established for only two years. The red bauxite from the opencast mine was transported by a giant conveyor (Plate 2 *bottom*), probably the longest in the southern hemisphere, for sixteen miles to the plant where the alumina (from which aluminium is made) was extracted and loaded at a rate of 2000 tons an hour into bulk-carriers lying at the jetty we had rounded. Half-way between the mine and the plant was the town of Nhulunbuy, built to house 5000 inhabitants. Very few towns are planned and then built; most are built and then planned if they are ever planned at all. Canberra, the Australian capital, is one of the exceptions and Nhulunbuy is another; a sort of 'instant town', it contained only one well-stocked shop of each denomination (supermarket, butcher, pharmacy, bookshop, haberdashery, hairdresser, and so on) and one hotel, the Walkabout; NABALCO ('the company') saw to it that prices were kept the same as those ruling in Darwin even though nearly everything had to come by air, for there was no road communication with the rest of the country. Most buildings, including the houses, were air-conditioned, and lawns and flower beds were kept green and fresh by sprinklers. That part of Australia, like much of the Northern Territory, is an aboriginal reserve, and the aboriginies were paid a royalty on every ton of bauxite mined. Only they had the right to kill wildlife in the reserve, and one result of this was that buffalo, which originally were introduced by early Malay traders, roamed freely—it was the footprints of these big creatures that we had seen along the track that morning. Shortly before our arrival a young doctor had been severely gored just outside the hospital in the heart of town while trying to photograph a buffalo. No doubt the creatures were attracted by that lush green oasis so surprisingly established in their harsh, dried-up domain. Medical and dental treatment was free, as was transport by bus between town, plant and mine, but many people had cars although there were only about twenty miles of road on which to use them; a house was rented for ten dollars a week including water and electricity. At the time of our visit there was no radio or television, and individual pursuits and clubs of all kinds flourished; indeed, the people entertained themselves and were happy and busy in doing so, but the unions insisted that television and radio must be provided, and it was widely thought that when that happened, within a year, the character of the place and the individuality of its people would change, and not for the better.

In our earlier, simpler, wooden yachts we had always said that there was nothing on deck that could be damaged by a mischievous child, and I often tried to reassure anxious parents as their progeny stamped about flat-footed overhead, that if the children tumbled overboard they would probably float and that anyway we would hear their screams. In our newer vessel we were not so sure about the former, and we had from time to time been inflicted with some terrible children, a few of which were not even house-trained. Shortly before leaving New Zealand a small visitor stuffed plastic clothes-pegs down one of the cockpit drains where they lodged much restricting the flow, and short of a cutting and welding job they could not be extricated. Another at Port Moresby put all his weight, which was not inconsiderable as he was a fat child, on the lever of the Morse control which, with precision, actuates the throttle and gearbox; repairs to that took me all of a day. The winding of winches with a clicking of pawls is only an irritation and is probably good for the winches, but the equally popular method of attracting the attention of those below by lifting and dropping skylights, is hazardous to little fingers as well as the owners' tempers. Susan says I ought not to mention these things as they might upset or antagonize the parents who had brought their offspring visiting, but I feel I am in good company as the following extract from *The Conveyor*, Gove's newspaper, will show.

Recently Building Services mechanics have found that the washing machines in the flats have been damaged by children who have been putting gravel in the machines. Would parents please keep a check on the kids to control this practice as it is causing inconvenience to flatters and the mechanics.

There is another difficulty that has sometimes arisen with visitors. We invite a couple aboard and arrange to pick them up by dinghy but, without warning us that they are going to do so, they bring along a couple of their friends—'they are longing to meet you'—or a large family; as our dinghy was small she could only carry safely two passengers, so such invasions involved making several journeys both ways, not only to bring them all aboard but to put them ashore afterwards.

With so big a ship as ours, of course, we ought to carry a larger dinghy, but our Souter-built GRP seven-and-a-half-footer (2·3 metres) is the largest hard dinghy we can comfortably lift aboard and stow. A big inflatable would solve this and several other problems, such as carrying it up a beach or flight of steps, but we enjoy rowing and no inflatable rows well, so we would be compelled to make use of the outboard motor most of the time; this we prefer not to do because with it running we cannot converse with other yachts as we pass on our way to and from the shore, nor can we talk to one another without raising our voices, and we know that is not a good thing to do as anything we might say would be heard all over the anchorage. That everyone is not aware of this was shown to us once when we were lying in the Beaulieu River and some people passing in an outboard-driven dinghy were discussing us; clear above the angry noise of the motor we heard one man say: 'He's a bit of an old bastard, but he's got a jolly nice wife.'

There are other things about dinghies, whether they have outboards or not, of which some people seem unaware. When using a landing at which the dinghy can be left afloat, she should be tied up with a long painter so that she can be pushed aside by others wishing to use the landing. Often painters are so short that one has to clamber through several (probably waterlogged) dinghies to get ashore. Rowlocks left shipped and oars not properly stowed inboard will surely foul the painters of the others, and make the confusion, which is all too common in harbours used by yachts, more squalid and frustrating than it need be.

We had none of these problems to contend with at Gove, however. The sand beach on which we landed was deserted, and the only footprints it bore were those of buffalo and the ones we had left on earlier landings and when, at the weekend, we moved to another bay and anchored off the sailing club so that some of the people who had been kind to us might come aboard (Plate 3 *top*), a launch ran a ferry service all day to bring off our guests, and we had the pleasure of entertaining forty of them.

Such a busy and social life did we lead at Gove that we felt it necessary to announce the date for our departure as the day before we intended to leave, so as to give ourselves a day in which to recuperate and prepare for sea and, although *Wanderer* must have been clearly visible, nobody came off to disturb our privacy. During the final night at our anchorage which, although within view of the brightly illuminated plant, was out of earshot of it, the only sound was the spine-chilling howling of dingoes—wild dogs with the habits of wolves.

Leaving Gove was easier than the arrival had been, for we had a known point of departure, and the northern approach is more straightforward than the eastern one. A fresh fair wind hurried us along for seventy-five miles to reach Cape Wessel (our turning-point for the west) just as the lighthouse tower on the cape was etched black and bold right in the orb of the setting sun. From that point on we had a wild two-day sail with a forty-knot wind on the quarter; we entered Van Diemen Gulf in the dark, spent a night at anchor there, and went on to Darwin under power in a calm.

We found that fast-developing city to have changed much from the rough, outback town that we remembered when its main job was to serve the missionaries and crocodile hunters; it had become a big bustling place with many new administrative buildings—the custom-house and harbour offices were now a twenty-minute walk from the port—and some industry and tourism. It had also become a base for a fleet of trawlers, big, expensive vessels which sometimes gathered 20 000 pounds (9120 kilos) of banana prawns in one haul. Darwin was good to us and provided all our needs with a smile, and it was with sad dismay that we learned a few months later of its destruction by a willy-willy, when forty-eight people were killed and 25 000 had to be evacuated.

* * *

From Torres Strait to Durban the Indian Ocean is nearly 7000 miles across, yet my mother, who knew about the Atlantic and the Pacific, seemed never to have heard of it; neither, it appeared, had some South Africans for, when we called there on our first voyage, a number asked if we had reached their country by way of the Atlantic or by Suez, and when we replied that we had come by neither but across the Indian Ocean they looked blank. Now the first long lonely leg of the crossing lay ahead: 1500 miles to Christmas Island. We made a slow start with very little wind for several days as we crept among the shoals which lay in the Timor Sea west of Darwin, where the brassy sun beat down from a hazy sky making the deck too hot for bare feet. But later the wind picked up and freshened, and *Wanderer* increased her gait to make day's runs of 140 miles or more. So in spite of the slow start we did not do too badly on that trip, though for the final eight hours we were reduced to the curious rig of mizzen only (under which she handled quite well) and then to bare poles, so as to slow down and avoid making a night arrival at Christmas Island, for the wind by then was blowing hard from the east; we began seriously to wonder if it would be possible to stop at the island with so much wind and sea from that direction, for Flying Fish Cove, which offers the only anchorage, is on the north shore and is not a big indentation, while the depth of water in it is great, leaving only a small anchorage area on a coral shelf close to the shore.

Considering the small range of tide, only about three feet (0·9 metre) at springs, the tidal streams round the island run with surprising strength. The stream was against us as we came up with North-east Point, and there the sea ran steep and crested, and into it many gannets were diving for their breakfast, and often were robbed of it in mid-air by squadrons of frigate birds. Now in full daylight we set the staysail and pressed on; the hospital and other buildings came into view, then the great cantilever phosphate-loaders, and suddenly we were out of the wind and in the cove which, contrary to our gloomy fears, was not at all rough, and to our surprise we found a party of four yachts lying there, the greatest number the island had ever had at one time. As we knew from earlier visits, there was only one good berth in which one lay moored fore-and-aft between the high pier (from which the barges helping to berth large ships were launched) and the buoy close north of it. As that was occupied by a yacht which had lain in it for more than a month, the other yachts were lying at anchor, some with lines to the buoy, and with difficulty we inserted ourselves among them; but it was an uneasy berth for there were squalls and enough surge to make our cable rasp on the coral.

Notwithstanding these disadvantages, Christmas Island always had been, and still was, a good stop for the voyaging yacht because all manner of stores could be had from the Phosphate Commission supermarket, including spirits and beer out of bond, though two of the cartons of beer we bought there were stale and almost undrinkable. The Australians running the phosphate mining and processing were welcoming. They had a tiny boat club at the one and only landing-place on the steep coral beach; the club had a bar but no barman, and all visitors were invited to help themselves, keep a tally of what they drank, and pay before leaving the island. How long the phosphate deposits can last I do not know, but we were told that much was now second grade, and that even the airstrip had been dug up and rebuilt to get at the material under it.

Our next trip was a comparatively short one, 524 miles to Keeling Cocos, and we did it in just over three days thanks to a strong wind and favourable current. The atoll is nowhere more than a few feet above the sea, but the tops of its palms may be seen from on deck at a distance of about nine miles, and because of the variable currents with which it is beset it is not the easiest of landfalls; we therefore felt a little anxious, particularly as we were carrying the mail from Christmas Island. The day before we expected to arrive, the sky became overcast and sights were not possible; however, we hoped for a star fix before dawn next day, and were fortunate to get an observation of Canopus, and a bit later one of the sun when it peeped out for a moment through a crack in the cloud cover. We were lucky, for that was the last glimpse we were to have of any heavenly body for the next three days. The resulting position placed us too far to the south and twelve miles from Cocos, so we altered course and very soon the faint grey line of palm-tops broke the horizon ahead as we lifted on the swell. Rain then drove down upon us, but we did not mind that now we knew where we were, and in little over an hour were sailing in the choppy but swell-free water of the lagoon, which we still considered to be the most beautiful that we had ever seen, and even under the low, grey sky, against which the breakers on the reef showed startlingly white, the colouring was superb. With Susan conning from up the ratlines we wove our way among the brown coral patches, crossed a bank where our keel had only a few inches under it, and came to the well-remembered anchorage in the sheltering, crescent-shaped embrace of Direction Island, where in crystal-clear, pale-green water over smooth sand we watched our anchor plunge to the bottom, turn over and dig in.

The rain came down more heavily then, the palms leant to the thirty-five-knot wind, the great swell thundered on the reef and on the windward side of the narrow island which protected us, and we experienced a wonderful feeling of cosy content, heightened by the knowledge that not for two whole weeks need we go out again into the boisterous ocean.

There used to be a cable station on Direction Island, manned on our first visit by Englishmen and on our second by Australians, and great had been the hospitality and magnificent the meals we had enjoyed in Top House and Long Mess. But advanced technology had made the station redundant, and the buildings, the garden and the pigsties, had all gone, and there was no trace of them except for the washbasins, complete with taps, placed on the ground for the chickens to drink from, and the big open-topped watertank which had thoughtfully been left for the benefit of visiting yachts. The island was now uninhabited, and young palms grew where once the busy cable station had stood.

Keeling Cocos was still owned by John Clunies Ross, whose grandfather had brought in some Malays and started the settlement on Home Island, one of the five major islands which, with several smaller ones all on the same reef, comprise the atoll. John had his establishment on Home Island, where his 500 people lived and were employed building boats and making copra. On West Island, the only other inhabited island, was a good example of Parkinson's Law. There was an airport there, but it was little used except by the fortnightly plane from Perth, which came only to bring food and other supplies for the people who maintained the airport. Including children, 175 people lived there; they had a hospital, school, golf course and other amenities.

As we could not take *Wanderer* across the shallows to Home Island, Jim Dixon, who was John Clunies Ross's right-hand man, sent a launch to fetch us over there for a curry lunch his wife had prepared and at which John and his wife were present. They told us how United Nations had recently sent a delegation to look into John's 'dictatorship' and to persuade the islanders that what they really needed was freedom and independence. But it turned out that the islanders, who apparently knew a good thing when they had it, were so disinterested that they did not bother to read the leaflets or to vote, so perhaps this apparently contented, obviously healthy, unique little community will be allowed to continue its peaceful existence under John's benevolent rule. The one law the

Home Islander did not like was that which forbade him to return should he choose to leave the island, as many had done to work on neighbouring Christmas Island. This might seem harsh, but it was difficult to see how else over-population could be avoided or disease or undesirable outside influences kept away. I asked if there was much theft or other crime, and was told hardly any, for a person caught doing something wrong was ostracized by his fellows, and with people so gregarious as the Home Islanders—they needed to be for theirs was a very small and overcrowded island—that was a severe punishment. The community had been dealt a hard blow five years back when a cyclone destroyed more than half the mature palms, for it takes up to six years for a young palm to start bearing. There was talk, however, of turning West Island into a quarantine station for breeding cattle and other livestock destined for Australia, and such a development might well be the shot in the arm the Home Island economy could do with.

Direction Island is not to everyone's taste. Alex Bell, American owner of the ferrocement ketch, *Alsanal Too*, wrote in a letter we had not long after his visit: 'It is a beautiful atoll but an overnight stop was all I cared to make of it.' You may, therefore, wonder how we occupied ourselves there for two weeks. Well, we swam and swam again in the lagoon which, when the sun was high, was an almost impossibly vivid green; we walked barefoot on the perfect little beach; we burnt our refuse, disposed of bottles and cans on the windward reef, ferried off loads of water from the tank and did the laundry, and with a water supply so handy and so brimming we had luxurious showers on board. In our smaller yachts we had at times suffered with skin infections which we believed were due not to not washing, for we washed frequently in salt water, but to not washing often enough in fresh. But now that we carried in our tanks about 200 gallons (900 litres) of fresh water we washed ourselves more often, and perhaps as a result of this unusual cleanliness did not in our bigger yacht have any of the skin troubles of the past. We split coconuts to feed the chickens on days when their keeper failed to come over from Home Island—an axe was provided, and the risk to the birds, which flocked in at the first chop, was considerable—and we watched a pair of herons fishing. Then we swam again, we walked, we . . . But I am sure you will understand that, in fact, we were rather idle, as we believe one should be on an uninhabited island; but we did some maintenance on board in the perpetual battle with rust, though that was not a good place to do it because of the salt-laden air from the ceaseless breakers to windward, and there was some writing and darkroom work to be attended to.

Sometimes we had company, for several yachts came and went during our stay, and one Wednesday a motorized barge brought many of the Australians across the lagoon from West Island to picnic on 'our' beach and offer us beer and a 'semmich', and Susan wondered if she might ask for the wastefully thick peelings off the cucumbers. When they had all gone home the evening sky was heavily overcast, there was rain to windward, and the only sounds were the roar of surf and the moan of the damp wind in the rigging. I had a momentary feeling of loneliness, perhaps of fear, as I thought of the long stretches of ocean that lay ahead of us. But with Susan, the best possible companion for me in that or any other mood, cheerfully busy in her galley, and with the familiar, easy comforts of our seagoing home around me, the feeling could not last, and soon, helped no doubt by the evening drink, was replaced by one of thankfulness that we could live this free and rewarding life, travel the world as we wished with few restrictions, stop at wonderful unspoilt places such as Cocos, make friends, and then sail on, and there came a pleasant tingle of excitement at the thought of what might lie ahead.

The day before we were due to leave, the kind Dixons came over from their island with all sorts of good things for us, including Cocos honey, which was some of the best we had ever tasted; the atoll seemed an unlikely place for bees, but a small, blue flower that grew there apparently provided all their needs. As we sailed out of the lagoon on 7 September we were sadder than I can say, for we both knew that never again would we see its exquisite beauty or enjoy its cosy shelter.

* * *

For the first three days of the 2300-mile passage to Mauritius we had good weather with a pleasant breeze on the quarter and not much sea or swell. We thought it so unlikely that we would meet any shipping on this little-frequented route on which, since the Suez Canal was still closed, there would be only one major shipping lane to cross, that from the Cape to Sunda Strait, that we did not keep watches and we spent most of each night in our bunks; if either of us woke up, however, we usually went on deck to have a look round, but we never met one another doing so. When sailing in frequented waters, however, we were not so casual because we believed the chance of being run down was the greatest risk a yacht was likely to be subjected to, for we knew that many ships, notably those under flags of convenience, posted no proper look-out when away from the land. I recall a tanker coming into San Francisco, and as she was berthing one of the line-handlers on the wharf called up to the officer on her fo'c's'le head:

'Say, what ya got there bud?'

Looking over the starboard bow the officer saw with horror the mast and rigging of a sailing yacht hanging on the anchor in its hawsepipe.

Long ago Susan and I abandoned the idea that in deep water power vessels give way to those under sail, as they are, by international rules, supposed to do. Often the power vessel does give way and in plenty of time to make her intention clear, but we do not bank on it, and if there is any doubt we take avoiding action ourselves, and then make a big alteration in course so that the ship, if she is looking, can see it and understand what we are up to. But before doing this, we have found it is wise to look over our shoulder, and often enough have found another ship coming silently up astern, and we had to take her into consideration; sometimes it was her presence that prevented the first ship giving way to us. When we consider that two 20-knot ships on reciprocal courses are approaching one another at 46 land miles an hour, we realize that they have to judge the situation with nicety, and that we, a sort of buffer state, are of secondary consideration even if we have been seen. Therefore, a yacht must act in her own interest and not necessarily obey the rules.

Upon sighting a ship we try to judge what her course may be. If her masts are well open and/or we can clearly make out one of her sides, she will probably go clear unless we are converging fast with her course, but if she is end-on and we can see her masts in line or nearly so, we watch her more carefully. The only way of being certain about the matter in daylight is to take a bearing of her and another a little later; if the bearing has changed she will go clear, but if it remains constant we are on a collision course and must take avoiding action before it is too late. When the sea is rough, however, it may not be possible to take sufficiently accurate bearings. By night the situation can often be assessed more easily. The two white steaming lights of a big ship are usually visible much in excess of the five miles stipulated in the international regulations, and it is easier to see if they are in line or are just open, than it is to judge the alignment of a pair of masts in daylight; and some ships, notably bulk-carriers and tankers, may have masts so short and thin that they are difficult to see by day, and some have no masts. On a clear night one can pick a star immediately over the ship and watch to see if she moves in relation to it; if she does move from under the star her bearing is changing and all is well.

But what about our own lights? By the regulations a sailing vessel shows from ahead to two points abaft the port beam a red light, and over a similar arc to starboard a green light; over the arc astern not covered by the red and green lights she shows a white light. It is well known, however, that red and green lights give only a small portion of the intensity of a white light of similar power. Another point that may not be so well known is that, unless the red and green lights are at least three feet (0·9 metre) apart, they combine to produce an orange light when viewed from ahead. A dioptric lens, which concentrates a light into a horizontal plane, is of little use in a heeled sailing vessel because the plane of light from the lee lamp is thrown down into the sea and that from the other up into the sky. However, the modern fresnel lens, with which I believe a vertical filament bulb is essential, does not have this disadvantage, yet it does appear to intensify the light. As a combination red and green lamp requires only one bulb, that can be of double the power for the same consumption of electricity; but often such lamps have a central column separating the two colour glasses, and this can cause an arc of invisibility or ambiguity of as much as fifteen degrees. The revised international regulations permit a sailing vessel to carry at her masthead a lamp showing red, green and white over the prescribed arcs; apart from a possible orange effect between the red and the green, this is a good and economical arrangement; the light being high is more readily seen, and it cannot be masked by any sail or obscured by spray.

I believe that the ordinary red and green lights made for yachts cannot be seen at a distance exceeding one mile, which gives a twenty-knot ship seeing them at extreme range only three minutes to assess the situation and alter course. For this reason, except when entering or leaving port or when in busy waters, we did not use our red and green lights; instead we showed an all-round white light, either from the masthead (this had a twenty-four-watt bulb) or from a paraffin-burning riding-light lashed in a position where it could not be masked by any of the sails but showed beneath them. In clear weather we hoped that either of these lights could be seen from a distance of five miles, so a twenty-knot ship seeing our white light at extreme range would have fifteen minutes in which to identify and avoid us. This practice may be considered to be cheating, for any ship sighting a single white light must suppose herself to be the overtaking vessel and her duty then is to keep clear. However, merchant navy officers have often said that they have no wish to sink yachts, and wish that all would show a white light so as to be seen. If they can see us in time they may be able to avoid us, for from their steady platforms they can obtain accurate bearings of us. Surely then the important thing is to be seen, and the further off we can be seen the greater is our margin of safety.

We have found that the life of twenty-four watt bulbs, when left burning for twelve hours at a stretch, is limited—those with extra-large glass envelopes appear to last longer than the normal ones—and if the bulb in the masthead lamp burns out I cannot replace it at sea because the motion is too great to permit me to go aloft with any degree of safety. So on a long passage we prefer to use the paraffin lamp which I have already mentioned. This, made by Davey of London, is a fine example of the coppersmith's art, and is almost a curio today; it weighs eight pounds (3·6 kilos), and with its three-quarter-inch (two-centimetre) wick and internal cone is gale-proof. At sea we lash it to the boom-gallows (Plate 3 *bottom*) in such a manner that the beam from its dioptric lens is parallel to the sea at our average angle of heel, and as we roll or pitch apparently the impression of a flashing lamp is given, for on several occasions ships have called us up by lamp, presumably thinking we were trying to signal to them; embarrassing though this was it did at least show that our light had been seen.

It is said that a yacht, particularly one of wood or GRP, does not show up at all well on a ship's radar display unless she carries a radar reflector at least fifteen feet (4·5 metres) above the sea; but for this to be effective I believe it needs to be fixed in the correct attitude, that is, not point up, and not single straight edge up, but in the attitude it would assume if it were placed on a flat surface. We carried one permanently mounted between the twin legs of the backstay, and because ships hull-down had sometimes turned off course to come and speak with us, we believe it may have been effective, or it could perhaps have been some part of our steel hull returning the radar waves to source.

Although we can see the big ships, for they stand up well against the sky, we often ask ourselves even in daylight, 'Have they seen us?' and in general I think the answer is 'No', for when at sea most ships do not use their radar except in thick weather, and a yacht is not easily picked out from high up against the ever-moving background of the sea. Once, when we were in the Coral Sea, the Swedish ship, *Tenos*, came out of her way to see if all was well with us, so she at least had seen us, and ranged up alongside, I thought uncomfortably close. Susan noticed that some people on her decks had cameras, and later I wrote to the master of *Tenos* asking if we might have a print of one of the photographs. He kindly had one sent to us, and in it our thirty-foot (nine-metre) *Wanderer III* looked very small and inconspicuous. She had her white twin running sails set at the time, and from the photograph we gained the impression that had her fore-and-aft working sails of tan-dyed terylene been set she would have been more conspicuous. Many a life-raft, those of the Robertsons and the Baileys naturally come to mind, has been passed unseen by ships half a mile away; but, as I have already suggested, that may have been because no lookout was being kept. Even in well-managed and properly-run ships, however, there are moments when, apparently, nobody is looking.

On an earlier voyage when we were at Mauritius in *Wanderer III* we met Captain Lloyd, master of *Tantallon Castle*. He was hospitable and he invited us to make use of his personal shower on board any time we wished but, as his ship lay on buoys far out in the harbour, that would have involved hiring a launch, so we never did avail ourselves of his offer. He left bound for Durban before we did, and when we arrived at that port we found that Lloyd had spoken of us, for we were greeted with the remark: 'So you are the Hiscocks, the people who never wash.'

It was some years after this that at about 4 o'clock one sunny afternoon we were crossing the Bay of Biscay bound south, when we met the liner *Durban Castle* coming the other way. We were on a collision course and, as the big ship did not appear to be looking where she was going, we had to take avoiding action, which was a bother because we were at the time running with spinnaker set. In what I intended to be a jocular tone I mentioned this meeting in a story I wrote, but there was a great fuss on publication. The Merchant Navy Officers' Association, I think it was, said that I had written disparaging remarks about Captain Lloyd—he now turned out to be not only master of *Durban Castle* but commodore of the Union Castle Line—and was about to sue the magazine for damages. It claimed that the ship was not where I had said she was, but when it was proved that she was there the matter was dropped, and we thought no more about it until three years later, when *Wanderer III*, having completed her second circumnavigation, was on exhibition at the London Boat Show afloat in the pool at Earl's Court. Each day she had many visitors, often a hundred or more crowding round the rails asking questions, and one day a voice I recognized came from among them.

'Hello, Hiscock! Do you remember one sunny afternoon in the Bay of Biscay?'

Looking up I saw Captain Lloyd leaning on the rail.

'You might like to know,' he continued, 'that the officer responsible is no longer with the company. But I should warn you, if you intend to go on with this sailing game, that 4 o'clock, like 8 o'clock, midnight, 4 a.m., 8 a.m. and noon are danger moments for people like you; we are changing watch at those times and nobody is looking.'

We became friends, and thereafter whenever his ship, outward-bound from Southampton, passed the little house on the Isle of Wight in which we then lived, she blew her siren and we from our foreshore waved yellow oilskins. His lesson has stuck with us. Now when we see a ship dithering, showing first her red light then her green, we look at our watches and as often as not find that it is one of those moments when nobody is looking or, perhaps, even steering. We were grateful for the hint, but as it turned out on this trip to Mauritius we did not see another vessel on the rare occasions when *we* were looking, and it was not until we came to round South Africa that the business of 'meeting steamers' called for all our eyes and our resources.

* * *

The third evening out from Cocos I felt so relaxed and content that I enjoyed a cigar before dinner, which we ate at the table in a civilized manner as our ship under full sail slipped effortlessly along. Later I was debating whether to bother to close the ports before turning in—chiefly to stop flying-fish from shooting themselves into the saloon—when we heard rain on deck and wind in the rigging. I suppose that had we not been dazzled by the riding-light we might have noticed black clouds gathering to windward. Quickly we closed the hatches and screwed up the ports, then we handed the staysail and mizzen, and as the suddenly arising wind continued to harden we rolled a reef in the mainsail. It had all happened so quickly that there had been no opportunity to put on oilskins, and by the time we had the ship snugged down we were sodden and shivering, for even in the tropics heavy rain by night strikes chill on one's bare flesh.

That was the end of the fine weather until we got to within 400 miles of our destination, and for the next ten days the going was rough. Crests frequently invaded the deck, and the cockpit although we had a weathercloth rigged there, and they found out the chinks in our armour. The skylight under the dinghy over the sleeping cabin leaked wretchedly; the rubber strips intended to seal the engine-room hatch had become perished, so some water got down into the engine-room bilge from which it had to be sponged out, for if as little as half a bucketful accumulated there it could sluice up the curve of the skin plating and get at the electrics and the machinery.

Although the wind, except in squalls, did not much exceed 35 knots throughout this period, the sea in steepness and confusion seemed out of proportion to it. The sea was on or just abaft the beam, a condition that always is uncomfortable, but we felt that this part of the ocean was a rough area, a view that is shared by others who have crossed it in small craft. We happened to have with us a National Geographic Society relief map of the floor of the Indian Ocean, and a study of this gave us food for thought. It showed that the seabed is not comparatively flat, as one might believe it to be from the scanty soundings on the chart—there is a line of soundings of between 2000 and 3000 fathoms between Cocos and Rodriguez, probably taken when the cable was being laid—but has mountain ranges rising from it. One of these, the Ninety East Ridge, starts in the Bay of Bengal and runs south to latitude thirty-four degrees, and this lay right athwart our course. Another, the Mid-oceanic Ridge, starts at the Gulf of Aden, passes east of Rodriguez, and then splits into two branches. Where all this information came from I do not know, and possibly a little of it is artistic licence, but presuming it to be true, such an uneven bottom to the ocean might deflect currents to the surface, and so produce the notoriously rough sea so many of us have encountered there (see also page 211). Incidentally, a recent correction to the southern sheet of the Indian Ocean chart showed an eight-and-a-half-fathom 'obstruction', surrounded by soundings of more than 2000 fathoms, lying in a position about sixty miles south-west of Keeling Cocos; was this, we wondered, another atoll in the making?

During the four years that we had been cruising in the Pacific we had been distressed at the lack of porpoises in that ocean, and had come to believe what many had told us, that Asiatic and other fishermen had killed most of them (see also page 227). We were, therefore, delighted to find a large number of these lively, warm-blooded creatures in the Indian Ocean, and night after night, for they mostly visited us during the hours of darkness, we heard them blowing, listened to their whistling talk, and watched from the bowsprit the silver gleams of phosphorescent light as they wove their intricate swimming patterns round us like luminous torpedoes. Their skill at steering was remarkable, for we never saw one touch another, and we knew they never touched our hull though often only a few inches from it—if only man could learn this skill, which of course is shared by birds, how wonderful it would be. Flying-fish were in abundance, too, and we observed that showers of these more often came aboard when porpoises were with us, as though the latter were determined that we should have a good fresh meal, and we did. One morning after Susan had taken and worked a round of star sights, she picked up thirteen of the gleaming creatures, big ones, from the deck and filleted them, and I fried them for our breakfast. Squid also we found on deck occasionally, but they were not so popular, and they left an inky stain wherever they fell.

So the days and the nights passed. We longed for a respite, if only a short one, from the jerky motion and the driving spray; we looked forward to a day when we would not have to put on oilskins each time we went on deck to check the course and the trim of the sails, to read the log, or while waiting, sextant in hand, to get an observation of the rarely seen heavenly bodies; but we did realize how fortunate we were in all that time never to have to steer, for had that been necessary we could not have made such good progress as we did without becoming exhausted. And our progress was heartening: the fifteen-degree time zones seemed to flash past, their 900-mile span crossed in six days and, at each zone crossing, we put our clocks back one hour so as to live our domestic life at what seemed (by the sun) to be the right time of day; and on one well-remembered occasion we made good from noon to noon a day's run of 190 miles, the best the ship had ever managed to achieve.

In the early hours of our seventeenth day at sea we made our landfall on Mauritius, and in the forenoon came to Port Louis on the island's western side, where we found many ships loading the sugar harvest, and others at anchor outside waiting their turn. The port had no facilities for yachts, but we tied up temporarily outside a big fishing vessel, and customs soon came to chip our paint, dirty our sea-scoured decks and seal up our Scotch. That was an interesting berth, full of life and noise, as was the town, and there were miniature tugs hauling strings of lighters between the ships and the wharves. But we felt vulnerable as there was so little room for the tugs and their tows to manoeuvre in, and when the owner of our neighbour offered to pilot us to Grande Bay, fourteen miles away, we gladly accepted, for the entrance to that place is shallow and reefy, and the leading marks for it shown on the chart were not visible, for one had fallen down and trees had grown up to obscure the other. At first we anchored off the thatched sailing club set amid casuarinas—quite a change from the palms of Cocos—but soon moved further in to where some other voyagers lay off a friendly little hotel at which we could land dry-shod and safely leave the dinghy. Our vivid green anchorage was landlocked by tree-shaded beaches, and a couple of near-by Chinese stores provided most of our needs; a delightful Mauritian family looked after us, invited us to their home, drove us to town whenever we wished to go, and took us by night on a tour of one of the steam-powered sugar mills which, in cathedral-like silence, was turning out eighteen tons of sugar an hour. At the end of an arduous passage all this was so pleasant that we were reluctant to leave it, but after a stay of two weeks we had to move on so as to be clear of the Indian Ocean danger area before the cyclone season set in. We were clear of it, and in South African waters, when we heard by radio the terrible news that Mauritius, just like Darwin, had been devastated by a cyclone, and we wondered anxiously what had happened to our friends, to the sugar mills and the town, and to that pleasant little hotel.

Early in the morning of the day set for our departure there was a knocking on our hull, and looking over the side we found a diver with a brush; he had been sent all the way from Port Louis to give *Wanderer*'s bottom a rub over as a kindly farewell gift from Captain Betuel who ran the shipyard. An hour later the diver tapped again and reported that our bottom, sacrificial zincs, and propeller were now all clean. We gave him a small present which he tucked away in his wet suit; he then submerged and returned to the shore as silently as he had come, his passage marked by a trail of bubbles. A local yacht led us out through the tricky entrance, and we coasted south past Port Louis, noticing how jolly Peter Both and all the other jaunty little mountains looked as the fertile, sugar-cane island slipped past to port, and we took our departure for a position south of La Réunion. The last time we came that way we made the mistake of passing to leeward of that high island, and got ourselves becalmed there for many hours in a confused sea; so on this occasion we passed to windward of it and held a steadier breeze.

We were now leaving for the first time in five months the region of the south-east trade wind, and for the rest of that passage the wind was variable both in strength and direction, and to keep the ship moving properly there was much sail-shifting to be done. One starlit night when we were running under main and boomed-out staysail, a change of wind called for a gybe and, while we were attending to that, we were startled by the blowing of a whale close off the port bow. Soon after, and while I was at the bow-sprit-end reeving the foreguy, the whale blew again, right ahead and apparently only a few yards away. It was an eerie sensation standing there with the bow-wave, a swath of milky phosphorescence, beneath me, the stars wheeling overhead, Susan's dim figure at the halyard by the mast, and suddenly that long, damp, soughing sound almost in my ear. It is strange how quickly memories flood through one's mind at such moments of excitement; I remembered the Pyes' *Moonraker* had struck a sleeping whale in the North Atlantic, the Baileys' *Auralyn* being sunk by an injured whale in the Pacific, and Bill King's experience off the south-west part of Australia. At least I concluded that this whale was awake, and I hoped that his or her sonor or radar, or whatever it is they use, was in proper working order.

A 274-fathom patch 100 miles south of the tip of Madagascar (Malagasy Republic) is shown on the chart. One might think this would be of no interest, yet people had reported a dangerously heavy sea in its vicinity; so we gave it a good berth before heading for the African coast. We were bound for Durban, and considered it wise to head for Cape St Lucia, which is 100 miles north-east of that port, so as to have plenty in hand when we came to the Agulhas Current, an enormous body of warm water which sets south-west along the coast at two knots or more in that area. Having read the section on currents in volume III of *Africa Pilot* we expected to have a fair current most of the way but, with the exception of some powerful oceanic arteries, such as the Humboldt, the Benguella and the Gulf Stream, currents are unpredictable, and for most of the 600 miles between our position off Madagascar and the edge of the Agulhas, we had sets of up to two knots in nearly every direction in turn. Fortunately, the sky was sufficiently clear for navigational purposes and, although towards the end of the trip we were headed off so that we never did get anywhere near Cape St Lucia, we sighted the loom in the sky of the lights of Durban in the evening of our fourteenth day at sea. There were twenty-five ships lying at anchor off the port, rolling slowly in the swell. We threaded our way among them, picked up the leading lights, and then under power in a calm made our cautious way soon after midnight through the narrow, breakwater-flanked entrance channel, and when the great harbour ablaze with lights opened out before us, a police launch came and politely led us to an anchorage among the big ships, where we felt dwarfed.

In the morning, after the boarding officers had done with us, we moved to the yacht basin and were given a berth outside four other overseas yachts at the rickety, wooden pier hard by the Point Yacht Club, and soon had three newcomers lying outside us (Plate 6 A). Inevitably that caused some coming and going across us, but this was mostly quiet and barefooted, for our neighbours understood that the correct way to cross an inhabited yacht is over her foredeck, never through her cockpit. Our immediate neighbour was the fine steel ketch *Williwaw*, sailed single-handed by Willy de Roos (Plate 4 A), one of the small and exclusive band of seamen who have sailed their own ships round the Horn; we could not have asked for a more pleasant, modest, or seaman-like neighbour, and we were to be fortunate enough to see more of him at other ports of call.

There can be but few places where visiting yachts have the privilege of lying among the high-rise buildings in the heart of a great city like they do at Durban; but when the southerly busters blew we were anxious, not so much for ourselves as we were protected by our neighbours, but for fear we might damage some of the smaller yachts lying in the next tier only a few feet ahead. It was not possible to get effective lines to the pier, so with the strong winds on our quarter each yacht depended on the spring lines of all the yachts lying inside her, and on the cleats or bollards to which they were made fast. The gear of the innermost yacht lying against the pier was none too good, and as her crew, who were for the most part not on board, seemed disinterested, we took our own spare ropes and doubled up on hers.

Our first afternoon in port we had forty-five visitors; most were just curious: dreamers, would-be owners, builders and the like; but some came to offer us assistance, hospitality, or the use of their cars. It was difficult to sort them out and, as we had been keeping watches all the way from Mauritius, we were tired, and we feared that some people might have thought us rude or ungrateful. We never have found the transition from the silent, empty sea to the noise and bustle of the shore at all easy.

From Mauritius I had written to our friend David Jolly in England asking him to send a six-pin electric plug and socket to replace a defective one. I had forgotten that David was a radio ham, and was, therefore, surprised to be met at Durban by two helpful experts, mechanical and electrical engineers; one of them, also a radio ham, had been asked by David to come to our assistance. These kind people, Bill Gurr and Rex Brink, did all manner of things for us, such as making and fitting a watertight junction-box to replace the faulty plug, welding a break in the bed of the generating plant and fitting new flexible mounts to it, and rewinding a drill to run directly off our batteries; all these things and others were done as gifts to a transient yacht. Then one day Rex said:

'I'm out of a job. Surely there must be something else you need?'

So I told him we had always wanted a high-quality eight-track tape-player, but the difficulty was that they all ran either off the mains or a twelve-volt battery; our supply was twenty-four volts, and I was reluctant to drill through a steel bulkhead so as to tap half of the bank of batteries in the engine-room.

'That's easily fixed,' said Rex. 'How big do you want the speakers to be?'

He got two ten-inch (twenty-five-centimetre) speakers at wholesale prices, and a handful of electrical parts, and went home to his workshop; next day he returned with a complete stereo set-up, all tastefully sheathed in black-and-silver nylon, and fixed it with four screws in one of the recesses in the saloon; thereafter we were able to enjoy splendid music whenever we wished. We felt that Rex had got some pleasure putting his skill and knowledge to such good use for us, but we believed he enjoyed even more the socialities, which sometimes quite astonished him, for he was rarely aboard for more than a few minutes without seeing and hearing a stream of visitors from all walks of life come and go with questions and invitations, and people from the other yachts discussing future plans.

The yacht basin at Durban, like those in many other ports round the world, was desperately crowded, and it was becoming increasingly difficult for berths to be found for the overseas yachts which in November and December were arriving at a rate of one a day. In addition, there were twenty-five yachts which had been built in or near Durban waiting for berths before they could be launched, and another 150 in the Johannesburg area. Durban is said to be the eleventh busiest port in the world, and merchant ships were having to wait outside so long for berths to be vacated that freight rates had been much increased; it was, therefore, not surprising that the harbour authority declined to make available any more space for yachts. The irritating thing was, and this was not peculiar only to Durban, that, of the local yachts in the basin, not a quarter ever left their moorings; of course, there was nowhere much for them to cruise to, but I fancy that many were regarded purely as a means of escape should the South African political situation become desperate; some had even sunk at their moorings without their owners noticing.

Yacht clubs in many parts of the world are welcoming and generous to the visiting yacht from overseas. They usually offer all their facilities, which may include a fine clubhouse with baths or showers, a mooring or marina berth, and sometimes even the use of a hauling-out slip, for which perhaps a small charge is made. It might be thought that this is good business, and that the voyaging fraternity will spend money in the bars and dining rooms, but I think little profit can be expected from this source as the voyager is often on a shoestring, and if he does drink in a bar he probably limits himself to a beer; but over that one drink he may spend many hours talking with the people off the other yachts in port and, as there are now so many voyaging yachts, we overburden the club so that the members who pay, sometimes quite highly, for membership, are hardly able to get into the place to have a talk and a drink with their friends. While we were in Falmouth we found the Royal Cornwall Yacht Club packed with the people from a considerable fleet of French yachts, and it was said that to preserve the amenities for members, the club might have to close its doors to foreign invasions in future seasons. It is not only the cruising and voyaging people who overcrowd hospitable clubs, however, but the ocean-racers. For example, the Royal Suva Yacht Club in Fiji times the finish of the Auckland to Suva race, and provides a temporary marina of moored barges to accommodate the huge fleet, which may number as many as eighty yachts. If each yacht has an average crew of six, there is a total of 480 people, plus the wives and families who fly up to join the yachts on arrival, and the little club was never intended for such an influx of visitors, some of whom do not always behave too well. There must surely come a time when clubs will, in self-defence and for the benefit of their paying members, have to call a halt to their welcome, or limit it in some way like the Panama Canal Yacht Club has had to do. Meanwhile the Point Yacht Club at Durban, and the Royal Natal just across the road, still kept open house. They offered the visitors full use of their facilities, which included fine dining rooms, lounges with magazines, and spotless showers, all free of charge for one month. This was remarkable when one considered the large influx of visitors, especially at the time we were there. I believe most of us were deeply grateful and appreciative, but a few people who had decided to stay a long time and work ashore were indignant when, after the first month free, the clubs made a small charge, and the harbour dues were increased. We thought that was quite reasonable for, if those people lived ashore while they worked, they would have had to pay rent, and if they wished to have the facilities of a club they would have had to pay an entrance fee and a subscription; meanwhile, their floating homes occupied berths which should have been available to genuine transient yachts.

One evening, a meeting of all visitors was called by the port liaison officer. He quite reasonably suggested that those who had been lying in the basin longest should move to the Silt Canal to make room for the new arrivals, but instead of insisting that they did so, he left it to the visitors to decide among themselves who should move. As the Silt Canal was in a remote corner of the harbour, had no facilities, no public transport for three miles in either direction, and a great reputation for break-ins and theft, naturally enough nobody volunteered to go there. So more and yet more yachts piled up alongside one another, and each year the number there and elsewhere will increase, as more and yet more yachts pour off boatyard slips, factory production lines, and out of countless gardens and backyards. New Zealand is a small and not overcrowded country, but yachts proliferate there and, when we were last at Westhaven, which is but one of many harbours, a new yacht was being launched every day of the year; there was a waiting list of 700 and accommodation for only 300. In the United States yacht production is on a grand scale in keeping with the vast population and, as yachting in that country is considered an important industry, apparently genuine and successful attempts are made by municipalities and other bodies to accommodate the ever-swelling fleet. In Britain there would no doubt be more marinas were it not for the strong opposition of environmentalists and property owners who, like myself, would not wish to look out on a marina sprawled across the saltings at the bottom of my garden, any more than I would want a garage as my near neighbour. Individually, sailing vessels are (well, most of them) pleasing, characterful creations; *en masse* they lose their attraction. Similarly, a Rolls, a Porsche, a Land Rover or a Mini, alone in a gracious setting is a delight to the (my) eye, for it has character and purpose; but with a hundred other cars in a garage it is just that much more pollution.

After a month of hospitality at Durban we felt we might be outstaying our welcome but, before leaving, we gave a film show to 300 seated and 100 standing members of the Point Yacht Club in a small attempt to express our appreciation. This was in the same room where twenty years before we had given one of our earliest colour slide shows.

I have many times been asked if it is possible to earn the expenses of a voyage by writing and lecturing about it and, as Susan and I have been making our living in that manner for a long time, perhaps it would not be out of place to recount here some of our experiences in that field to show what is involved if one is to make a success of it. I must say at once that we were lucky in that at the time we completed our first world voyage such a feat was regarded as something quite remarkable, and that the interest in yacht cruising and voyaging has been steadily increasing throughout my writing career. But those readers who are not interested in this, and the small amount of trumpet-blowing and name-dropping that inevitably goes with it, are recommended to turn on to page 61 where the voyage narrative resumes.

* * *

My first book came out in 1939 at a time when publishers usually restricted the printing of yachting books to 500 or 1000 copies, and not very many of mine had been sold when the remainder were destroyed in an air-raid on London. After the war was over I worked with Adlard Coles, who then owned, edited and published *The Yachtsman*, the oldest-established yachting magazine in the world. One day Adlard showed me a letter he had received from the Little Ship Club in London, inviting him to give a talk in the club's winter lecture programme on a subject of his own choice. Although Adlard was a highly entertaining speaker if he could be persuaded to talk, he was shy; he said he did not want to give a talk and suggested that I give it instead. 'It would be excellent publicity for your books,' he added, and as I had just revised and republished my first book and written another which Adlard had published, I agreed to speak, and the Little Ship Club, which then had its headquarters in the Hudson's Bay Company's Beaver Hall on Garlick Hill, agreed to the change of speaker and accepted my chosen subject; this was single-handed cruising, something I believed I knew a lot about, for Susan and I had married in 1941, and prior to that most of my sailing had been done alone.

Led by Commander W B Luard, president of the club, I entered the hall and saw with surprise that the curved rows of seats rising in steep tiers to the back were full; a buzz of conversation filled the place, as I subsequently learned nearly always happens when boat people get together. I had never before made a speech or given a talk to an audience, and I had an awful feeling of panic at having to address this noisy, virile gathering, and a strong desire to run away. On the platform stood a lectern with a shaded light, and on this I placed my notes; having introduced me, the president sat in a chair close beside me also facing the audience, which now was hushed. As I have never been able to read ordinary print or writing without the help of a magnifying glass, and, as it embarrassed me to use such an aid in public, I had written my notes in enormous letters on foolscap sheets of paper; these I laid on the desk before me, and cleared my throat. Then out of the corner of my eye I noticed Luard looking with evident astonishment at my poster-size words, and, realizing that he would know what I was going to say before I said it, I was so upset that I crumpled the sheets into a ball, stuffed them in my pocket, switched off the light, and gave my one-and-a-half-hour talk from memory. I have never since tried to make use of notes. Fortunately for me, the members of the audience were kindly; my talk was well received, and when a great gust of laughter greeted some remark which until then I had not thought was particularly funny, I warmed towards them, gave them something more to laugh at, and began almost to enjoy myself.

It was on this occasion that I met Frank Eyre, a member of the club and later one of its vice-presidents. Frank worked for the Oxford University Press in London, and later was appointed manager of the Australian branch. He had read my two sailing books and suggested that I now write a big and as complete as possible one on cruising under sail which OUP would publish. This project occupied two years, and Susan and I took more than 1000 photographs from which to select the illustrations, each of which was coupled to the text in an intimate manner that had not been tried before. When we had finished correcting the proofs and doing the layouts for the plates, we made a voyage to the Azores and back in our twenty-three-foot (10·3-metre) gaff cutter, *Wanderer II.* It is amusing to consider that at that time such a trip was thought to be a very bold venture, yet today the island of Fayal alone is visited by about 150 yachts each year and when, in 1976, *Yachting Monthly* sponsored a single-handed race to San Miguel, there were more than fifty entries.

I had heard of people giving illustrated lectures and, although I was of the opinion that slides would be a hindrance rather than a help as well as a distraction for the audience, Susan persuaded me to move with the times. So in my darkroom I made a set of black and white slides on glass from the more suitable negatives with which to illustrate a talk about our Azores adventure. Audiences were enthusiastic and actually seemed to appreciate the rather poor slides, of which I believe there were no more than twenty-five.

In connection with *The Yachtsman* I had communicated a lot

with the Clyde photographer Ian Gilchrist, many of whose fine photographs we had used in the magazine. Shortly before we left on our first world voyage, Gilchrist, who for some time had been trying to persuade me to take up colour photography, kindly sent me a spool of Kodachrome together with some hints on its use. This we exposed largely on the tulips in our garden, and we were so impressed with the results that we bought a second camera body (we already had one Contax and a set of three lenses for it) and from that time on we photographed everything in colour—for the slide shows we hoped to give if we safely returned—as well as in black and white for illustrating the magazine stories I proposed to write as we went along. *Yachting World*, then edited by Group Captain E F (Teddy) Haylock (the Walrus), serialized the story with lots of our photographs and, when we reached South Africa and were asked to give talks there, we bought an Aldis projector. Until then we had regarded talks solely as a means of getting publicity for my books, so it was with pleasant surprise that we found on leaving Cape Town that we were ninety-five pounds richer, thanks to the generosity of the South Africans.

Today, so many long voyages are made in small craft that little is thought of them, but when *Wanderer III* returned to England in 1955 she was, I believe, only the fourth yacht from the British Isles to have circumnavigated, having been preceded by O'Brien's *Saoirse*, Muhlhauser's *Amaryllis*, and Tom and An Worth's *Beyond*. Telegrams came in batches as well as letters of congratulation; one from Sir William Haley, editor of *The Times*, who, throughout the voyage, had been publishing what he called my 'dispatches', said: 'They opened up quite a window out of a dark and gloomy world.' Nine yacht clubs made us honorary life members, and the *Daily Express*, in conjunction with Laurent Giles and William King, *Wanderer III*'s designers and builders, exhibited her at the London Boat Show. This was held in Olympia where a staging was rigged up so that people could file by and look on to the deck and into the brightly lighted cabin; it was said that 100 000 people took advantage of this. Sir Max Aitken thought up, had made, and presented to me the Yachtsman of the Year trophy, which has since been awarded annually, the recipient being chosen at a lunch party by guests comprising representatives of the press and the earlier holders of the trophy, but Max had to cut down a bit on the latter because they became too many as the years went by. Throughout the show Susan and I were in attendance to answer questions, and our replies were often drowned by the loud voices of animals in Bertram Mills's menagerie, which was berthed next door and separated from us only by a wooden bulkhead; visitors often remarked on the smell, which we hoped they did not attribute to us. I supposed that somewhere around were copies of my books, though I did not see them, and, of course, there had not been time to write and publish a book about the voyage we had recently completed.

The BBC invited us to make a number of broadcasts, and the most exciting one for us was a television appearance in a popular half-hour programme called *In Town Tonight*. It went on the air 'live' on Saturday evenings, and the one we were to be in was scheduled for Christmas Eve. This raised a problem, for we lived on the Isle of Wight and, although we could catch a late train to Brockenhurst and arrange a taxi on to Lymington, the last ferry would long since have departed, and there would be no more until after the Christmas holiday. But our friend Harold Hayles had promised to collect us at Lymington by launch, which he did, and as we bashed our wet way across the Solent late that night with the engine racing as the launch dipped her bows in the steep little sea, Harold turned to us and shouted above the general din: 'You two have just sailed round the world, and I'm cox'n of Yarmouth lifeboat. It'll be a proper charlie if we sink out here tonight.'

Invitations to give lectures, speak at dinners, open this and that and attend all sorts of functions came pouring in, and we agreed then, and have kept to it since, that no matter how small the audience might be or insignificant the event, we would never decline, for one thing might lead to another. But all that we did then was amateurish, for we were beginners and did not know much about gaining publicity for books. However, each time we gave a show—we preferred to use that term rather than the word 'lecture', which sounded too serious and dull—we tried to improve on the last one and, instead of the twenty-five black and white slides of the past we now showed in a space of one-and-a-half hours about 300, all in colour. Susan worked the projector while I stood facing the audience beside the screen, at which it was my boast I never glanced, for having selected, mounted and arranged the slides I knew the sequence by heart, and I had plenty of opportunity to see them, for, before every show, we went through them in their boxes to make sure that each was upside down ready to be slipped into the projector and, depending on the audience, sometimes to make deletions or changes. Communication between us was a difficulty to begin with. A tap on the floor with a stick worked well enough in small places until we gave a show in a deeply carpeted room where it made no sound; 'next please' or a buzzer was too distracting for the audience, and so was a flash from a torch. Finally, I made a signalling device consisting of a small wooden box in which was housed a torch battery and a bulb painted with red nail varnish; a thin flex connected this to a bell-push in my hand. When I pressed the push the little red light glowed beside the projector on Susan's table, and this was so inconspicuous and successful that many people were mystified by the apparent telepathy between us.

If the hall was not too large we preferred to use our own projector, so wherever we went, and we went everywhere by rail because we had no car, we carried with us a suitcase of suitable clothes, the projector with its two lenses, a canvas bag holding in boxes our 300 glass-mounted slides, and a case containing a wide selection of plugs and bulbs, for we had learned the hard way that types of electric fittings and current varied. In some parts of London the current was direct instead of alternating, and was thus capable of damaging the fan-motor in the projector. The first time we met this hazard was at the Cruising Association's headquarters in Baker Street and, while the audience waited, a lead had to be run out of a window and down to the nearby underground station to get the necessary alternating current.

The first winter after our return we gave only twenty-five shows to a total of 7000 people, but there were some other events, such as a ball at the Savoy (tails and decorations) to collect a trophy presented by the Royal Corinthian Yacht Club, and the terrifying ordeal of having to open the exhibition of the Royal Society of Marine Artists at Guildhall. A very exalted person had been booked to do that job but had to cancel because of state affairs, and I was ordered by Charles Pears, the president, to take his place. I knew nothing about art, but fortunately I did know the marine artist David Cobb and, when I told him of the fix I was in, he kindly suggested some things for me to say. Then, and this was

---

3 *Top* Some of our bauxite-mining guests at Gove. *Bottom* Indian Ocean lookout; the flash from the camera has almost eclipsed the gleam from the big riding-light lashed to the boom-gallows.

another tails affair (Moss Bros. were doing well out of me), we attended the annual dinner of the Royal Cruising Club, of which we are both members, to receive the Blue Water Medal presented to us jointly by the Cruising Club of America; Hank du Pont, commodore of that club, had flown over from America to hand it to us. The dinner was in Middle Temple Hall, where we sat at long refectory tables surrounded by portraits and coats-of-arms of benchers and, as the lovely old hall was floodlit, we within could enjoy the beauty of the stained-glass windows.

The following year my account of our circumnavigation was published, and again we got into our swing, giving shows to audiences of about 20 000. For most of these, except a few we gave for charity, we received between five and twenty guineas, but much of this went on travelling and hotel expenses. To reduce the former it was clear that we needed to consolidate and give as many shows as possible in one area, or at least in some sort of geographical order. So we went to see Miss Whalley who, from a small and cheerless office at the back of Foyle's bookshop in the Charing Cross Road, ran a lecture agency. We explained to her what we had been doing and asked if she thought by now we might have saturated the market.

'Not at all,' was her reply. 'If you care to put yourselves in my hands I think I can organize for you more engagements than perhaps you want.'

And that in her remarkably efficient way she proceeded to do. Unknown to us there were throughout the land a great many lecture societies, libraries, schools, ladies' luncheon clubs, literary and philosophical societies, army, navy and civil colleges, teachers' and parents' associations, and even prisons, all apparently crying out for someone to go along and talk to them. There was yet no colour television, and we found, particularly in industrial areas, that people were prepared to turn out in their hundreds, even on a black January night with driving sleet, just to listen to me talk and to look at the colour pictures Susan threw on the screen, and sometimes before or after to treat us as a rather special couple. We did not mind the dinner or supper party after

---

4 *A Top left* Willy de Roos, one of the exclusive band of seamen who have sailed their own ships round Cape Horn. *B Top right* Susan takes an amplitude. *C Bottom left* The Aries vane gear at work. *D Bottom right* Crocodiles galore, but nobody can find any affection for them.

the show, but when this was held before the show some problems arose. At ladies' luncheon clubs we ate first; this usually meant that I sat beside the chairman, who for want of something closer to us both asked many questions about the voyage, where we went, what we did in bad weather, which country we liked most —all these and others were questions with which I would be dealing shortly, and in an increasingly hoarse voice. There were also the coffee cups which were still being rattled long after we had started to perform. When we were asked to dine before an evening show the meal was in a hotel or someone's home, with enjoyable conversation, and plenty of wine which I had to sample sparingly. Often these over-ran the set time and, although in advance we had asked for our simple needs by letter, a stable table of a certain minimum size at a set distance from the screen, and so on, when rather late we arrived at the hall to find the audience already seated and growing impatient at the delay for which they thought we were to blame, we sometimes found that the table was too small or had been incorrectly placed; so we had to change it or move it towards or away from the screen, with a resulting disturbance to those members of the audience who had already positioned themselves in the best seats. There were also problems with screens and public address systems. Sometimes the screen was too small or had dirty marks on it or, as in the Pump Room at Bath, was made of such thin material that most of the projected picture vanished through it; in one place there was no screen, but we were assured it would be fine if we projected on to a wall, and so it might have been had the wall been white, but it was green. Loudspeakers often had to be moved and their leads and the position of the microphone rearranged. I found that moving furniture and equipment and arguing with people were not the best preparations for a show—for that one needs to feel cool and clean and on the best of terms with everyone.

The third winter after our return we were still doing the rounds, and on one tour gave sixteen shows in ten days, usually each in a different town. But no matter how many we gave each was a fresh experience, each audience had a different character, and every time I mounted the platform and looked at the indistinct sea of faces, I had a hollow feeling in my inside which even the best of meals could not allay. It was a bit like making a landfall, something which, no matter how often one has done it, still provides in anticipation a feeling of inadequacy mixed with tingling excitement. And again, like making a landfall, there were sometimes surprises and even shocks in store: one evening Susan was taken ill with gastric 'flu near the end of a show; in the dark I could not see what the disturbance was about, nor could I understand why the final few slides came on so slowly, until as the lights went up I saw she had handed over to another projectionist. One afternoon while trying out the public address system in a darkened theatre at Torquay, I mounted a flight of twelve blind steps in front of the stage, stepped off the top and fell heavily to the floor. There was the occasion when a big thunderstorm put out the lights of the town, including, of course, that in our projector, and in absolute darkness violently stabbed now and then by a flash of lightning, I gave the bulk of the talk without slides; then when at last the lights came on the audience insisted that I go back to the beginning and do it all over again. I remember, too, an evening when H.M.S. *Caroline* in Belfast Harbour started to roll while we were giving a show on board, and I had to explain to the uneasy audience that this always happened when the night ferry to Heysham left at high speed.

To keep our expenses down we put up at the cheaper hotels, many of which were warm, friendly, and clean, but for future reference we kept a list of the other sort, with brief remarks: 'frosty reception; room next to heads which flush at regular intervals all night; breakfast served late and cold by cold and late waitress.' But there were wonderful breaks in the routine, when people connected with the club or society for which we were to perform invited us to spend nights in luxurious comfort in their homes. One of these was situated on an island in the middle of Derwentwater, so we came and went by boat; another was a manor house in Cheshire where we dined by candlelight as the electrics had fused, and we did not see the lovely old house until the morning. A night was spent in 'Wylie Warren', the remarkable red, pinnacled home of the famous marine artist, Harold Wylie, standing so close to the water's edge at the entrance to Portsmouth Harbour that we could, as it were, have tossed a biscuit upon the deck of a passing ship. Other nights were spent as guests of the commanding officer at Sandhurst and at Dartmouth, and in many public schools, including Charterhouse where Susan was born, Bromsgrove where I was educated, and Benenden, which produced the most appreciative feminine audience we had ever had.

Each audience, as I have said, differed from all others, and that was the main fascination of our job. We had been for a week visiting remote places in Scotland where we found some of our audiences a little dour. After one show somebody who had asked me a question said, rather with awe: 'I see you are in Caird Hall tomorrow.' That meant little to me for, although I knew we were due to appear in Dundee next evening I had not yet taken in where we were to perform, and I had not heard of Caird Hall. On arrival in Dundee we got a room at a hotel in which to rest and change, and then went to have a look at the hall. It was huge, and we could not believe that enough Scots would come out of their homes that chilly evening to fill more than a quarter of it. But when we returned in the evening we found our names in lights above the entrance, and the hall packed—I believe it held 2000. We started and, as the first slide came on the screen, there was much clapping, so with the second, and the third . . . This began to worry me, for I could not continue until the applause had died down, and we had our usual 300 slides to get through, and after that needed to catch the *Aberdonian*, the night express for London, to keep another engagement. However, by hurrying, and by getting Susan to run some slides in very quick succession, I got over to the audience the idea that they were not meant to clap until the end, and then the show went normally. So we caught the train, slept indifferently on it, gave a midday show near London, and reached Dover College in time for an evening performance. A boy, probably the senior monitor, had been told to propose a vote of thanks, which always seemed ridiculous to us when we were being paid to do a job. He got up and said:

'I am a cricketer. I have listened to Mr Hiscock talking for more than an hour about his voyage round the world, and my wish is to remain a cricketer.'

So up and down the country we went, and I see from an old British Rail map on which I had traced our routes that on our tours we travelled on every main line in the country and on lots of branch lines, too, for in those days one could go almost everywhere by rail. I enjoyed this, particularly thundering in some named express through big towns where level-crossing gates held back impatient road traffic, gliding with an effortless click-click of wheels across the countryside, through cuttings and tunnels and over the bridges and embankments, for it gave me a sense of urgent importance as I sat in my corner wondering what kind of an audience we would have that night and what the practical problems would be. But, of course, that was with a great steam locomotive hauling; my enthusiasm for rail travel waned with the coming of the diesel locomotive, and with headless electric centipedes, cleaner and quieter though they are, the thrill expired.

As the next Olympic Games were to be held in Australia, a country we had visited and for which we had formed a high regard and affection, we offered to give a show so that the Royal Yachting Association might raise a little money to help with the organization of the British yachting entry, for sponsorship of yachting was almost unheard of then. We did not suppose that much would come of this, for racing and cruising people have little in common but, in the capable hands of Francis Usborne, secretary of the RYA, it turned into a rather grand occasion, for H.R.H. the Duke of Edinburgh graciously consented to come along and introduce us and make the 'thank-you' speech. Francis received directives from the Palace, we received directives from Francis, and the Dean of Westminster kindly allowed us the use of Church House.

At a small cocktail party before the show we were presented to Prince Philip, and we were both with him on the platform during his introduction. He then made his way to his seat, from where I could hear laughs and chuckles from time to time, while Susan hurried up two flights of stairs, pulling off her long white gloves as she went, to reach the projector in the balcony just as I finished my preliminary remarks and was ready for the first slide.

Nigel Warington Smyth, who was then president of the RYA, gave a dinner party for Prince Philip at the Bath Club immediately after the show, and I was fortunate enough to be one of the guests. As this was a stag party Susan was not invited, so she went home with Francis and Bridget Usborne with whom we were staying and when, late that night, I joined them in their cosy Chelsea home, I was so puffed up with my own importance as to be almost insufferable; but that was knocked out of me the following evening when we were booked to give a show at Lewisham. Instead of, as on the previous evening, being whisked up Whitehall and across Horseguards in a car to which police were giving priority, we travelled with our usual impedimenta by suburban train, failed to get a taxi at the station and had to walk, arriving only just in time. The chairman, unlike the previous evening's, had not done his homework properly. Reading from a scrap of paper in his hand he said:

'My task this evening, ladies and gents, is to introduce Mr and Mrs Itchcox. They sailed round the world in an open boat and have come here tonight to tell us why.'

We were in the middle of yet another lecture season (our fourth) and found ourselves at Leeds. The weather was thick and the sky appeared to be raining soot as we came out of our cheerless hotel to stretch our legs after the journey from Bradford. In the murk we chanced upon a cinema, an oasis of light with gay posters proclaiming that *South Pacific* was showing within. Our intended walk forgotten, we bought tickets and much enjoyed the film, of which the Bali Ha'i scenes appeared to have been shot in Moorea, an island we had visited.

'Why don't we make a colour movie like that on our next voyage?' asked Susan as we groped our way back to the hotel. 'We could put sound on it; then if anyone asked us to show it, you would not have such a talking marathon to endure. Besides,' she added thoughtfully, 'we might even get it accepted for television.'

The idea certainly had its attractions; it would be a fun thing to do, and I was beginning to have had enough of slide shows.

'But we haven't got a movie camera and we don't know how to make a film.'

'Well, let's buy a camera and learn.'

And so it was that when we set out that year to attempt a second circumnavigation by a different route, we carried with us a recently bought second-hand cinecamera and a stock of expensive sixteen-millimetre Kodachrome film. As each 100-foot (thirty-metre) spool was exposed we sent it back to England for processing, and it then went to our friends Peter and Susan Guinness who were experienced and skilful film-makers. They ran our films through their projector and wrote to tell us what we were doing wrong and to make valuable suggestions, but we did not see any of the one-and-a-half miles of film we had exposed until we returned to the Isle of Wight at the conclusion of our three-year voyage. Much was then repetition; again we were invited to give illustrated talks, again we did some broadcasting, and once more little *Wanderer* was on exhibition at the London Boat Show, this time afloat in the pool at Earl's Court.

But our immediate priority was to edit the film and put sound on it—my voice and some tape recordings we had made in the South Pacific—a job which took us about four months. We then showed the finished film to the BBC; they made a black and white copy, shortened it a little, and got me in for two exhausting days at Shepherd's Bush to make a new commentary for it; they then split it into two half-hour programmes and used them in the *Adventure* series which, produced by Brian Branstone, was televised on Friday evenings. The first one went on the air while *Wanderer* was on exhibition at Earl's Court and was said by BBC audience research to have been viewed by twelve million people, and the second half followed a week later. We were deluged with letters all of which (except for a poison-pen one) we answered. Many were kind and of a congratulatory nature, others sought information:

'After seeing your film my wife and I have decided to sail round the world. Please tell us where to get a suitable boat, which way to go to avoid bad weather, and let us know what it will cost.'

If only we could have sold those people copies of my latest text-book, a treatise on voyaging under sail, we would have done very well. But as it was we did not do too badly, for the BBC used the film a second time, and it was televised in most English-speaking countries throughout the world, and each time it was used we were paid a royalty; also, of course, it helped to publicize my books. We showed our version of the film in colour in many places in England, Ireland and Holland, and at my publisher's suggestion and expense we flew with it to Canada and showed it there.

Though the trifle of fame that came our way through books, talks and films was at times pleasing, it was often a disturbance, but we derived great pleasure from being able, in a simple way, to provide a little excitement and entertainment for others who in a more humdrum way of life were not so fortunate as ourselves.

But I must not risk boring you with further accounts of these affairs which have little to do with this voyage, but at least what I have written here may serve to give some idea of what was involved in our way of making a living, though of course it does not answer the question, 'Can I make a living that way?' To give financial details would be worthless because of inflation, but I would say that today with more and more long voyages being made in small craft, publishers may not be quite so ready as they were to publish accounts of such voyages, though it has to be remembered, when thinking of the market, that sailing people tend to buy books to take along with them rather than borrow from a library, as people are more likely to do if their interest lies in, say, gardening or bee-keeping. An account of a voyage may have only a short life before being eclipsed by a new voyage story and, although I am fortunate in that my publisher has so far kept all my books in print, the most successful ones, which have continued to sell in considerable numbers year after year, were not my accounts of the voyages that Susan and I had made, but my two text-books. There are many more yachting magazines being published now than there were when we made our first voyage; but again there are more people writing for them, and unless an arrangement can be made with an editor for publishing a regular series of articles, I think that earnings from this source should not be relied upon. I believe that the stories I wrote regularly as we went along may have appealed to editors because they were generously illustrated with our own black and white photographs, which we developed and enlarged on board (see page 187).

Perhaps it might, therefore, be better to employ some other skill at which one is already adept, or for which one has been trained. Doctors and dentists need have no difficulty in earning as they go; for example, the Boots family in *Spencerian* from California spent two years in New Zealand while Don worked in a hospital and the three boys went to school, and then sailed on their way. Bill Howell, to whom we sold our *Wanderer II*, took with him his dental tools, and it was said there were some toothless islands along his route from England to Hawaii, for Bill was pulling teeth at a dollar a time or three teeth for two dollars, and few people can resist a bargain. Schoolteachers, shipwrights, and carpenters also seem to fall on their feet as do diesel and electrical engineers, but as many countries insist on work permits, which are not always easy to obtain, most of the artisans we met confined their activities to working on other yachts, or perhaps building houses for people who were prepared to keep quiet about their labour force. There must be many ways of earning as you go, and one of the more unusual was practised by a Canadian couple in the yacht *Silent Echo*; they told Susan that they earned 400 dollars a month collecting and selling shells, and when we met them in Antigua they were searching for a particular shell which it was said had come from Africa on the bottoms of slavers, and for which there was suddenly a market.

PART II

DURBAN TO ENGLAND

WITH SOME THOUGHTS ON

Shape of keels—Rhodesia—Ground tackle—Navigation—Fresh water and catchments—Reefing—The barograph—Charging batteries—Slips—Marinas—Showers—The modern yacht—Tapping halyards—Building materials

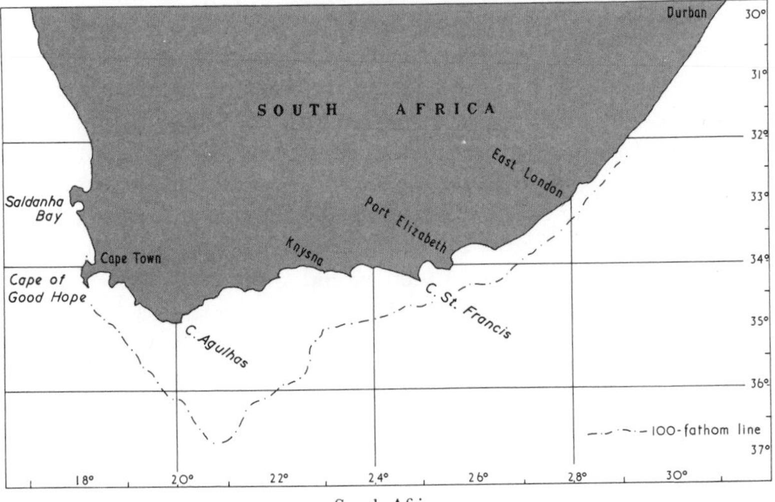

South Africa

WITH the exception of Knysna, there is no good natural harbour along the 900-mile stretch of coast between Durban and Cape Town. We hoped to put in at Knysna and wait there until well on in January, when the percentage of gales off Cape Agulhas should drop, but there was an element of chance about this, for, in some conditions of wind and sea, the entrance to Knysna is impassable. Before we left Durban, however, we were visited by Leighton Hulett, a sailing man; he owned, and was developing for housing, a large area of land near Cape St Francis, which lies about half-way between Durban and Cape Town, and was digging and dredging a network of canals so that most of the plots would have a water frontage, and the owners of them, that desirable thing, a boat at the bottom of the garden; the canals were connected to the Kromme River, which flows into St Francis Bay. Leighton invited us to put in there and lie as his guests for as long as we wished at the tiny marina he had built among the sandhills. A study of volume III of *Africa Pilot* had convinced me that there was no river on the south coast that we could enter, for all have bars, and in the summer most are closed, and water from the rivers flows under the sand or shingle to reach the sea, and of the Kromme River the *Pilot* said: '. . . is not navigable, and has a bar over which there is a depth of less than one foot and is impassable for boats; shoal depths extend about three-quarters of a mile offshore near the mouth.'

Leighton, however, assured us that we could enter with our seven-foot (2·1-metre) draught provided we did so at the top of high-water spring tides. This idea shocked us, for Susan and I belong to what we call 'the low-water club', by which we mean that we prefer to attempt a tricky piece of pilotage just after low tide and with the flood making, so that we can be sure of getting off easily if we should run aground. But Leighton was persuasive; he said there would be sufficient depth over the bar, and that either he or a competent friend would pilot us in, also that he would have a launch standing by in case we needed a little help. So we decided at least to go and have a look at it provided the wind was off the land when we got there; the bay is open from north through east to south-east.

I have mentioned earlier that there are certain stages on a voyage to which one looks forward with apprehension, and one that we regarded as the most hazardous now lay ahead, for the South African coast is notorious for its sudden changes of weather, the frequency and violence of its gales, the steepness of the sea found along the continental shelf, and the effect on it of the Agulhas Current, which may at times attain a rate of up to five knots. Also, the passage would be made in one of the busiest shipping lanes in the world.

The Department of Oceanography at the University of Cape Town had made a study of the freak seas which occur in the area, notably along the 100-fathom line between East London and Port Elizabeth. These seas, which have long been regarded as sailors' exaggerations, can reach a height of fifty to sixty feet (fifteen to eighteen metres); many ships have been sunk, and others, including giant tankers which it is said are capable of maintaining full speed with seas running twenty-five feet (nearly eight metres) high, have been damaged, and naturally enough some yachts have been capsized. It seems that these freak seas can build up or subside within minutes, and that the dangerous time is after a fresh north-east wind has been blowing and one of the sudden changes of wind direction, which is commonplace here and can occur in a few hours, happens, and a gale blows from south-west. The seas raised by the new wind meet the weather-running Agulhas Current—a sort of wind against tide situation—and immediately grow steep and become superimposed on the Cape rollers, the long ocean swell which usually runs from south-west. The current, which is said to reach its maximum velocity of five knots just outside the 100-fathom line, contributes to the drama, and, by tugging at the foot of a superimposed sea, may create an abnormally high and steep wall of water. Of ten ships sunk in the area eight were two to three miles outside the continental shelf in the above-mentioned weather pattern. I have an idea that all this has for a long time been known to masters of the Union Castle ships, which for many years have plied their trade along this coast, for, so far as I know, none of the fleet ever suffered sea damage there. While we were at Durban, *Notices to Mariners* mentioned the likelihood of freak seas occurring twenty miles offshore between the longitudes of East London and Richard's Bay, that is, north-east of the above-mentioned area, where recently two ships had been damaged and a third lost.

Durban's narrow entrance channel had one-way traffic control, and we were held up inside for half-an-hour while a tanker entered. Outside, there was hardly any wind and, as we were anxious to get on our way before bad weather pounced upon us, we motored along at our economical cruising speed of five knots but, with the help of the current, we made good seven knots over the ground. To reduce the risk of collision between ships in those busy waters separation zones had been established, but as so many ships ignored them they proved to be more a danger than a safety factor and were soon abolished. We found the general trend was for ships bound east and north to keep inshore, where perhaps they might benefit from the counter-current which sometimes runs there, and those bound south and west to keep further offshore where they gained the benefit of the main current; but unfortunately, giant tankers of the sort that cannot quickly alter course could be found anywhere going in either direction. The shipping kept us on our toes, and often both of us had to be on deck together to identify their courses and sometimes to take avoiding action; but for the most part the ships behaved well, holding steady courses or giving way in good time.

Not until the second day out was there sufficient wind to make it worthwhile to switch off the engine and carry on under sail, and, on the third day, the glass began to fall and the wind, at east, to freshen. That night, when we were well past East London, the ore-loading port off which the danger area of freak seas is said to start, we hove-to on the offshore tack, not because of stress of weather but because we did not want the current to sweep us past our destination; also we might then work out of the shipping lane and get some rest. In the night, a row of brilliant and apparently stationary white lights inshore mystified us; we thought they might be on an oil-rig, but no such thing was shown on the chart or mentioned in the sailing directions, and we concluded the lights might have belonged to a depot ship servicing a fishing fleet.

By dawn our position was uncertain; there was no sight of land, and for the past few hours we had seen no ships, so we let-draw and headed north-west for where we hoped Cape St Francis lay. An early shot of the bleary sun placed us forty miles west of where I thought we were; I did not believe this, but another sight taken an hour later gave a similar result. Not until noon did I get a fix by crossing a noon latitude with a bearing of Cape St Francis's radio beacon by putting the ship's head on it, for in a steel vessel, the hand-held direction-finding aerial and compass combined, such as we had brought with us from our last wooden yacht, cannot be used for taking radio bearings in any other way; this is not only because of the magnetic effect on the compass of the ferrous metal, but because of the closed-loop effect on the aerial. The fix placed us thirty-six miles *south-west* of St Francis instead of south-east of that headland, showing that the current, for which I had been allowing a rate of two knots, had been running at something over four knots.

We altered course accordingly, but now, after so much watch-keeping, navigating and worrying, we had grown tired, almost dangerously so; there was to be no rest for either of us yet, however. All afternoon, the barometer fell steeply while the wind which, since the forenoon, had shifted right round from east through south to west continued to freshen, and we had to take in the mizzen and reef the main, and still we roared along at eight knots. The sun shone, but indistinctly, and visibility became poor. We had a worrying encounter with a fishing vessel, which repeatedly changed her course and finally came uncomfortably close presumably to edge us away from a clutch of plastic buoys she had dropped, each joined to the next with a floating orange line.

By mid-afternoon we were once more in the shipping lane and crossing it obliquely. The first we saw of each ship was a faint gleam in the sky where the light caught her white-painted superstructure, and, unless she had conspicuous masts, and some had not, minutes which could be vital for our safety passed before we could be sure of her heading, and it was too rough to take bearings. Then, with breathtaking speed, the great hull appeared, faint, grey and menacing as the ship swept past to vanish in the haze, the whole business from first sighting taking seven minutes or less; and there were ships large and small going in both directions. By now we had a full westerly gale on our hands, and we should have made a further reduction of sail as that would have enabled us to alter course more easily when we had to, but only by pressing on at our utmost speed was there a chance that we might be able to reach an anchorage before dark, and in our tired state the thought of another night out there among the ships scared us.

Not until 5 p.m. did we sight a faint smudge of land ahead, and in time identified the ethereal, all-white tower of the lighthouse standing on surf-girt, rocky Cape St Francis—how much easier it might have been to see in those conditions had it been painted with a red or black band. There was no counter-current to help us, and the west-going Agulhas stream was strong against us right up to the shore, from which that day a child was swept to his death by the sea, and, in spite of our high speed, we seemed to crawl only slowly over the ground. With some caution because of the motion, I made my way forward and lifted the anchor off its chocks on the foredeck and made it ready to let go, and I took in the jib before we came on the wind. It was a wonderful relief to double the cape and come at last into the comparatively smooth water in its lee but, as we beat into the bay, spray from the bow-wave drove aft to hit the helmsman cruelly, and one could not look to windward with eyes unshielded. By sunset we had reached a depth of three fathoms, and there, with great care because of the strains involved in such wild weather, we let the anchor go, and link by cautious link veered thirty fathoms of cable.

We lay steadily and well in the bay, where there was not a lot of swell, with the low, rocky finger of the cape to port, and a long, smooth beach backed by sandhills—from among which peeped the thatched roofs of some houses and a larger building which proved to be an hotel—stretching across our bows and curving away to starboard to vanish in the haze. The wind continued to savage the rigging with undiminished fury, and the national news on the radio reported that near-by Port Elizabeth was closed and was experiencing a gale of 106 kilometres per hour, which according to my reckoning is fifty-eight knots, or sixty-six miles an hour.

The gale subsided in the night, and we slept well. We had been seen from the shore, and in the forenoon at high water they came for us: a scarlet rescue launch (equivalent to the R.N.L.I. inshore boats) manned by three young men in scarlet wet suits, and the twin-screw launch *Spray* to act as tug if needed. Leighton Hulett was away, but Ken Jones, a retired airline pilot and local resident who knew the river well, boarded us to act as our pilot; he and the skippers of the launches could communicate by walkie-talkie radios. We weighed and started on a traumatic experience.

The entrance to the Kromme River was not easily made out from seaward, for the whole shore was fringed with breakers, the bay being open to the Indian Ocean; and, after crossing an outer bar, we had to turn to port behind a spit running parallel to the shore and on this there were also breakers (Plate 5 A). Ken was confident, but Susan and I were more anxious than perhaps we had ever been in our sailing lives, and when we struck the hard sandbar with a dreadful, tooth-jarring thud, I realized what a fool I had been ever to have allowed myself to be persuaded to enter such a dangerous trap. There was no possibility of turning back now, however, and the swell lifted us on and over; but twice more we struck with shuddering thuds before reaching slightly deeper water within the spit. Soon we left the river and, turning sharply to port, entered the narrow dredged channel which wound its way for half a mile to the marina. On its eastern side, the channel was flanked by a thin ridge of steep sandhills hiding it from the ocean, and on the west by a wide sandbank on which a party of flamingoes waded. We had gone but a short way up this channel when we came to a complete stop on a shoal, and from this our engine, even with assistance from *Spray* and the rescue launch, failed to shift us (Plate 5 B). It was still high water, and it was now abundantly clear that since it had been dredged the channel had silted up at that spot. The launches could do no more, so they left us, and that evening at low water we lay over at forty-five degrees, and life on board came to a standstill. Neither heads, sinks, cooker nor refrigerator could be used, and movement below was almost impossible. Susan and I, head to tail like sardines in a tin, shared the lee berth, or rather its backrest, and listened to music on our new tape-player; Tchaikovsky, Paganini, and Rachmaninov helped to ease the tension and drown the roar of surf on the beach just behind the sandhills.

Leighton returned that night, and in the morning came by Land Rover to take us to his lovely home, which, like all the others in the settlement known as Sea Vista, was whitewashed and thatched, to meet his wife Ann and enjoy a bath and a civilized breakfast. Because of our discomfort on board, he offered us accommodation and meals as his guests in the attractive hotel, which Ann had largely designed, until such time as *Wanderer* could be got to the marina; but we felt unable to accept his generous offer, because we wished to stand by our ship and make certain that she came to no harm each time she sewed on the falling tide.

Originally, we had found she was too tender, burying her lee deck in anything of a breeze from forward of the beam, so we gave her two extra tons of ballast. As her existing ballast of lead had been poured into all the available spaces, the only way of adding more was to have it welded to the underside of the keel, and as the yard could obtain steel plate only five inches (thirteen centimetres) thick, to get the weight amidships where we needed it, the plate had to be a bit wider than the original keel; so now we were landed with a keel which was, at its widest, twenty-eight inches (seventy-one centimetres) across and quite flat. In some ways I thought this might be an advantage, for I remembered once seeing the yacht *Patronita* dried out for a scrub on the Jolly Sailor hard at Bursledon. She had a wide, flat keel, and I noticed that daylight was showing under the feet of both her legs, and that her owner walking about on deck did not upset the balance. So a yacht with such a keel ought to be easy to slip; but then I remembered something else. Kindly Maud Weeding, who used to take impecunious youngsters like myself away cruising, was a fine, big woman probably weighing about fourteen stone. Her father, with whom she sailed in a pretty little Linton Hope cutter called *Polestar*, was even bigger—one could tell from a distance if they were both at one end or at opposite ends of *Polestar* by that yacht's trim. One day while they were sailing in the Solent on a falling tide they ran aground on the Brambles Bank, that patch of drying sand off Cowes on which the late Uffa Fox used to organize a cricket match around low water equinoctial spring tides. The Weedings were great card players, and when their attempt to kedge-off failed, they went below and became engrossed playing patience. Time passed quickly until Maud suddenly realized that the yacht had not heeled over, and on going into the cockpit was shocked to see that, although the tide had fallen, *Polestar*, with no other support, was balancing on her wide, flat-bottomed keel with the hard sand drying all round her. Maud crept below and neither she nor her father dared to move, hardly even to shuffle the cards, until the tide eventually rose to float them.

A flat-bottom keel may make hauling out easier and be kinder on the cradle, but for stranding, intentionally or otherwise, such a keel may pose a risk. While on a cruise round New Zealand's South Island, our rudder became a little stiff and, to investigate the cause, we decided to dry out at Nelson, which had a convenient range of tide. We selected a berth alongside a wharf where, the locals assured us, the sand bottom was quite flat. Of course, we took the customary lines to the wharf in case of accidents, but in spite of them, *Wanderer* persisted in leaning out from the wharf as the tide fell. In something of a panic we put out more lines, thirteen in all, and set them up as taut as possible; but she continued to list outwards until, mercifully, she stopped at an angle of about five degrees. At low water, of course, we found that the sand was not flat but sloped away from the wharf at five degrees.

I now believe, though I have no proof, that any vessel with her ballast low down and a wide, flat keel will insist on sitting squarely on that keel no matter what efforts are made to restrain her and keep her upright. In my view this could create a dangerous situation should she stand on an athwartships-sloping bottom when the tide is dropping. In any future yacht I would certainly have the bottom of the keel rounded or vee-shaped so that, in the above situation, the yacht would heel over gently whichever way I wanted her to as the tide fell, so that she would settle gently on her bilge instead of, as I suppose might happen—

and it was this that worried us in the Kromme River—remaining upright for a time and then falling over suddenly. Incidentally, an important merit of the rounded or vee-shaped keel is that nearly all of it can be scrubbed and painted. This is not possible with a flat keel, not even when the yacht is hauled out in a yard, for large areas of the flat part resting on the bearers of the cradle will be inaccessible. Another disadvantage of a wide, flat keel is this: if a yacht with a normal keel has run aground and cannot be got off in any other way, her draught may be reduced by heeling her, perhaps by setting up a halyard to an anchor laid out on the beam; but with a wide, flat keel such an action is scarcely possible, and even if it were it would, to start with, increase the draught instead of reducing it.

Leighton arranged for a small suction-dredger to be put to work just ahead of us to deepen the channel (Plate 5 C), and a day or two later further attempts were made in a vicious south-west gale with heavy rain to move us upstream. But we stuck again almost at once, and two tractors were then summoned by radio. They came lumbering over the submerged sandbank up to their axles in water to take a line from each bow, but the only result was a parted two-and-a-half-inch (six-and-a-quarter-centimetre) nylon rope, which went at the bowline on the tractor, proof that just like the text-books say, a bowline does weaken a rope; the parted rope acted like a piece of shock-cord under tension, and its end came flying back to hit our topside with a loud report, and on its way narrowly missed the head of the second tractor driver. We found afterwards that so great had been the strain that three strands of part of that rope had fused together.

At last it became obvious to all concerned that without wheels or skids you cannot drag a twenty-two-ton ship up over a hill. For one more day the dredger worked round us in an attempt to make a hole in which we might remain more nearly upright at low water; but then with Christmas drawing near the men who worked the dredger departed with their friends for the Transkei, and we were left to stand on our keel or heel over at low tide as *Wanderer* felt inclined.

The weather was rugged, with hard winds blowing alternately from the east—when they brought a blinding storm of fine white sand from off the dunes—or from the west—when they brought almost as much sand, but it was mixed with lime which was used for consolidating the unsealed roads; from either direction the sand was well laced with spray. Twice we had gales in excess of sixty knots, and one dreadful day a sou'wester blew at a horrifying eighty knots, which is well up the hurricane scale. Our brightwork and enamel soon looked as though it had been rubbed down with coarse glasspaper, and the flying sand penetrated everywhere, seizing up the blocks and winches, plastering the masts, to which it stuck like cement, and getting below deck so that the hinges of all the doors grated harshly when the lockers were opened or closed.

After each of the gales, and before washing down, we removed something like a sackful of sand from the lee scuppers and the cockpit, and we began to understand how it was that the channel had come to be so silted up. Everyone assured us that such weather was unheard of at that time of year; but all over the world they tell you that, and statistics usually prove them wrong; we held our peace, for we knew that we were almost on the latitude of, and not very far from, the Cape of Storms.

The residents in that sandhill country (about thirty families, mostly retired, lived permanently there) were extremely kind to us, and two of them made it their business to bring us bread, milk and ice each day simply by walking out to us across the sandbank at low tide; others had us for meals, drives, shopping expeditions, and even flights over the area to take photographs. The press at Port Elizabeth (seventy miles away by road) gave our stranding so much publicity that the day when the tide rose high enough and sufficient dredging had been done to allow us to move upstream, a friendly crowd gathered on the sandhills to watch.

After eighteen days aground, we finally reached the tiny marina, where we were as cosy as could be (Plate 5 D), but we could not do much to repair the ravages of the gales on our paint and varnish because there was so often sand in the air. By a rough road we were about two miles from the one-and-only store and post office and the road out of 'town', but we had a remarkable number of visitors, including the Prime Minister of South Africa and Mrs Vorster, who were on holiday in the area, together with their burly bodyguard; they showed much interest in the galley and the wind-vane gear. It was while we were lying there that we received an invitation to go to Rhodesia. Someone from that country had seen our film at Durban, and the Amateur Boatbuilding and Cruising Association (it seemed strange that there could be such a thing in a country so far from the sea) said that if we would show the film twice at Salisbury they would fly the pair of us both ways, put us up for as long as we liked to stay, and show us something of the country and its game reserves. Of course, we accepted, for such an opportunity was far too good to refuse, and it had been agreed that we must wait until the spring tides towards the end of January, which were predicted to rise a trifle higher than the tide on which we bumped our way in, before attempting to get out across the bar; we looked forward to that event with trepidation, and we hoped the Rhodesian break might ease the tension.

* * *

Extracted from my journal
Thursday 16 January In the dark silence at 4.45 a.m. Ann Hulett in her Mercedes picked us and our cans of film up at the marina and drove us to Port Elizabeth; having misunderstood the time of our flight by half an hour, she took us on a sightseeing tour and then lost her way, so we arrived at the airport only a few minutes before take-off. Our return tickets were waiting there for us. Stopped at East London, thereafter were served with a fine breakfast, had to wait two hours for our connection at Johannesburg, and reached Salisbury at 12.45 p.m.—about 1200 miles from *Wanderer*. Immigration thoughtfully suggested we might prefer they did not put a Rhodesian stamp in our passports—presumably this could be an embarrassment if we wished to visit other African countries. Malcolm Russell (chairman of the association) and our host Morris Benetar with his friend Veronica, and others, met us—bouquet for Susan and bottleowine for me. Drove to Morris's A-frame house with swimming pool and games house in the garden, and alsatian Rex and beagle Georgie, to dump our gear and wash, then drive round the attractive town, interview with press, tape-recorded broadcast, and a live t.v. appearance by me. A splendid roast cooked by Ricky, and afterwards a lot of boatbuilders in to meet us—it seems most boats are of a size to fit a railway truck so they can get to the sea by way of Mozambique.*

Friday 17 January After late breakfast, drive up the Kopie for the view. When United Nations imposed sanctions the Rhodesian government had built huge warehouses in which to store tobacco and other produce, but in spite of sanctions Rhodesia did so well exporting elsewhere that the warehouses were dismantled and sold, mostly to farmers. More press interviews, then a lunch in a Chinese restaurant as guests of a chap who

*Soon after this Mozambique closed her border with Rhodesia, and I do not know how all those boats ever did get to the sea unless they went via Durban.

had bought the Van de Wieles' famous *Omoo* and wrecked her on Ras Hafun on Africa's east coast, the whole meal being devoted to a slow blow by blow account of this disgraceful affair, enlivened only by a terrific thunderstorm. Technical troubles p.m.; on visiting the theatre where we were to show the film, found the speakers had been placed at the back of the auditorium instead of by the screen, and there was no public address system through which to give the introduction and answer questions. Much telephoning and help by kind Morris and all was straightened out, and after steak-and-kidney dinner we arrived to find the theatre packed and a long queue (some said 800 strong) in the street. The audience a good one, ready to laugh at anything.

Saturday 18 January Bruce Andrews, a farmer, drove us early to the flying club where we met Rod Bater, our pilot for the day, and Bruce flew with us in the four-seater Mooney. Rod, an amateur but experienced pilot, had a little trouble with the plane; its engine, fuel-injection type, tended to stall when on the ground, and there was some difficulty in lowering the undercarriage, which needed so much force that it almost seemed the little plane would be wrenched apart.

Arrived at Kariba at 9 a.m. and were there met by another Rod, who, I think, shared the costs of the flight with Bruce. He drove us to see Kariba Dam, the town built to house the Italians who built the dam, and the open, circular Catholic church. After breakfast of toasted cheese and tomato sandwiches at a hotel, we flew on across the huge (150-mile long) man-made lake, which this overcast morning was smooth and the colour of pewter. It was thought a storm was brewing, but nothing came of that, and soon we were over the south shore and approaching the short and difficult grass airstrip of Matusadona game reserve. We bounced twice, heavily, so Rod took off again, circled, and made a more successful landing. Land Rover driven by Richard Ailward, park ranger, met us and took us to the warden's house for tea. Richard had lost a leg when he stepped on a landmine laid by the Zambians, but seemed to manage very well on an artificial one. He took us on a two-hour drive round the reserve where we saw elephant, one paddling in the lake and close enough to be photographed. Richard had built the Land Rover himself out of parts from discarded ones—he said an LR normally did 100 000 miles before needing a major overhaul—and whenever we got out I noticed the black boy sitting in the back handed him a rifle. The reserve was closed to visitors because the Cabinet was having a conference there, but permission had been granted for our visit, and we met the ministers in the warden's house at the end of our drive.

We took off from the grass without trouble, and a few minutes later touched down on another grass strip—this was largely occupied by zebra and impala, which were not much disturbed by our noisy arrival—and had a late lunch at the Bumi Hills Hotel, from the observation platforms of which game can be watched along the nearby shore of the lake.

We then flew back to Salisbury, steering an S-course to dodge thunderstorms, and were cheerfully welcomed back to our resting place by Rex and Georgie. After another of Ricky's splendid but rather hurried meals disturbed by several visitors, we showed the film for the second time; again the house was full, again there was a long queue outside, and again the audience was an enthusiastic one and the question session spirited. There were gifts for us both, and we learnt that the sale of tickets had paid all the expenses and left a small profit.

Sunday 19 January Up early, Morris and Ricky driving us to catch the 7.15 plane, a Viscount, for Victoria Falls. So well and thoughtfully has everything on this tour been arranged for us, and so insistent were our hosts that we should pay nothing, that even the bus tickets for the thirteen-mile drive from the airport had been provided. A room had been booked for us at the Victoria Falls Hotel, a lovely great rambling, colonial-style place. Were met there by Peter Nicholls, regional tourist officer for the district, who at once drove us to the falls and left us there for a while to stroll about. It is very well done with pleasant footpaths to points of vantage, but no fences, litter bins or postcard kiosks. Amazing that Livingstone could have come downstream by canoe and landed on the island named after him right at the very brink of the falls without disaster, but at least he did it in the dry season. The falls were in great form (Plate 6 C) and there was much spume as the river was high, so high indeed that within a few days sluices at Kariba will have to be opened though some work there has yet to be completed. On the way back we came upon a party of baby baboons playing in the road. 'Good morning,' said Peter softly as we drew up; they gave us a glance and continued with their game.

Back at the hotel, changed hurriedly—the only time, apart from the film shows, that I felt it necessary to wear a tie on this tour—to lunch at another hotel with members of the SKAL Club, people connected with travel and tourism, and had to make a speech. The afternoon was hot and humid, we strolled in the garden of the Falls Hotel and at 5 p.m. Peter took us on the 'sundowner cruise' on the Zambezi River above the falls. It was wonderfully peaceful, could not even hear the engines of the boat, but of wildlife we saw nothing, except the tops of some hippo swimming; drinks, as many as one wanted, were free. Later we watched native dancing; one big chap picked up from the ground with his teeth and held aloft a length of railway line which was said to weigh 200 pounds (90 kilos). And, thinking of railways, there is a rail bridge over the gorge at the falls into Zambian territory. Rhodesia mines coal which Zambia needs, but the locomotive pushing the trucks has to stop at the bridge or its driver will get shot, and a Zambian loco then takes over and pulls from the other end.* Got early to bed, turned off the air-conditioning and opened all the windows, and the croaking of frogs almost drowned the music of the dance band; but, oddly, as soon as man had stopped making a noise not a frog croak was to be heard.

Monday 20 January Up early again, and while shaving watched a party of monkeys investigating the scraps left after last night's garden barbecue. Went on the 'dawn patrol'. Pilot drove us, along with three American tourists, in a minibus to a nearby airstrip. We flew in a six-seater twin-engine plane with low wings, not the best for viewing game. Saw some herds of buffalo under the gloomy, wet sky, but the best part of the flight for us was the circle we made over the falls on the way back.

After breakfast Barry Bell, a National Parks warden, took us by Land Rover to a crocodile farm round which a young woman showed us. Eggs are brought in from nests and hatched, and the reared crocodiles are killed at about five years old when four to five feet (1·2 to 1·5 metres) long. But some are returned to areas which are short of them, for the crocodile, like all other creatures, is an essential part of the ecology, keeping the numbers of some predatory fish down to the right proportion. We handled a baby. One-way flaps seal nostrils, tongue seals throat, so food can be caught submerged without becoming waterlogged. The creatures can hibernate for long periods in the mud, and do so when food is in short supply, and during those periods its metabolic rate drops. Remarkable reptiles (Plate 4 D), but even the people who rear and look after them can find no affection for them.

Barry drove us round his reserve and, although we saw little except secretary birds, which eat snakes, it was most enjoyable because of his personal charm and the many things he told us in simple language about his job and tales of the elephant's sense of humour: one watched a farmer digging in fencing posts, and when the job was done went along the line, lifting each post out and laying it on the ground; another had the habit of making its way silently into a camp and then trumpeting, and when the campers in fright had taken to the bush, he retreated as silently as he had come. Elephants, of course, have a big intake of food, and being chaotic feeders do a lot of damage, tearing bark from trees, and often uprooting a tree simply for a few mouthfuls of shoots. Sometimes when numbers become too great or food is scarce herds have to be culled; an unpleasant job for nearly everyone loves the elephant. It seems the reason why we saw so little game everywhere is that this is the end of the rainy season, food and water are plentiful, so game is scattered and has

*It was in a railway coach placed in the middle of this bridge that Mr Smith, Prime Minister of Rhodesia, was later to hold his unproductive meeting with other African heads of state.

no urgent need of the waterholes in the reserves. Barry spotted a chameleon crossing the road, stopped, and brought it into the LR; beautiful, delicate, gentle, might, like a wife, be a good seagoing companion.

We caught the 1.30 plane. Karl, son of Ingrid Adolphs who had in her own plane flown us over Sea Vista, met us at Jo'burg airport. On the way to his parents' home for the night he showed us a new shopping and office complex with its free underground parking, well-designed arcades, splendid lighting, and goods of every kind; here the shopper never has to carry anything, for all is delivered to a pick-up area. In the maze of highways, clover-leaves, and bridges, distances—in typical South African fashion—seemed great, and we caught only a distant view of the 50-year-old city.

Tuesday 21 January Karl got us to the airport in good time to catch our plane, and we arrived at Port Elizabeth at 11.15 a.m. Chris and Alice Rosslee, who we had contacted by phone last night, were there to meet us. Did all the shopping we needed to do and were back aboard *Wanderer* by mid-afternoon. Blazing sun, fierce south-west wind, sand and dust blowing, and an ominous rumble of surf from beyond the sandhills.

This has been a whirlwind trip, every bit a pleasure, and we have the kindest feelings for the enthusiastic and hospitable people we met in Rhodesia, coupled with an embarrassment at being British. They spoke well of their black fellow countrymen, appeared so far as we could see to be giving them every reasonable opportunity to share in the running of businesses, farms, broadcasting, and there was no obvious apartheid. But whether those charming and efficient whites mostly of British origin, who have developed the resources of their productive country and achieved such a gracious way of life, can possibly survive, who can tell; they seemed confident enough, but perhaps their heads were buried in the sand.

* * *

The highest tide was predicted for 28 January in the afternoon, and as that day drew near Susan and I became increasingly apprehensive. It was reported that the bar at the mouth of the river had shifted its position since our arrival, and that there might perhaps be an inch or two more water over it. We hoped that the weather would be fine with an offshore wind and little swell, and that the barometer would not rise high, for an increase of pressure could depress the tide; we knew that should we strike the bottom at the unprotected entrance and come to a stop, the next roller would knock our head off towards the shore and then our ship would almost certainly be lost, while if she survived but failed to get out to sea she might be imprisoned indefinitely. We even thought of having her lifted out by crane no matter what the cost might be, and transported to some safe launching place; but there was no hard standing anywhere near the water for a crane. That Leighton had taken out insurance on any vessel he was responsible for while navigating the entrance showed that he, too, had misgivings.

The day was fine with a light offshore wind; Ken came aboard at 4 p.m. to act once more as pilot, and Leighton brought *Spray* round to take a line from our bow. I had persuaded him to fit a towing post amidships so that *Spray*, like a proper tug, could now be steered while a strain was kept on the towline. The rescue launch stood by, and we left the snug marina among the sandhills and cautiously made our way down the narrow and now familiar channel, past the place where we had been aground for eighteen days, and near which most of our friends had now gathered on the sandhills to wish us luck and watch us leave; Ann was at a point of vantage with her cinecamera. Where the channel met the river, there was a shallow spit and a sharp turn which we failed to negotiate, and even there, still well protected from the sea as we were, we began to feel the swell; but *Spray* was able to pull our head round and we came off.

The next few minutes were fearful, because we had to keep parallel to the shore and very close to the breakers on it, and there the swell was higher than it had been the day we came in. Five times in the trough of the swell we struck the hard sand with a shuddering jolt, but with our engine running and *Spray* straining ahead we never quite lost way, and so avoided the desperate situation of having our head knocked off towards the shore by the next swell as it came surging in. But at last, and after what seemed more like hours than minutes, we were able to turn and head offshore. Ken removed the pipe from his mouth, gave us a grin and, in the manner of a dentist reassuring a worried patient said:

'There, we're in deep water now.'

I wondered how often in his flying days his quiet and confident voice coming over the public address system had reassured his anxious passengers.

Out in the bay in front of the hotel we anchored in four fathoms for the night, and I thought Leighton looked a little strained as he came alongside to pass us his farewell gift of a case of red wine, and the load of water in cans he had brought out, for we had emptied our tanks to lighten ship before leaving. We gave Ken three telegrams to send to people who had been worrying for us: '*Wanderer* safely crossed bar Tuesday.'

A long time later we learned that all hands, having safely re-entered the river, went to the hotel bar for double Scotches, and our relief at having escaped with the help of our competent friends from a situation which in a moment could have become a disaster, was profound; our own drinks that evening did not have too much water with them.

We rolled increasingly in the night as the swell grew heavier. At breakfast time rain set in and the wind shifted to the south. We were still covered by Cape St Francis, but only just, and we felt we ought to leave, but the morning weather forecast assured us that we could expect a freshening westerly. If we put to sea that would be a headwind for us, while at our anchorage we would have an excellent lee; also we thought that the wind shift was probably caused by the rain and might be only temporary. But we, like the weather office, were wrong. By 10 a.m. the wind had shifted round to south-east so we no longer had a lee, and with remarkable speed the sea was rising. There was no question about hanging on now—we must get out, and quickly.

To help the rather feeble electric windlass heave in the chain, we motored towards our anchor in short bursts, but on one occasion did so for a little too long and over-ran the cable, which then fell slack. At that moment a squall blew our bow off to port, and when the strain came on the cable, the latter was leading off the starboard bow (the side where the chain roller was) at an angle of ninety degrees. The sudden sideways strain was so great that the steel cheekplate supporting the pin on which the nylon roller turned was bent outboard like a piece of cardboard. The chain jumped over it and slid aft so that it led sharply over the side where the bulwarks began and, as it no longer had a fair lead to the gipsy of the windlass, the remaining ten fathoms had to be got in by hand, a link or two at a time, using a rope stopper. This was a difficult job and dangerous for the fingers, because again and again the chain snubbed heavily as we lifted on the sea, suggesting that the anchor was foul of some obstruction. But eventually the anchor, a seventy-five pound (thirty-four kilo) CQR, came free, and on sighting it we found it was badly bent; we lashed it down on deck, where it no longer fitted its chocks, set the mainsail, and motor-beat out of the bay, the shore of which had now become alarmingly close.

Off the cape, to which we gave a berth of more than a mile, we shipped a sea which was almost a breaker, steep, higher than the others, and unstable. It came aboard solid over the bows and swept the full length of the ship, washing away the forward ventilator cowl, ripping the spray-hood and twisting its stainless steel supports into an absurd shape, and left only a trace of a lifebuoy housing. Much of it crashed into the cockpit, thrusting Susan, who was at the wheel, hard against the after bulkhead and, as we had been too busy to ship the washboards, a good deal got below.

When, at last, we were clear of the rugged cape, on which the sea was breaking high with a roar that was much too loud even at our distance, we turned and ran with the wind on the port quarter, steering to cross the shipping lane diagonally and get outside of it. With the wind blowing onshore at thirty-five knots, it would have been foolish to attempt to cross the bar and enter Knysna, which harbour lay ninety miles to the west, as had been our original plan and where we were expected.

Throughout the following twenty-four hours the wind increased in strength and shifted to the east, while the barometer rose steeply to 30·3 inches (approximately 1026 millibars), and next afternoon the wind was by our estimate blowing at fifty knots; but we learned from the news on the radio that it reached a sustained sixty-five knots, that much damage was done to fruit throughout the Cape Province, and that *Queen Elizabeth 2* had been unable to dock at Cape Town. At least the wind was blowing with the current, but even so the sea had grown high and steep, and steering under the close-reefed mainsail, which by then was all the sail that we had set, was becoming difficult, and we had already shipped some heavy water aft. So we took the mainsail in, which was not very difficult to do as it was so small in area because of the deep reef, and the high, wide gallows was ready to accept the boom in either of its three notches; we ran on more easily then under bare poles. When I went aft to find out why the vane gear would not steer, I discovered that its plywood vane had been snapped off, leaving a jagged stump only two inches (five centimetres) high. We carried a spare vane, but there was some other trouble with the gear which I could not stop to investigate then, and at Cape Town was traced to a broken stainless pin allowing one of the toothed wheels to slip on its shaft instead of being held firmly to it. We did not know when this damage was sustained, but it must have been due to a recent heavy dollop of water aft because the gear had been steering until only a short time before.

Both of us will remember for a long time the night that followed. We stood two-hour tricks at the helm, keeping the ship stern-on to wind and sea, for that seemed to us the safest thing to do. This was not physically hard, for she steered quite easily, but it called for alert concentration and a sensitive response to the feel of the wind on one's ears and the back of one's neck. There were moments when her stern was flung up high, her bow was tilted steeply down towards the black void of the trough, and as the crest of the overtaking sea passed beneath and beside her, a great roaring wave rose several feet high each side abreast the main rigging—that was the closest *Wanderer IV* had ever come to planing. Now and then some heavy water fell aboard amidships and poured into the cockpit, and on one occasion, after a particularly heavy inundation, I realized with astonishment that the two massive teak boards on which I was standing were floating like water-skis, and clanging against the steel sides of the cockpit. In a glamorous tropic anchorage that large, centre-cockpit was a pleasant place in which to relax on soft, white-covered cushions under the awning, and entertain our friends, but it was far too big and vulnerable for the rugged conditions we were encountering just then. For once I was glad it was not placed aft because there that night it would have been much wetter than it already was, perhaps dangerously so. It did occur to me that if this wind increased much more we might need to tow some form of drags to reduce our speed, and then I remembered that all our heavy lines and fenders, which we might need for the purpose, were stowed in the locker right aft, to which the only access was through a hatch on deck; with so much water coming aboard it would have been risky to open that hatch to get the gear out. But no matter what happened that stormy night as we approached the southern tip of Africa, we both felt lighthearted at no more having to worry about crossing the bar of the Kromme River, and we said so to each other—often.

By noon next day the gale was over, and we found that under bare poles only for most of the time we had made a day's run of 156 miles; but no doubt some of the credit for that should be given to the Agulhas Current.

We had been running dead before the wind and altering course with it as it shifted towards north-east, so that we had come a long way offshore. We had seen no ships after the first day, and had seen nothing of Cape Agulhas, and when the gale had finished with us we were ninety miles south of the Cape of Good Hope, and just where the chart informed us icebergs had been sighted at that time of year. But we saw no icebergs and we saw no ships so far south and, when the wind died away, we turned in and slept, and after that we pumped and mopped out our several bilges. From there it took us four days to reach Cape Town, for when the wind sprang up again it was ahead, and after two days of that we had another calm, in which we did not use the engine much because the temperature gauge insisted it was overheating. I did not entirely believe it, thinking that as the gauge was electric it might have suffered from the water which at one time had been sluicing round in the engine-room, but I felt it was there for the protection of the engine and that I should not entirely ignore it. So we progressed slowly, and, shortly before dawn of our sixth day at sea, were just about to creep into Table Bay when we were enveloped in fog, which is common there where warm air flows over the cold Benguella Current.

Until then all had been silent; but now out of the fog there came a roaring of diesels as an inshore fishing fleet got under way and passed so close that ghostly shapes were sometimes briefly visible; there were the deep notes of ships' sirens, and the grunt every thirty seconds of the diaphone at Green Point lighthouse. For two tantalizing hours we lay stopped in the fog, and when it started to disperse it did so from the top. First the grey above us changed to pale blue, then the flat summit of Table Mountain and the heads of the Twelve Apostles stood in black silhouette; as the tide of fog dropped lower, the tops of masts and funnels of ships at anchor in Table Bay materialized, as well as the upper storeys of high-rise buildings, and finally the red-and-white-striped lighthouse tower, still grunting away, appeared. As the splendid scene was unveiled we saw that cloud, thin at first but quickly thickening, was forming on Table Mountain, and soon the well-remembered 'tablecloth' (Plate 6 D) was spread there with its edge draped over the northern face. We knew what that portended, but we did just manage to reach a berth in the yacht basin before the expected sou'easterly gale began to blow.

The chief thing we had learned in those few adventurous days was the importance of having everything in connection with the ground tackle strong enough to withstand the great strains imposed on it in bad weather by a yacht of *Wanderer's* heavy displacement and considerable windage. When she was building I specified forty-five fathoms of half-inch (1·27-centimetre) Lloyds-tested chain, and a sixty-pound (twenty-seven kilo) CQR as bower anchor. This chain had a test load of three tons, but it was clear that I should have ordered a larger size, for it had stretched a little and now no longer exactly fitted the gipsy of the windlass. Neither was the anchor heavy enough, for in New Zealand waters we had dragged it on several occasions, and finally bent the curved part which lies between the plough and the pivot-pin. I therefore asked Fosters, the big chandlers in Auckland, for one of seventy-five pounds (thirty-four kilos); this they did not have in stock but were shortly expecting a shipment from Scotland. Several months later the anchor was delivered and we noticed that it was faulty. Near the pivot-pin of the CQR anchor are two stops, their purpose being to limit the swing of the shank to an angle of less than ninety degrees each way; with the anchor lying on its side on the ground, if the shank is able to swing more than ninety degrees there could arise a situation in which the anchor might not be able to turn over and dig in. We found that the web of the H-section shank of our new anchor had been stopped too short by half-an-inch (1·27 centimetres), so that it passed over the stops and allowed the shank to swing to an angle of about 130 degrees. On enquiry, Fosters disclosed the fact that although the smaller anchors in the shipment appeared to be correct in this respect, all the seventy-five-pounders had the same defect as the one they had sent us. A friend put ours right by welding a piece to the web, after which we had the anchor regalvanized. We had excellent service from this anchor but now, as I have said, it was badly bent and at the same place as the earlier one.

When considering what sort of windlass to have I thought of those quiet mornings when it is a pleasure to steal away noiselessly under sail from an anchorage, so I chose an electric model which the makers claimed had a pull of 1200 pounds (544 kilos); in the event of an electrical failure it could be worked by hand-lever, though very slowly. However, as the drain on the batteries was heavy (up to sixty amps) we preferred to put something back into them while the windlass was hauling and, therefore, ran the main engine which drove an alternator; and, as the windlass was not powerful enough to haul the ship up to her anchor in a fresh wind, the engine was sometimes needed to help the windlass, as in St Francis Bay. In addition, we had the luxury of a deck-wash pump, which was used for cleaning the cable before it went into the chain locker; originally, this also was electric, but we had so much trouble with it that we replaced it with a Jabsco pump, belt-driven by the engine. Therefore, it turned out that we hardly ever did get under way without the engine running, so we might just as well have installed an hydraulic windlass instead of an electric one, and this I believe would have given us better service and more power. But at least the electric windlass, operated by Susan, could hoist me aloft in silence when I had work to do on mast or rigging, and it was able to handle my weight without putting a big drain on the batteries.

It was, however, not so much the windlass as the stemhead fitting that had been the cause of our recent trouble. The headed stainless pin on which the big nylon roller turned passed through two steel cheekplates, an outer one (it was this that had got bent back like cardboard) and an inner one alongside the bowsprit. Instead of having a nut and washer on its end behind the inner cheekplate, the pin was held only by a split-pin, which collapsed, thus allowing the outer cheekplate to take all the sideways strain. I am sure, too, that the cheekplates should have been made much higher, and/or that a drop-nose pin should have been provided to act as a keeper because, when weighing anchor in shallow water, the chain sometimes grew almost horizontally, and a puff of wind on the wrong bow could cause it to jump off the roller.

A chain compressor (a bedplate fitted with a lever-actuated eccentric) secured on deck between windlass gipsy and stemhead roller is a fitting rarely seen in yachts today, but I believe one should be provided in any vessel displacing more than ten tons. As things were arranged aboard *Wanderer*, as aboard most other yachts of her size, the chain when running out was controlled only by the clutch on the windlass, so when she dropped back in a strong wind to snub her anchor in, all the strain came on the windlass; the chain was apt to jump the gipsy then, which was bad for both chain and gipsy, and due to this ill-treatment the shaft of the windlass became slightly bent. When riding at anchor in a gale we usually put a rope spring on the chain and secured it to one of the big bollards on the foredeck so as to take the strain off the windlass, but a compressor would have saved the need for that, and would as well have taken all weight off the windlass when letting the anchor go, which was when the greatest strains were involved. I now appreciate that anchors, cables, windlasses, and other gear associated with them, need to be like *Dulcibella*'s in Erskine Childers's *Riddle of the Sands*, so big, strong and capable as almost to look absurd, then when conditions are bad there need never be any doubt about them.

Incidentally, we did have, in *Wanderer IV*, an arrangement which might be of interest to other owners of yachts with bowsprits and chain bobstays. As they will know only too well the noise of the anchor chain grinding on the bobstay, as the yacht sheers from side to side when puffs of wind catch her on one bow or the other, is not restful and destroys the galvanizing on both chains. We had a simple way of overcoming this. We had a rather larger bobstay plate than is usual on the stem, and had a second hole drilled in it just below the hole for the bobstay shackle; to this we secured a length of nylon rope long enough to reach the bowsprit and be made fast there when not in use. Having anchored and veered almost as much cable as was required, we unhitched the rope from the bowsprit and, with a rolling hitch, made it fast to the cable outboard of the stemhead roller, and then veered more cable until the rope, now all under water, took the strain. Lying to her anchor like that, the yacht lay much more steadily than she did when the cable led from the stemhead roller six feet (1·8 metres) above the water, and as the cable could not touch the bobstay there was no noise. The only drawback to this arrangement was that, if for some reason we needed to veer more cable, we had first to heave a little in until we could reach the rolling hitch and release it, so we did not often use it in a gale.

The Royal Cape Yacht Club accommodated us at its marina and looked after us very well. From that berth it was a long hot walk through dockland to the city, but Denzil Penny, a member, made it his business to call every morning for our 'orders', and when he returned to the club for lunch brought with him the things we needed. The other drawback, about which nothing could be done, was the dirt. I am sure that only those who have lain in the basin at Cape Town (Plate 6 B) can have any idea how bad it is for a respectable yacht. Often there was oil on the water, for this was a big and busy port, and the motor-tyre fenders of the marina ground the oil in between wind and water. But far worse was the soot and grit from the coal-burning locomotives, which day and night were at work in the big shunting yard just behind the clubhouse, attempting to haul, with wheels spinning, trains which were much too long. When the sou'easter blew, which it did with violence nearly every day we lay there, the filth was almost indescribable: masts turned black; the gloss on paint and varnish soon vanished; any rope left in position became ingrained with soot (we stripped to a gantline to avoid this), and down below, as in the Kromme River, there was dust and grit everywhere, for the heat made open doors and skylights desirable.

But the people of the club treated us so well that we had a pleasant feeling of being wanted. Rarely did a day pass without someone quietly putting into the cockpit a carton of grapes or a bottle of wine. All our requirements, including the righting of our defects and damage, such as the distorted anchor, the stemhead fitting, the inoperative vane gear, the wayward temperature gauge, and the twisted hood supports, were quickly, and at very reasonable cost, attended to by Jacko Jackson, another club member, who had access to various workshops, and the ability to find within a few minutes things that might have taken us weeks to lay our hands on.

We were delighted to have again *Williwaw* as our near neighbour, as well as the fine old wooden yacht, *Fia*, owned and sailed by two young Swedes, Hans and Carl. They had such charm and good looks that we wondered how they had managed to sail two-thirds of the way round the world (they subsequently completed their circumnavigation) without being dragged to the altar, and we were touched by the interest they took in us and the help they gave. They were astonished at the number of our visitors, and not a little sympathetic, for well they knew that we, like themselves, needed to press on with our jobs if we were to leave on time, and they only smiled—instead of being angry, as I would have been—when strangers boarded their ship to take photographs of ours.

The club had one of the best and cheapest slips in the world,

---

5 *To view A Top left* The exposed mouth of the Kromme River; the bar is at the top left, and the narrow channel leading to the marina at the right. *B Top right* We came to a complete stop on a shoal from which *Spray* and the rescue launch failed to shift us. *C Bottom left* At low water we lay over at forty-five degrees, and a suction-dredger was put to work to deepen the channel. *D Bottom right* After eighteen days aground, we at last reached the marina among the sandhills.

and we hauled out on it one Sunday evening when the vile sou'easter had eased a bit, and scrubbed the bottom. Early next morning we were mixing up the antifouling paint by floodlight when Carl and Hans arrived to lend a hand. They efficiently used our two rollers, one on a long broomstick, while Susan and I plied brushes, and by 8 a.m. with their kind help we had put on two gallons (nine litres) of paint and finished the job before the sun rose over the wall to reach us. This was as well, for the day turned out to be the hottest the Cape had experienced for seven years. The sun beat into the concrete bay of the slip, and by eleven o'clock the cabin temperature was 108 °F (42 °C), probably the highest we had ever known. By the time we had cleaned the brushes and rollers and serviced the sea-cocks, we were dehydrated. Between getting up and lunch (which we had in the club with Denzil, Carl and Hans) I had consumed two cups of coffee, three tumblers of health salts, three tumblers of water, each with a salt pill, two beers and a glass of wine (this was a mistake), and four tall glasses of orange juice with ice; even so I felt dried up. We launched off in the cool of the evening with Jacko's help, and returned to our berth which the secretary had kindly cleared for us, because at Cape Town, as in any other marina, you have only to leave your berth for a minute and someone will nip into it.

Our final day was the usual hectic affair to which we had become accustomed each time we were about to leave port. Having topped up our water tanks and filled every available container, I cleaned the worst of the filth off the decks and sides, and rove the running rigging, which we had stowed down below to keep clean; meanwhile Susan was taken into the city by Ken Jones's nice young niece Sheila, to do her final shopping and arrange for stores out of bond to come aboard at eleven o'clock; but these did not arrive until much later, by which time we had been invaded by a family that had been good to us. They came by appointment to 'take photos', but it was a movie sequence they wanted, and they brought along a great deal of equipment, including some 1000-watt lamps for which a special lead from the shore had to be arranged. They then filmed each other sitting round our table, while Susan and I held their floodlights and

---

6 *To view A Top left* The congestion of overseas yachts at Durban. *B Top right* The basin at Cape Town. *C Bottom left* The Zambezi was high and the Victoria Falls were in great form. *D Bottom right* Not another waterfall, but the 'cloth' spread on Table Mountain in a sou'easter.

suggested little things for them to do to get a bit of action on the film. While this was going on, a customs officer arrived to seal up the stores, and a little later the Commodore and Mrs Penso came with a club plaque and an armful of paperbacks as farewell gifts, and we persuaded them to stay for drinks. Meanwhile Jacko, assisted by me in my spare moments, was working in the engine-room fitting a new thermostat, and a chap from the South African Broadcasting Corporation came to make a tape-recording. When everyone at last had gone it was too late, and we too tired, to cook and eat the chicken Susan had prepared, so we dined off cold bully and grapes.

* * *

About sixty miles north of Cape Town an extensive inlet thrusts its way into the wild and almost barren coastline of South Africa, which here is a hard and lonely terrain baking under the summer sun, and across it the searing sou'easters roar. Frank Wightman, who lived there aboard his yawl *Wylo*, is quoted as having said:

'You endure it for a time, you become sated with it, and then the feeling of revulsion sets in . . . here there is nothing to see but those white cliffs, those sand dunes . . . this is a sun-bleached desolation without shade, not a thumbnail of shade. You feel like an ant on a griddle . . . in the summer it is like someone holding a burning-glass over you.' [Lawrence Green, *A Giant in Hiding* (Timmins).]

This inlet is generally known as Saldanha Bay, though Saldanha, where there is a small town and fishing boat harbour, is only a part of it, and it is said that, had there been a supply of fresh water, it might well have become South Africa's major port instead of Cape Town, where the harbour had to be made by man. But one day soon Saldanha should become a port for big ships; in 1975 suction-dredgers were at work day and night gathering sand with which to build a breakwater connecting the island in the entrance with the northern shore, and already a railway had been built to bring ore from the mines inland. When we were there, however, the place was still untamed; fish and birds abounded, the great ocean swell exploded on the outer beaches and had repeatedly washed away the foundations for the breakwater, the sun beat down from a clear blue sky, and the harsh, hot wind rushed over it.

It was to this strangely exciting place that we sailed when we left Cape Town because, although we had obtained our clearance and therefore were supposed to leave the country, we needed a quiet anchorage for a day or two while we cleaned up, prepared for the long ocean passages which lay ahead, and got some undisturbed sleep. Accompanied by porpoises and seals, and with long, thick skeins of unidentified black birds overhead, we passed inside Dassen Island—low, yellow and featureless except for the lighthouse on it—and, in the evening, reached an anchorage in Salamander Bay on the south side of the inlet, where we found smooth water in the lee of the low land but could not escape the wind; nevertheless, we slept soundly, for there were no shunting engines to disturb us. We remained for several days, using the containers of water we had brought with us for the purpose, to wash the soot of Cape Town from the masts and standing rigging; also we cleaned the oil from the sides and scrubbed the filthy dock lines. The only inhabitants of the peninsula in the lee of which we lay were Basil and Mary Livingstone, who lived in the white house above the abandoned whaling station which once they used to run. They brought us gifts of their precious home-grown grapes, crusty home-made bread, crayfish caught in a nearby wreck, two valuable whales' teeth, and their delightful company. Their nearest village was thirty miles away by rough track.

When we left on 3 March we were bound towards England, and we intended to make only three stops on the way, at the South Atlantic islands of St Helena and Ascension, and at Horta in the Azores. The total distance would be nearly 6000 miles, and we were leaving rather earlier than we might otherwise have done because we wished to reach England in May so as to have the whole summer before us there.

After we had got well away from the land the South Atlantic treated us well; one glorious sunny day and star-filled night followed another, the fair wind blew warm and steady and, as we ran easily on our way under main, mizzen and boomed-out staysail we did not have a single squall or even a shower of rain. Once when Exy Johnson was asked where after her many circumnavigations in the two big *Yankees* she would most like to return to and settle, she is reported to have replied: 'The trade wind area of the South Atlantic.' We felt inclined to agree with her. The vane gear, which Jacko had fixed in Cape Town, now steered as reliably as before, so after keeping watches for three nights, by which time we believed ourselves to be well away from the shipping lanes, we spent nearly all night every night in our bunks with ports and hatches wide open to the breeze. With so much good sleep we felt wonderfully fresh and energetic, and by day enjoyed attending to many maintenance jobs, which we cannot often do at sea because of the motion, and I even got some writing done. Navigation presented no problem, for the sea was not rough, and usually the heavenly bodies and the horizon were sharp and clear; indeed, it would have been a fine opportunity for a beginner to learn and practise the art.

* * *

I suppose that anyone wishing to navigate by means of observations of celestial bodies, which is still the most widely used and most accurate method available to the ocean-going yacht, would endeavour to learn some of the theory behind it from one of the many books on the subject, though I have to admit that I never got very far myself with logarithms and spherical trigonometry. But fortunately for me and people like me the modern method that most of us use today (unless we have been taught by some old seadog who does not approve of simplicity and time-saving) requires little understanding of such things; all that is needed is an elementary knowledge of geometry, and the ability to add and subtract degrees, minutes and seconds of arc, and hours, minutes and seconds of time.

It may be of interest to recall that the simplified method of obtaining position lines from observations was devised by the late Sir Francis Chichester for his solo flight across the Tasman Sea in his little seaplane, *Gipsy Moth*. For the success of the flight, it was essential that he should, without delay, be able to find the two small islands of Norfolk and Lord Howe, as he would need to refuel at both of them, but as pilot/navigator he could spare no time for working his sights in the old cumbersome way. Tables for aircraft navigation, based on his method, were published in 1939 under the title *Astronomical Navigation Tables*. These have since been replaced by *Sight Reduction Tables for Air Navigation* (H.O. 249) which most yachtsmen use, and *Tables of Computed Altitude and Azimuth* (H.O. 214), which are similar but of greater accuracy, to 0·1 of a minute. One or other of these, together with the current edition of *The Nautical Almanac*, is all that is required.

Obviously a single observation of a body can result in only one position line, on some point of which the observer must be. Simultaneous observations of two celestial bodies are needed to provide a fix—the point at which they cross on the chart—though a slightly less accurate 'running fix' can be had by carrying a position line forward with the parallel rules along the known course steered and distance run since taking the first observation, until it can be crossed by a second position line obtained from the same body when the azimuth of that body has changed sufficiently to enable the lines to cross at a satisfactory angle. Theoretically, the ideal angle is ninety degrees, but in practice the error caused if they cross at fifty degrees is very small, and a cross of forty degrees is quite acceptable. But I am sure all this is widely understood, and here it is not my intention to attempt an explanation of the working of sights, but rather to mention some of the practical points of navigation which frequently arise on any voyage of more than a day or two.

So far as I am aware only two worthwhile improvements or accessories have been devised for the mariner's sextant since the micrometer replaced the vernier and made it easier to read; they are the stella lenticular and the polarizing filter, but they are refinements which still are found only on the more costly instruments. It will be appreciated that to measure the altitude of a body accurately the sextant must be held vertically to the plane of the horizon, otherwise the angle measured will be too great. With sun or moon sights this is easily achieved by swinging the sextant slightly out of the vertical from side to side, when the reflected image of the body will be seen to describe a shallow arc, and the observer adjusts the micrometer until the edge (or limb) of the body just kisses the horizon at the bottom of the swing, at which moment the sextant is vertical. With stars and a dim horizon this is not so easy, but the lenticular makes it so. The fitting consists of a glass screen in a frame which is pivoted along with the coloured index shades, and can be turned up into position just like a shade. It has the optical property of converting a point of light (a star) into a horizontal streak of light at right angles to the plane of the sextant. One can thus see instantly if the streak is or is not parallel to the horizon.

When observations of the sun are being taken on a cloudy day when the sun pops out only now and then for a few seconds, it is not easy to choose a shade of the correct density and have it in position at the right moment, for in such conditions the intensity of the sun is constantly varying; by the time one has tried a shade, found it unsuitable and changed it for another, the chance of getting a sight may have been lost, and there may not be another opportunity that day. The polarizing filter replaces the (usually four in number) coloured index shades, and a half turn of its adjustable rim will dim the light of the sun from minimum to maximum; the adjustment can be made in a moment without the need to remove the sextant from one's eye.

New sextants pour out from all manner of seemingly unlikely sources, and what a pity it is that so few of them have the above refinements or are arranged to stow in their cases ready for instant use, that is, with any telescope shipped and with any shade swung up; usually the largest telescope or monocular has to be unshipped and all shades turned down before the lid can be closed, so that the instrument is not ready for instant use, and the delay in getting it ready may cause one perhaps to miss the only chance of a snapshot sight that day.

With the exception of meridian altitude and Polaris observations, it is of course essential to know Greenwich mean time (G.M.T.) at the moment an observation is taken. Until fairly recently, a clockwork chronometer was used for the purpose, but that instrument was expensive and bulky, and did not take kindly to the often violent motion of small vessels. The dry-battery-operated quartz crystal movement has overcome these drawbacks, does not alter its rate with changes of temperature, and is remarkably accurate. However, the wristwatch of today is generally so good that it may serve quite well as the navigator's timepiece, and its daily rate of gain or loss is of little significance provided it remains constant, for so long as the radio receiver does not fail, the watch has only to carry the time from one time signal to another; as radio stations WWV and WWVH normally provide world coverage, and there are many other radio stations from which time signals may be had, there need be little risk of the navigator's watch being much in error without him knowing about it. On this voyage I used a Rolex wristwatch known as a G.M.T.-Master. In addition to the three normal hands, this watch has a fourth hand which makes a revolution every twenty-four hours, and it indicates the hour on an outer bezel marked in the twenty-four-hour notation. The bezel can be rotated, and I turned it on or back one hour every time I shifted the hands on entering a different time zone; thus I could read G.M.T. instantly anywhere in the world, and found that very convenient. Soon after I had bought it the watch needed adjustment, so I took it to a Rolex agent, only to be told it could not be dealt with for several weeks as they had so many requiring attention. Crossly I wrote to the head office in Switzerland, suggesting that they might spend a little less on advertising and a bit more on after-sales service. Their reply took the wind out of my sails, for they politely agreed with me and said they would have to do something about it. That was good psychology, for when Susan needed a new watch she bought a Rolex. Of course it required attention, but when she sent it to the agents they dealt with it immediately.

The need for accurate time is clear when we consider that four minutes of it equal one degree of longitude (sixty nautical miles at the equator), so an error of one minute in the navigator's timepiece could cause an error of up to fifteen miles, depending on the latitude. Incidentally, our masters who have decided that we must go metric are going to have some trouble if they try to include the nautical mile in their rearrangements. As we know it the nautical mile is one-sixtieth of a degree measured at the equator, making the Earth's girth 21 600 nautical miles; so unless they are prepared to change the 360-degree circle to one of 100 or 1000 degrees, and then split the degree into 100 minutes, they are going to be stuck with it. And while they are stuck with it, perhaps it might be more sensible when giving the visibility in weather reports or forecasts, to do so in nautical miles instead of in kilometres, for which the seaman at present has no use at all.

Ship's noon, that is, the moment when the sun bears true north or true south, is by tradition the time of day when the ship's position is marked on the general chart and the run from the previous day's noon position is measured and recorded. I found this a satisfying moment, and liked to regard it as the end of my navigational day unless I was growing anxious at the near approach of land. Weather permitting, I took a sun sight in the forenoon, carried its position line along the course and distance made good, and crossed it with the position line obtained from the meridian altitude sight, commonly known as a noon lat. Susan usually joined me on deck with her sextant to take the noon sight—this was a good check on me—and it was rare for our sextant readings to differ by as much as one minute. If in the early morning the day looked as though it might become overcast, I took the forenoon sight as soon as possible, but I knew that unless I had to it was not wise to observe any body with an altitude of less than about fifteen degrees, because the lower the body the greater is the refraction (bending of light rays as they enter the Earth's atmosphere), and although this is allowed for in the altitude correction tables in *The Nautical Almanac*, it is subject to changes due to temperature, humidity, and atmospheric pressure, for which we cannot always make allowance. Indeed, abnormal refraction may often have accounted for the discrepancy most of us have, on occasions, found between a.m. and p.m. sights, a difference greater than could be accounted for by bad steering or an error in the patent log (Lecky makes quite a point of this), and that great sailor, the late Peter Pye of *Moonraker*, once told me in a whisper that when taking afternoon sights he always 'pulled the sun down a bit into the sea'.

The noon lat has four advantages over other methods of obtaining position lines. First, an exact knowledge of G.M.T. is not required, for one can start observing several minutes before ship's noon, and continue to do so until the sun hangs stationary before starting the afternoon descent. However, this is a point of real value only in the event that G.M.T. has been lost through failure of the timepiece or the radio receiver; normally it is more convenient to obtain in advance from *The Nautical Almanac* the G.M.T. of the sun's meridian passage. The second advantage is that as the sun becomes increasingly slow-rising as noon draws near, one stands a much better chance of getting an accurate observation, especially in rough weather, than when the sun is changing altitude fast; one can repeatedly check the observation each time the ship lifts on the highest sea running, making tiny adjustments to the micrometer, and go on doing so until the sun rises no higher. The third advantage is that the working is simple and quick, and no tables except those in the almanac are needed. The fourth advantage, of which I have seen no mention elsewhere, is that on a cloudy day there is a better chance of seeing the sun at noon than at any other time because, being then at its greatest altitude, its rays pierce the cloud more directly and so have a shorter distance to travel through it. I have repeatedly found in weather when a forenoon or afternoon observation has not been possible, that the sun has shone, though perhaps only faintly, at noon.

It has been said that if you ask a young merchant navy officer where the ship is, he will take a pencil, sharpen it, and make a precise dot on the chart; if you ask an older officer he will sketch a circle round the dot, and the greater his age the bigger is the circle likely to be; but if you ask the master, who has been finding his way about the oceans most of his life, he will probably stab a horny finger at the chart and say: 'Somewhere around here.'

Most sextants can be read to one-fifth of a minute of arc, some to one-tenth, but to me such small measurements seem pointless when, except perhaps in the quietest of weather, one cannot take an observation from a small vessel with an accuracy greater than one minute. Also, if I do bother with these fractions or decimals I am likely to make some stupid mistake, especially if I am tired. For the same reason, when looking up the declination and the hour angle in the almanac, I do so to the nearest whole minute. I reckon that any position I may fix on the chart will lie within a circle four miles in diameter; I hope it will be in the centre, but I do not bank on that.

I did not take a course in navigation or go to evening classes or night school, but learned what I needed to know from Lecky, Worth, the instructions in *Astronomical Navigation Tables* and *The Nautical Almanac*, and from one or two cruising friends; so perhaps some of the things I do are unorthodox, and maybe there are others that I ought to do but don't, chiefly because I wish to keep my methods as simple and foolproof as possible. The authors of several navigation books I have looked at recently insist that it is not good enough to take just one observation of a body; they say that five or more should be taken, plotted on squared paper against their times, and that those that lie more or less in a straight line should be averaged. I think those authors ignore two things: the voyaging yacht, unlike the ocean racer, is usually short-handed, and her navigator will have other things to do besides navigating, such as standing a watch or cooking; even if he or she can spare the time to take a chain of sights he/she is quite likely to make some error when adding or dividing (especially dividing) the figures. The other point is that the occasion when one is most likely to obtain a poor observation is when there is much low cloud and one can get only a hurried snapshot; it may be the only one that can be obtained, or one may have to wait ready on deck for an hour or more to get another. I am of the opinion that with practice, and one gets plenty of that on a voyage—during this circumnavigation I took 581 observations and

Susan 215—the navigator learns to judge whether or not his/her observation was a good one.

While we were at Keeling Cocos I met the master of a freighter in from Singapore to load copra. Over the years a number of yachts had failed to find that low atoll, so I was particularly interested when he told me that he had himself failed to find it once or twice and had to turn and try again. He also confirmed something I had long believed but felt shy of stating: any observation, no matter how poor it may seem, is better than none.

As was only to be expected, the electronic calculator has been brought into the field of navigation and is used by a few people for solving the spherical triangle. No doubt it does this very well, but I do not understand why anyone should want to solve the triangle, as the modern tables provide the solution on inspection, and to make the calculator do it one has to turn everything into trigonometrical functions; and, of course, just as with any timed sight, one has first to look up in the almanac the declination and Greenwich hour angle. If one is fond of calculators no doubt the ability to find jobs for them and put them to work is satisfying, but I do wish calculator addicts would not try to get me involved.

* * *

As planned, we made stops at St Helena (1653 miles from Salamander) and at Ascension (700 miles further on), but at each the anchorage was so uneasy because of the swell, and landing so difficult, that we did not stay at either island for long. St Helena, which from seaward looks like a great fortress but has some fertile valleys hidden within the ramparts, struck us as being the most pathetic of Britain's few remaining overseas possessions. As passenger ships did not call there any more and the island had no airport, there was no income from tourism and, because of the widespread use of synthetic materials, flax was no longer exported; the only earned money came from St Helenans employed on Ascension, where there was a cable station, a BBC relay station, and a well-staffed American tracking establishment. Jamestown seemed just the same as on our earlier visit, with its one long street of very English-looking houses straggling up the valley, its citadel where the harbour officials sat at their office desks among the dusty files with nothing much to do, and its lovingly tended public garden, ablaze with flowers round its central fountain; a smart squad of men and women police were drilling on the quay well below the mark showing where, in 1878 during a run of phenomenal rollers, the sea reached a height of about twenty-five feet (7·5 metres) above normal. We bought bread, Irish butter, a chicken and some green beans, the only fresh food we could find, and we filled our water breakers at the tap near the flight of stone steps at which, we reminded ourselves, everyone on the island who had not been born there must at some time have landed from small boats, steadying themselves as we did by grasping the thick ropes hanging from an iron bar overhead.

Then in continuing fine weather we sailed on, life out at sea being much more comfortable than it had been at our rolly anchorage and, on the sixth day, raised ahead the colourful ash-heap of Ascension. In Clarence Bay we were happy to find Willy de Roos and, at his suggestion, tied up to a vacant buoy in the lighter anchorage, for the holding ground is poor. When the wind died in the night, however, we bumped the buoy so heavily that we cast off from it and anchored, and we felt a bit happier then for we do not trust old moorings. We learned later that shortly after our departure from St Helena, the German yacht, *Lotus II*, (Dr Gunther) put in and lay to a mooring; the chain parted, the yacht drove ashore and became a total loss, nothing from her being saved. Another German yacht came into Clarence Bay while we were there and anchored close inshore; her single-handed owner apparently carried no charts, had been blown ashore in a cyclone in the northern part of New Caledonia, and the night he approached Ascension woke from a sleep to find himself only a quarter of a mile from the land. While he was ashore his yacht started to drag, and we were just about to weigh and attempt to take her in tow when her anchor at last got a hold. At St Helena there was a lifeboat (she looked like an old R.N.L.I. boat) which often went out to bring back the small local fishing boats when their engines broke down, otherwise they would have blown away towards South America. But Ascension had nothing like that, so yachts lying there kept an eye on one another as they usually do in an awkward or dangerous place. Willy, who now was alone again as the two girls he had picked up at Cape Town had returned there by air, was waiting for a spare part for his autopilot to come in *Cape Hope Castle*. We had him aboard for dinner, and when he left we watched his white-shirted figure until we saw he had safely reached his ship, for Clarence Bay, with its strong offshore wind, was no place from which to go adrift in a dinghy. He told us that the night we shifted from the buoy he had heard our anchor chain run out, and had kept an eye on us for two hours to see we did not drag.

Not so long ago the visit of a ship to a small island was an event to look forward to and enjoy; people from her landed, islanders went aboard, drinks and gossip were exchanged. But that was no longer so at Ascension. When *Cape Hope Castle* put in for a brief stop she announced her arrival by siren, but apart from a barge which went out to collect a container from her, nobody showed any interest, and the same applied to the visiting yachts. Perhaps this was due to the security regulations—no cameras might be taken ashore, passports were held by police, and so on—but I believe travel by air was so commonplace there that a ship no longer had for the islander an atmosphere of romance, nor was she any longer a welcome break in a monotonous routine.

Too high a swell was running to permit us both to land together as there was no place at which to leave the dinghy, and we felt we could not drag her up the steep and narrow stone steps without doing her some damage—an inflatable would have been just the thing there—but I was able to back in so that Susan could jump ashore, and again she bought butter, English this time, which she salted down; it kept perfectly through the hot weather and we ate the last of it three-and-a-half weeks later.

Williwaw left the same day as we did bound north, and together we passed out from under the long banner of island-generated cloud into the sunny ocean, but there our courses separated as Willy was heading first for St Paul Rocks (to the west and just north of the equator) before going on to Horta.

The passage from Ascension to Azores is interesting from a sailing point of view, and can be divided into four parts: first the fair wind run to the equator (about 650 miles); then the doldrums with their calms and squalls; next comes the belt of the north-east trade wind, perhaps 1500 miles in width, and finally the area known as the 'horse latitudes', where one may be long delayed by calms and light winds, probably from ahead. In April, when we were there, the recommended sailing route from the Cape to the Channel crosses the equator in twenty-four degrees west, and we followed it for, although there is a temptation to cross further east so as to be more up to windward when meeting the north-east trade, the doldrum belt rapidly widens in that direction; also, further east there is a likelihood of finding the wind more north than north-east after getting through the doldrums. The chief factor deciding the distance that will be sailed and the time taken over the passage is the direction of the trade wind, for naturally the more north there happens to be in it, the further will it push one away to the west. When we made this same passage twenty years before in our thirty-foot (nine-metre) *Wanderer III*, we had the interesting experience of *sailing* through these doldrums, as we had only a small engine and little fuel, and we took two weeks over it and fifty-two days for the whole passage; this time, having a good engine and plenty of fuel, we motored right through the doldrum belt in thirty-six hours. We found the area not at all as we had remembered it, for the sky was clear, the sea was smooth, we never had a squall or any thunder, and, most surprising of all, not even a drop of rain; yet it was with this passage particularly in her mind that Susan had fabricated a water catchment with which to replenish our tanks.

Having carried that catchment round the world and used it very little, we felt such a thing was not worth its quite considerable stowage space. In trade wind areas where, because of the length of some passages, we would have liked to collect water for luxury purposes, we found that most of the rain fell only in showers of short duration, and as they were usually accompanied by a sudden though temporary increase of wind, we were too busy reducing sail to bother with the catchment, and even when we did spread it, the wind usually got under it and spilt the water out. A much better way was to make use of the mainsail, on which the slides along the foot were on a track recessed into the boom; the recess acted like a gutter, and rain from off the slanting sail ran along it to pour from the forward end where it could be caught by way of a big funnel, and once the sail was washed completely free of salt the water could be put straight into a tank. In port, too, we found the special catchment was not worth bothering with, and that it was better to collect rain from the awning which was probably already spread and, in a tropical downpour, we caught an astonishing quantity in a very short time. Apart from saving us the bother of ferrying off water from the shore, this provided pure water, whereas shore water in some places was polluted or heavily chlorinated, and sometimes had to be paid for. However, we rarely thought it necessary to purify shore water with the Halazone tablets we carried for the purpose, though in some places we refrained from putting the local water into our tanks and used it only for washing. By careful measurement on our first ocean trip we found that for drinking, cooking, and teeth cleaning, five gallons (twenty-three litres) lasted the pair of us for a week. In *Wanderer III* we carried a total of seventy gallons (318 litres) and never found any need for rationing. The 200 gallons (910 litres) we carried in our bigger *Wanderer IV* seemed very generous, but, although her water-pressure system was convenient it could be a cause of wasting water, and even I, who am parsimonious in that respect, occasionally found myself absent-mindedly washing my hands under a running tap. It is a pity that shore-bound people, who seem to regard water as one of nature's inexhaustible gifts, do not have to spend a few months in voyaging yachts, for they might then learn to have a greater respect for it. According to a report presented at a United Nations conference in 1977, a human in the semi-arid lands of Africa used no more than 0·8 United States gallon (three litres) of water a day, while a Londoner used sixty-eight gallons (257 litres), and a New Yorker 270 gallons (1022 litres) a day. A delegate expressed the rather extreme view that the day was not far distant when a drop of water would cost as much as a drop of oil, but I quite understood what he meant.

The trade wind was light to start with but slowly freshened, and although according to the pilot chart the average force should be no more than four to five on the Beaufort scale (ten to twenty-one knots), for one whole week it breezed up to force seven (twenty-two to thirty-three knots) with gusts of up to forty knots, as measured by our very conservative anemometer at deck level. This was too boisterous for us, as we had for so long known only the easy lift, surge and roll of sailing with the wind aft. As *Wanderer* disliked being close-hauled as much as we did, we eased sheets a trifle and let her sail a good point free, and for a heavy floating home with a middle-age spread and all our worldly goods aboard, she did not do at all badly and made good an average of 125 miles a day; but of course it was wet and uncomfortable sailing (Plate 7) and we spent a lot of time chocked off in our bunks reading.

It was while looking through some yachting magazines then that I came upon a letter asking whether a barograph could be used aboard a seagoing yacht, a question that had cropped up before. We used a very old one with complete success for some twenty years, first in our thirty-footer (nine-metre) then in our forty-nine footer (fifteen-metre). Marine opticians sell a little spring gadget so that the barograph may be suspended to guard it against vibration caused by rough weather or machinery, but this would appear to be unnecessary in a sailing vessel. Our instrument was securely screwed down in such a position that its nib-holding arm lay athwartships, and I believe this to be important, otherwise a leeward lurch might throw the nib momentarily away from the chart. In rough weather, such as on this leg through the trade wind belt, the line traced was thicker than normal; nevertheless, the diurnal movements, which are a regular feature of the atmosphere within the tropics except perhaps when a storm is brewing, could be clearly seen, as could movements as small as one-twentieth of an inch (which is approximately one and a half millibars). A thick trace might also be caused by engine vibration or overfilling the nib. Of course, a barograph is not essential for, if the height of the ordinary barometer is noted, say, every hour and marked on squared paper or a barograph chart and a line drawn through the resulting dots, one has the equivalent of a barograph trace; but I doubt if many people would bother to go to so much trouble.

For this long leg of the passage we put a deep reef in the mizzen and kept it there. The chief reason for this was that when we fitted the wind-vane gear we had to move the mizzen sheet blocks further forward along the boom so as to permit the vane to swing down in any direction; with the whole sail set close-hauled in a fresh wind, this arrangement put such an alarming bend into the rather flimsy boom that I feared the boom might break, whereas with a deep reef tucked in, the strain came at just the right place. We kept the staysail set all the time and usually the small jib (though not in force eight gusts) and our quickest, easiest and most efficient means of reducing sail further when we needed to was by rolling down some of the main.

Today we hear so much about 'slab' or 'jiffy' reefing that we might almost suppose this to be some wonderful new invention, instead of the method everybody used before the advent of roller-reefing gear, and simply referred to as 'reefing'. Having been shipmates with this and with roller-reefing, I chose to have the latter for the mainsail of our ketch, because I knew how quick and easy it would be with the worm gear to revolve the boom and wind down round it as much of the sail as I wished, to be able to do all the work from a safe position by the mast, and on any point of sailing without having to haul the boom inboard. The fact that the resulting reefed sail might not be quite such a good shape as one reefed in the old manner did not much concern me, for I knew that if the boom had the correct taper the reefed sail need not set all that badly. I did not give the mizzen much thought then, supposing that we would not often need to reef it and, as its boom overhung the stern, I knew that if we had roller-reefing for the mizzen we would have to use that abomination, a claw-ring, for the attachment of the sheet. As it turned out, however, we often did need to reef the mizzen, for it was a large sail and, in some conditions, upset the balance of the ship. We did not usually bother with the first reef and, when reefing, we made a worth-while reduction of sail by pulling the second reef down straight away; but the pendant for this was so long that there was hardly length enough along the boom for the reef tackle. Obviously what we needed was a small winch mounted on the side of the boom, and later in England I tried to get one; it had to be of the ratchet type, for, at times, it might not be possible to wind the handle full circle. I could not find that type of winch in the small size required, but salesmen were not slow in pointing out that to get the ratchet effect all I had to do was buy a ratchet handle. The price of the winch was about five pounds, but the price of the ratchet handle for it was more than twenty pounds. For a modern racing yacht with perhaps eight winches arranged round the cock-pit, no doubt there would be some saving in cost by having single-action winches and a single ratchet handle to work all of them (not that I have heard of this being done), but that expensive handle would for us have worked only the one small winch, so I would not buy it. Then Susan had one of those simple ideas which always so impress me. She suggested we fit a jam-cleat on the boom, lead the pendant by way of a fairlead through it, and set the pendant taut on the halyard winch; then the cleat would hold the pendant while we cast the turns off the winch and used the latter for its proper purpose of tightening the luff. This simple idea cost us less than two pounds to put into effect, and its only draw-back was that the jam-cleat, like most of its kind, was hard on the rope it held. We tidied up the bag of sail along the foot with reef points, which we found quicker and more convenient than reeving a lacing, but even so that was always a long, hard struggle, for the boom was high and the upturned dinghy lying beneath it got in the way. We often said when we read those glowing descriptions in yachting magazines of the joys of 'slab' or 'jiffy' reefing, that their authors would be welcome to come aboard and have a go with ours. Were it not for the high cost of replacing the rectangular and too-flimsy boom with a new one, round in section and stiffer, we would long ago have changed over to roller-reefing for the mizzen, and put up with the claw-ring.

Originally the yacht was fitted with a triatic stay connecting the heads of the main-mast and the mizzen-mast, an arrangement I do not care for as I believe the masts of a ketch should be independently stayed and not have to rely on one another. But it was necessary because the mizzen mast rigging was incorrectly arranged. The lower pairs of shrouds went to the root of the crosstrees and were well spread to give the mast good fore-and-aft support as far as that. The upper half of the mast was kept straight fore-and-aft by a jumper stay which started at the root of the crosstrees and passed over a strut half way up that part of the mast. The mast, therefore, had no proper fore-and-aft support just above the crosstrees, at which point it could have snapped were it not for the support provided by the triatic stay. So we removed the jumper strut, doubled its length, and fixed it at the root of the crosstrees; we doubled the length of the jumper stay, and led it from the masthead over the strut and set it up to a point on the mast low down near the boom. We were then safely able to dispense with the triatic stay.

Whereas the South Atlantic had bathed us in sun- and starshine, the North Atlantic sky was gloomy. Always the forenoon was overcast, but it was usually possible to get observations of the indistinct sun if one waited long enough on deck with sextant in hand, though this usually resulted in the instrument getting deluged with spray; sometimes in the afternoon the sky did clear partially for an hour or two, but only to cloud over again before nightfall, thus defeating Susan's attempts to take star sights. Humidity was high, and most days the saloon sole remained dark with damp; rust began to seep from the ports and other places where the paint was weak; and the new varnish, a polyurethane which was all we could get in South Africa instead of the old-fashioned oil-base type which we preferred, peeled off in long, dead strips like plastic tape. For two days we sailed through what appeared to be an harmattan; visibility was poor, and our masts and rigging turned a pale stone colour where the dust, fine like talcum powder, and presumably blown from the Sahara 1000 miles away, settled—two weeks later at Horta the coating was still intact on the upper parts of masts and rigging where the spray of our passage had not reached.

On the chart we crossed several of those lines which are of such interest to the navigator: the southern limit of the trade wind belt and, 1600 miles later, its northern edge; the Tropic of Cancer, after which we found the days grew longer and cooler. And there were our own special lines marked by coloured crosses and dates, showing our noon positions on earlier voyages: three west-bound trips of *Wanderer III* and one of hers coming north from the Cape, and, surely the most important of all to *Wanderer IV*, her own outward track made seven years before—so she, too, had now put a girdle round the globe. When at last we sailed out of the region of the north-east trade in about twenty-nine degrees north, thirty-three degrees west, we were extremely fortunate for, instead of the calms and light headwinds of the 'horse latitudes', the wind continued fresh and conveniently hauled round to south-east, so that, with sheets well eased, we were able to head direct for our destination for the first time in many days.

On this passage we saw very few ships, having sighted only four all the way from Salamander Bay; but you may well draw my attention to the fact that as the vane gear had been steering all the time we did not keep much of a lookout. However, we did have one mysterious visitation. It was at supper-time—we found that most of the things that needed attention, such as a change in the strength or direction of the wind, occurred then—when Susan's special dish of canned tuna with mushroom sauce was ready, and the chips were browning nicely in the pan, that we sighted the lights of a ship astern coming directly at us. We were showing our usual white light as we reached along under all plain sail, but whether or not the ship had seen it, of course we could not tell, and as she did not alter course we assumed she had not seen it and took avoiding action ourselves, gybing for the first time since leaving Ascension. But the ship then changed her course, too, continuing to follow us, and shortly afterwards she switched on her searchlight, which so dazzled us that we could no longer see her navigation lights, but at least we presumed she could now see us. She came close under our stern, still playing her searchlight on us, and kept station there. This vessel, which was not large and had the shape and sheer of a tug, remained with us for two hours while our supper congealed; then she stopped and switched off her searchlight and, as we gybed back on to our course and sailed on our way, her lights eventually dipped below the horizon. If she had wished to speak with us we wondered why she did not do so, and we felt her intrusion on our privacy and the spoiling of our supper was unforgivable. In daylight the following morning a bulk-carrier crossed our bows steering west; then she turned and headed for us, but had come no closer than a mile when, seemingly satisfied with what she saw, she resumed her original course. The two incidents caused us to wonder if a search for some small vessel was under way, but at Horta we could learn nothing about any search or any vessel in trouble.

Early in the morning of our twenty-fifth day at sea the dark mass of high land materialized ahead, and we hove-to until dawn showed that we had made a good landfall on Fayal. Pico, the neighbouring island, was hidden in mist and cloud; but, as we approached the port of Horta, where the colourful little town skirts the waterfront, with a backdrop of steep, hedged, green fields topped by a row of windmills, the splendid volcanic cone of O Pico lifted its head clear of the clouds as though to bid us welcome to the Azores.

On earlier visits we had lain either to an anchor or a mooring, but this time we were directed by the pilot to lie alongside the great stone breakwater which, nearly half a mile long, protects the harbour on its eastern side. The bollards were so far apart that we had to use very long lines, and although these were of large size, they had enough elasticity to allow us to surge backwards and forwards a distance of four feet (1·2 metres) on the scend that was running throughout most of our stay. The wear and tear on our lines and fenders and on our nerves was considerable, but two kind men, evidently understanding our situation, produced from somewhere and helped us rig an enormous cylindrical, floating, rubber fender, which was a great help, though it held us so far from the wall that getting ashore except at high water was difficult; also the debris thrown overboard from a ship to windward—mostly bottles and cans—drifted down on us and got trapped by the floating fender, so that day and night our waterline was hammered and the noise reverberated through the steel hull. It was not very restful, and I thought how good it would be if the harbour authority at Horta could lay a trot of moorings for the use of visiting yachts—about 150 put in each year, as I have mentioned elsewhere—and make a small charge to defray the cost. At Ponta Delgada this was done for the safety and convenience of the yachts taking part in the single-handed race from Falmouth, but it is commonplace that, though much may be done for a sponsored racing fleet, little is done for the unsponsored voyager.

A feature of the inner side of the protective wall of Horta's breakwater was the great array of painted records of the visits of many yachts; some were only names and dates, others were artistic portraits of the yachts under full sail. But the area of wall abreast of us was completely filled with the word 'MAYFLY', done in quite enormous orange letters on a green background, leaving no room for anyone else; it was like lying alongside an advertising poster. We had noticed similar displays of exhibitionism in other places: at the old post-office barrel on Charles Island in the Galápagos it has for many years been the custom for vessels putting in there, mostly yachts, to leave their names discreetly painted or carved on small pieces of wood attached to the barrel; but when we were there the name of a Japanese vessel had been smudged repeatedly in big letters all over the place. Again, on the ruins of the old whaling station at Whangamumu, yachts painted their names, but always there was one who outpainted all the others.

At Horta there were other displays, for Portugal was just about to have a general election, and the hammer and sickle of the Communist Party was everywhere to be seen. Some buildings were stuck over almost entirely with posters, the emblem had been painted repeatedly on the grey cobbles of the streets, and the buoys in the harbour and the upperworks of some of the ships were plastered with them. But all this seemed to have made little impression on the islanders, who were just as kind, gentle and quiet as ever, and Peter Azevedo, friend at the Café Sport of all voyagers, went out of his way to do us many kindnesses. There were shopping expeditions in the charming little town, walks out to the remarkable circular Caldeira Inferno—what a splendid harbour that would have made were it not open to the south—and there were pleasant meetings with other yachts, including our old friend *Williwaw*. Willy had been unable even to sight St Paul Rocks, let alone land and dive there as had been his intention, for bad weather had prevented him from getting closer than twenty miles to his goal. He kindly gave us his *Reed's Nautical Almanac* which we needed for the lights and tides and separation zones of the Channel, and radioed his wife to bring another when she flew out to join him.

Being a radio ham Willy needed plenty of electricity, and this he got by way of his free-spinning propeller when under sail. He had the same engine and gearbox as we had, a four-cylinder Ford diesel and hydraulic Bourg Warner with two-to-one reduction, but his propeller was larger than ours. By means of a lay-shaft and belts, the propeller drove an alternator which, when the ship was sailing at six knots, charged the batteries at a rate of twenty-five amps. So he rarely needed to run a generating engine, and it is these which cause so much disturbance and irritation in many anchorages; the worst offenders are those yachts with electrical or mechanical refrigeration and deep-freeze chambers, which sometimes call for four to six hours charging daily. If only the people who make use of generating plants could all agree to run them at the same time of day, life would be less unpleasant for their neighbours, who then could grit their teeth and bear it or go ashore during the noisy period; but each of the generators seems to run at a different time of day so that they overlap, and from dawn until dusk, and often long after, there is in many anchorages which should be peaceful havens, a burble or rattle of diesel exhausts. The mote in my own eye?—we charged our batteries once every two or three weeks, but then we ran a paraffin-burning (kerosene) absorption-type refrigerator, and did not have deep-freeze facilities, nor did we ever find any need of them.

Also in port was the Danish training vessel, *Danmark*, a beautiful full-rigged ship. Some of her cadets called on us one evening, pleasant young men who spoke excellent English and, at their suggestion, we went to their ship before leaving port to get a weather forecast. After a few moments waiting at her gangway we were invited aboard—snowy decks, large areas of gleaming varnished teak, and overhead an intricate tracery of rigging—and taken to the chartroom on the upper deck to meet the ship's master, Captain Hansen. He showed us the latest synoptic chart and explained it to us: a very high 'high' was moving south-west while a very low 'low' was going in the opposite direction, and the riddle was to guess what might happen when they met. On the morning of our departure, Captain Hansen came in person and in mufti along the wall to hand us the latest synoptic chart. How remarkable that so busy a man with sixty cadets and twenty officers in his charge could spare the time to be so kind, but I have learned that often the more important a man may be and the greater his responsibilities, the more time does he seem able to spare for individuals. *Danmark* was due to leave two days after us, and I said what a pleasure it would be if she were to overhaul us at sea under full sail, but the captain replied that if there was a headwind, and he thought there would be, his ship would be not under sail but under power, for he had a date to keep at Copenhagen.

When we were ready to leave we had difficulty in recovering our forward line, for a ship which had berthed ahead of us the previous day had dropped the eye of her after line on top of ours on the same bollard, instead of first passing it up through our eye, when either could have been cast off without disturbing the other—something I had thought that every seaman understood. It took the combined efforts of two bystanders and the harbour policeman to get it free.

For most of the passage from Horta to Falmouth we had a headwind. It is well known that the fruit schooners which used to trade between the Azores and England, when confronted with a headwind, stood away with the wind on the starboard side until in higher latitudes they met the westerlies. But those passages were made later in the year when westerlies are more prevalent further north than they are in May; also it was likely that consideration for the unrefrigerated cargoes made the skippers anxious to get quickly into cooler water. The pilot chart for May showed that on the direct route, there were more winds with a westerly component than an easterly; therefore, we continued turning to windward, always hoping for a change, and did not deviate far from the rhumb line. So it was that *Danmark* did overhaul us, and unfortunately she *was* under power; she spoke to us by signal lamp, but we could not reply.

As it happened, our tactic proved to be the correct one; the large 'high', of which we had been told, became stationary and, because of it, there were no westerlies there or further north at that time, and, had we stood away to the north or north-west, following the traditional route, we would, according to the weather reports, have found that the headwind was much stronger there, often reaching gale force and sometimes more. The nor'easter continued for about two-and-a-half months.

Accustomed as we were to life in the tropics, we found the weather cold, especially the nights, and needed four blankets on our communal bunk in the saloon even though we had the diesel heater going for some of the time, and when on watch we needed so many layers of clothes topped with oilskins and boots that getting dressed took all of five minutes. With so much clothing and bedding around, Susan remarked that the place looked more like a girl-guide camp than part of a seagoing vessel. Of course, our progress was slow, and in one twenty-four-hour period, when the wind was so strong that we hove-to for a rest, we actually lost thirty-four miles of easting. That evening, two swallows came aboard, and, one embracing the other with a protective wing, they huddled together precariously on the windward seat in the cockpit, a pathetic little bundle of feathers. We thought that they, like ourselves, must be feeling cold, and fearful that a dash of spray might knock them over, Susan picked them up in a soft duster and put them in a corner of one of the bunks in the sleeping cabin where at least they would remain dry. We wondered if they could survive, for there was no food that we could give those insect-eaters, and we felt they ought not to have been 300 miles from the nearest land; we supposed the strong offshore wind had blown them out to sea, or that they had transhipped from some other vessel. At dawn we opened the cabin door so that they might go on their way if they wished, and they did, though we never saw them leave.

We no longer slept all night, but kept a lookout for shipping since we were approaching crowded waters. However, the route-ing chart showed that the transatlantic lanes sprang out on their great circle courses from the Bishop and Ushant and, by limiting our activities to one degree of latitude (forty-eight degrees thirty minutes north to forty-nine degrees thirty minutes north) as we approached the Channel, we managed to keep between the lanes, and apart from fishing vessels we saw only two ships until we neared the Lizard on our sixteenth day at sea. That we made this same passage many years ago in an engineless twenty-three-footer (seven-metre) in twelve days, shows once again that passage times depend not so much on the ships and the people in them as on the weather. How good the Cornish countryside looked, and how lovely it smelt, as we sailed past the familiar landmarks, Black Head, Coverack, the Manacles, Helford and St Anthony, and so came to an anchorage off the old, grey waterfront at Falmouth (Plate 8 A). Since we were last there we had made good about 50 000 sea miles, 18 000 of them since leaving New Zealand.

* * *

We found the West Country in the spring delightful, and we spent some time in the area attending to the ravages of the voyage, scraping, painting and varnishing, and meeting old friends. The holiday season had not yet started, so my dawn walks through the narrow streets of Falmouth were protested only by flocks of gulls screaming from the rooftops. We went to Helford to see Nigel and Bobby Warington Smyth, now finished with the city and happily settled in the house on Frenchman's Creek where the late P C Thurburn had painted many of his splendid marine pictures. We rowed up Abraham's Bosom and were sad that Bevil, who had been so helpful with one of my books, was no longer alive to welcome us at Rose Cottage. It was a nostalgic pilgrimage, and much had happened in the seven years we had been away.

When we felt *Wanderer* was sufficiently respectable, we moved on to Fowey to attend a meet of the Royal Cruising Club, where all the other yachts looked so very smart and shiny. It was the first West Country meet that we had taken part in, and I noticed a difference between it and the much bigger meet held at the end of the season in the Beaulieu River: at the former everyone was saying where he was going and at the latter telling where he had been, but a feature common to them both was that no one really listened. The supper party at the Royal Fowey Yacht Club was over, and most of us had safely reached our bunks by the time the old church clock, mentioned in McMullen's *Down Channel*, struck midnight.

Then we went up Channel, mostly under power because there was so little wind and we were impatient, for the summer of 1975 was the finest and calmest that anybody could remember. We arrived in our old home port of Yarmouth in the Isle of Wight (Plate 8 C) to find it pretty full, and the same landing places still choked with the same semi-waterlogged and tightly tied up dinghies. Again our walks filled us with memories, for we had been married in the village church, and for many years had owned a house overlooking the Solent. But nostalgia gets one nowhere and is dull for those who are not involved, and we had many friends to see, a refit to undertake, and eventually a departure date to keep. It had never been our intention to stay beyond the summer, for the winter is too long and dark to make year-round living aboard enjoyable, and the Solent area, where we might have wished to stay, was so crowded that we would probably have had to rent a marina berth at high cost. Nevertheless, it was a surprise to find that *Wanderer*, having been built abroad but not imported into the country, was still subject to duty. We had thought that over the seven years of her absence the duty might have been written off, but on the contrary, it was still ten per cent, though not on what we had paid for her but on the current cost of replacement. That was a large sum, and on top of it there would have been value added tax, which at the time was twenty-five per cent. Although this was interesting it did not directly concern us in fact, for we had every intention of returning to the less-congested waters of New Zealand where, provided we did not sell her within two years, our ship could be imported duty-free.

When I owned my very first boat I used to lay her up for the winter at Moody's yard on the Hamble. On one occasion she lay in solitary state in what was then called the Meadow, an area of marshy land just west of the yard, where she stood on her own legs, and Mr Alf Moody used to come along and tell me what I was doing wrong when I plied my inexperienced caulking mallet or my amateurish paintbrush. Today the Meadow has been developed. There now is hard standing for many laid-up yachts, together with huge sheds into which they may go if they wish to get out of the cold and wet; there is a well-stocked marine store, workshops, an ablution block, and, of course, the big marina. We decided to do our refit there.

Among other things I thought we needed was a set of new batteries, as ours seemed to be getting tired and no longer held their charge so well as they used to. Therefore, I 'phoned Mr Eric Moody (although now a big affair the yard was still run by the Moody family), told him what sort of batteries we had, and asked if he could provide a new set.

'Of course we can,' he replied, 'but they are very expensive now, so are you sure you really need them? How long have you had yours?'

When I told him they had been in use for seven years he laughed. 'Most owners don't get them to last half that time.'

On the way to Moody's we put in at Newtown Creek for a night or two, and George Seabroke kindly provided us with a mooring. As the evening tide stealthily receded to uncover the mudflats (Plate 8 B), we listened to the haunting cries of waders and watched the light fade over the swelling curve of the downs, but we missed the fine stands of elm which used to be such a feature of the place before Dutch elm disease killed them. As it was still early in the season, there were few other yachts to share that wonderful, unspoilt place with us, but when we wanted to put in there after our refit was finished and 'phoned George to see if we might again have the use of a mooring, his reply was: 'Yes, but I don't recommend it. Last night there were about a hundred yachts in and it was bedlam.'

Wanderer had been taken out of the water on a number of occasions, once by synchrolift at Grenada (that was easy and pleasant), and once on an old bus chassis, but the other times she had been hauled out on slips of varying efficiency. For we who reckoned to do our own work, the average slip presented one big problem: because of the rails, and the wheels and bearers of the cradle, our ship with her seven-foot (2·1-metre) draught stood so high that some form of staging had to be erected to let us reach all of her underwater body with our scrubbers and paintbrushes, and it was rare to find a yard provided with light-weight trestles and planks which we could handle comfortably; and even when we had collected what we needed, the ground was often so unlevel that we had to search for wedges with which to prop up the feet of the trestles. The slip at Cape Town was good in that respect, for it was on smooth concrete, and there were some light planks and a plentiful supply of empty oil drums on which to put them. Apart from slipping there, the last time we hauled out was at Whangarei where, because the underwater paint put on only three years before had lifted in countless tiny blisters, we had to embark on a whole new bottom-painting programme.

We had heard good reports of an antifouling paint called Jet Black, and when I wrote to the makers (PGH Industries) for particulars and told them about our trouble, they showed much interest in us, and spent most of a day with a sensitive voltmeter searching for a possible electric leak or a wide difference in electric potential, which could have caused the blistering. They found neither, but they did come up with the interesting idea that our aluminium neighbour, with which we had been sharing a marina berth for some months, might have been acting like a giant anode and throwing our paint off. (Three years later we knew that was not the cause, for again the bottom paint was blistering, and we had not lain near any alloy vessel during that time.) The paint people recommended sandblasting the underwater body to their high specification, and this to be followed by two coats of tar-epoxy paint to protect the hull and insulate it from the copper content of the two coats of Jet Black that were to follow; and to ensure that everything was done to their satisfaction their sales manager spent nearly a week at Whangarei supervising the work, lending a hand himself when needed, and dispensing beer generously.

Having once before had the bottom sandblasted—that was when the filler with which it had originally been covered was removed—Susan and I knew what to expect, and to stop the sand and dust from getting below we sealed every crack in doors, hatches and skylights with masking tape, and, as we could no longer live aboard, two families took it in turns to put us up in their pleasant homes. The weather at Whangarei is apt to be wet, and the morning the final sandblasting was done we watched anxiously as cloud built up to windward, for the first coat of epoxy paint had to follow the sandblast within two hours, and if it did not, then the steel would have to be blasted again. The paint, five gallons (twenty-three litres) of it, was of the two-pot-variety, and before blasting had finished, we were mixing it up and still watching the clouds, for had it then rained not only would there have the delay and expense of another sandblasting, but the paint might have had to be thrown away, for once mixed it had a working life of only eight hours. But it did not rain, and the first coat was sprayed on without incident, except that the gusty wind carried the fine spray up above the topsides, which had been masked with paper, to adhere in tiny specks to the varnished rail-capping and the stainless guardrail staunchions, and later many hours of work were needed to remove it. The painter had obviously done this kind of job many times before, and with speed, dexterity, and the grace of a ballet dancer up on the staging, got the first coat on quickly. The second coat soon followed and this had to be covered by the first antifouling coat within twenty-four hours, a job we planned to do ourselves to save expense. Then the rain came, not hard, but enough to dampen everything; our night-time hosts turned up without being asked to lend us a hand, and brought plenty of rags with them, so each section was carefully dried before the paint was put on. Some special paint had been specified for the narrow band of bare steel along the waterline between bottom paint and topsides, and clearly this did not like the rain, for within a few weeks of starting the voyage rust began to show all along that vulnerable area between wind and water, and it was this in particular that we wanted Moody's to attend to as it seemed to be beyond our own capabilities.

Wanderer, being of heavy displacement type and with a long straight keel, presented a huge area of bottom when she was hauled out. We looked forward to painting the bottom with misgiving, for when confronted with so much we felt puny; but with this, as with so many other things, we found fellow cruising people helpful: the Swedes at Cape Town, our friends at Whangarei, and on other slippings people have come to our aid even when professional help might have been available. On a recent painting occasion we were joined by Eve Wright, a slight, fair woman whom we knew to be a prodigious talker. And talk she did, but she was a wonderful worker, hardly pausing through the long hot day, not only scrubbing thoroughly and painting well, and getting in a dreadful mess, but alone she searched the yard and came staggering back with planks and trestles.

But at Moody's our ship with both masts standing was plucked gently out of her natural element by Rennerlift (Plate 9 *left*) and carried smoothly to the chosen spot near the paint shop, where she was lowered to stand on her keel quite level fore-and-aft, so that we were able to continue living aboard in style and comfort. An experienced painting gang set about the rusting waterline, ground it until the steel was clean, painted it, filled it, and painted it again and again. The job took a long time, but two years later the waterline was still in perfect condition.

Meanwhile Susan and I worked on deck, chipping and painting the coamings and the bulwarks; we shopped in a big way, went to see Francis and Bridget Usborne who had now given up Chelsea and lived at charming old Bursledon, and other of our friends, and a notable thing about them all was that, although they were at least seven years older, and some of them showed it, their voices had remained unchanged. We kept cleaner than we had ever done before during a refit, for within a few yards of us were the immaculate showers in the ablution building. The only trouble there was an unusual one: the water was so hot we could barely stand it, and emerged pink like cooked lobsters, for since something had gone wrong with the master thermostat there was no means of regulating the temperature. I sometimes wonder if I have now gathered enough copy for a story on 'baths I have baked in and showers I have shivered under'. In our time we have used all types of shower, from the grand tiled affairs of Florida and California to sleazy ones in Tahiti and the Canaries, where we hardly cared to remove our shoes; at some we first had to light a fire under a boiler to heat the water, and at others had to insert coins in a slot, then, unless we hurried, the water became icy before we had done; there were bush showers in Queensland, a gendarme's shower in the Gambiers, and a prison shower on the island of Rodriguez. A common failing of most was that there was nowhere to hang ones clothes or put the soap.

When the work was finished, we were launched as effortlessly as we had been lifted out, and for a few days lay in Moody's marina while people with whom we had business came from London to see us. As with showers, so we have had experience of many marinas, and this one was California standard, by which I mean one of the very best. From our own private tap, water flowed generously—in some marinas it was no more than a trickle, and even that might cease if someone up-pipe turned his tap on—and I am sure that only those who, like ourselves, spend most of their time when in port at anchor, fully appreciate what a great luxury an occasional freshwater supply is; in our water-using habits we temporarily left the ranks of the Arabs and joined the New Yorkers—we washed almost everything. By night the walkways were discreetly lighted by low, non-dazzling lamps, and there was none of the groaning and squealing of ill-fitting pontoons working on the piles, such as had often disturbed us elsewhere, for this marina was in a well-sheltered situation. At some in exposed places, or subject to wash from passing vessels, it may not be safe to lie alongside a pontoon; lines then have to be run off to piles to keep one away, and getting ashore may be difficult, though it need not be if the marina is well planned. Also at Moody's there were no late parties, loud radios, shouting children, barking dogs or generators running, such as we had sometimes had to endure elsewhere, but this was probably because, although the marina was filled, mostly with yachts of a very fine order, ours was the only inhabited one. This was sad, for yachts ought to be used as often and as much as possible to give their owners pleasure and justify their fantastic cost, but Mr Alan Moody told us that not more than about ten per cent left his marina at weekends. I believe this may have been due not so much to lack of enthusiasm as lack of anywhere suitable to go. If an owner whose yacht lay at Moody's wished to sail, say, to Cowes or Lymington, then he would be wise first to 'phone and see if there might be a marina berth vacant; however, if there was he would probably have to pay for the use of it, while still paying for his own berth. And if he took a chance and tried to sail for Yarmouth on Saturday in the height of the season, unless he arrived early enough he might well find the 'harbour full' red flag flying and the harbourmaster waving him away. Over one fine weekend we were berthed at the extreme end of one of the marina piers, and sat on deck enthralled by the constant stream of small craft—the river looked like a motorway on a bank holiday—and it was noticeable that the majority of those that went downstream in the morning returned before nightfall.

We wished to go to Lymington to see Roger Pinckney, Adlard Coles and other old sailing friends, and to be in a convenient place for members of our families to visit us. We were able to get a berth at a marina in which the emphasis was on the medium- and smaller-size yacht, rather than the larger and more costly incumbents of Moody's domain. There were about 300 of them, and we supposed that they provided a fair sample of the modern yacht; but we did wonder a little about some of the fragile-looking creations. It was obvious that many had been designed and built solely with racing in mind, but it did seem strange that even those intended for cruising incorporated so many of the racing yacht's less desirable features.

I have no quarrel with the fin keel except that in rough going it may lack directional stability, and so is hard on the helmsman whether human or wind-operated; but the separate and unprotected rudder that sometimes goes with it surely needs some form of skeg or rudder-post immediately ahead of it, not only for protection and added strength, but to ensure that the rudder is made more effective by having a straight flow of water directed to it. The fin and separate rudder also poses a problem, not only when slipping or drying out alongside, but in waters where there are obstructions, such as floating ropes in congested harbours, the buoy lines of lobster or crayfish pots, or the live kelp which is a feature of many coasts in temperate climates; then the rudder or skeg may become fouled, or the unprotected propeller be at risk. Nevertheless, I have often been envious of such yachts when I saw them working their swift and efficient way to windward, and felt sure they must have been much more fun to sail than was our heavy-displacement ship with her great area of wetted surface.

I take it that the fashionable forward-sloping stern, which with very few exceptions the modern racing yacht possesses, suits the rating rule, but I consider it to be an unsuitable end for a cruising yacht, though many of the latter copy it; the sharp edge near the water where skin meets transom, is vulnerable to damage in marinas or by dinghies, and the concept reduces the deck area aft just where the cruiser needs it, for she may wish to carry lifebuoys, a danbuoy, a liferaft, or even an outboard motor there, as well as a wind-vane steering gear with its connections to wheel or tiller. This type of stern also reduces the space in the after locker, where the cruiser may need to stow lines, fenders, and other bulky gear.

For racing the forward-sloping bulkhead at the forward end of the cockpit does provide a trifle more elbow-room for a crew working winches, but such a feature permits rain to fall vertically into the cabin unless the door is closed or washboards are shipped. For a similar reason, tumble-home or coachroof coamings should be avoided if they are provided with opening ports. I noticed that very few of the yachts did have opening ports, yet if they were seriously going cruising they would have needed them, for those expensive items make a lot of difference to the ventilation, which is often left to a couple of small water-trap vents; at times the ports on the lee side can be left open at sea and, in a calm, if all are open the motion of the yacht will cause air to flow to and fro to keep the accommodation cool and sweet.

Today a big selling point appears to be a large number of sleeping berths, the more the better, even though there may be little space left for the belongings of the people who are going to occupy them; six berths in a thirty-footer (nine-metre) are not uncommon, and it is noticeable that at least two and perhaps four of them are toed-in so that they are not parallel with the centre line. This means that a person sleeping on a lee berth will have his head lower than his heels (he cannot end for end himself because such berths are usually tapered), and one sleeping in a windward berth will have the blood run to his feet; so on neither tack is there any comfort to be had, and headaches are endemic.

Of course, the alloy mast has come to stay, for it is light and stiff and almost maintenance-free, but how strange it is that so few owners stop their wire halyards from beating against the masts in a breeze causing wear and fatigue. The manager of the marina at which we lay told me that originally he had made it clear to owners that if they did not silence their halyards he would have it done for them at a cost of £1 a time, but added that his solicitor had now advised him that he should not persist with this. On that account alone it is not surprising there is such strong local opposition whenever plans for a new marina are being made. When Roger Pinckney, like others there, built his house at Lymington, it overlooked the saltings and nothing was to be heard but the cries of birds; now, with a marina at his doorstep, he could not sleep on windy nights for the noise of steel halyards slapping alloy masts. We, too, have suffered, and have used up many yards of string in attempts to silence the halyards of near neighbours. I mentioned this to the owner of a nearby yacht, and he astonished me by saying that tapping halyards were music in his ears, and on windless nights he missed it so much he could not sleep.

The majority of yachts we saw in England were of glass-reinforced plastics, the most widely used boatbuilding material of today. At the time when Susan and I were considering having a new and larger yacht built, we would have accepted a hull of GRP had one suitable for our purpose been available, for we believed that material to be free from any of the forms of decay such as affect wood, steel, or ferrocement, and we naively supposed it would call for no upkeep; but time has proved us wrong. Some hard-driven yachts built of GRP have shown weaknesses, and there have been cases of osmosis, in which the gel-coat lifts in tiny blisters due to water getting in behind it, or perhaps having been there all along; if this is not attended to, delamination of the glass moulding may occur. I have seen several cases of osmosis in yachts built by what were believed to be first-class firms, and suspect it may have been due to lack of humidity- and temperature-control during the moulding process. Apparently osmosis is not fully understood, but it seems that a GRP yacht should be taken out of the water now and then so that she may dry out, and that if osmosis appears the only cure is to grind the blisters away

---

7 *Top* It was wet and uncomfortable sailing in the north-east trade wind; *Bottom* but with the sheets eased a trifle we averaged 125 miles a day.

8 *To view A Top left* Falmouth waterfront. *B Top right* The evening tide recedes from the mud-banks in Newtown Creek. *C Bottom left* Our old home port of Yarmouth in the Isle of Wight. *D Bottom right* The distant island downs peep over the marshes of the Beaulieu River.

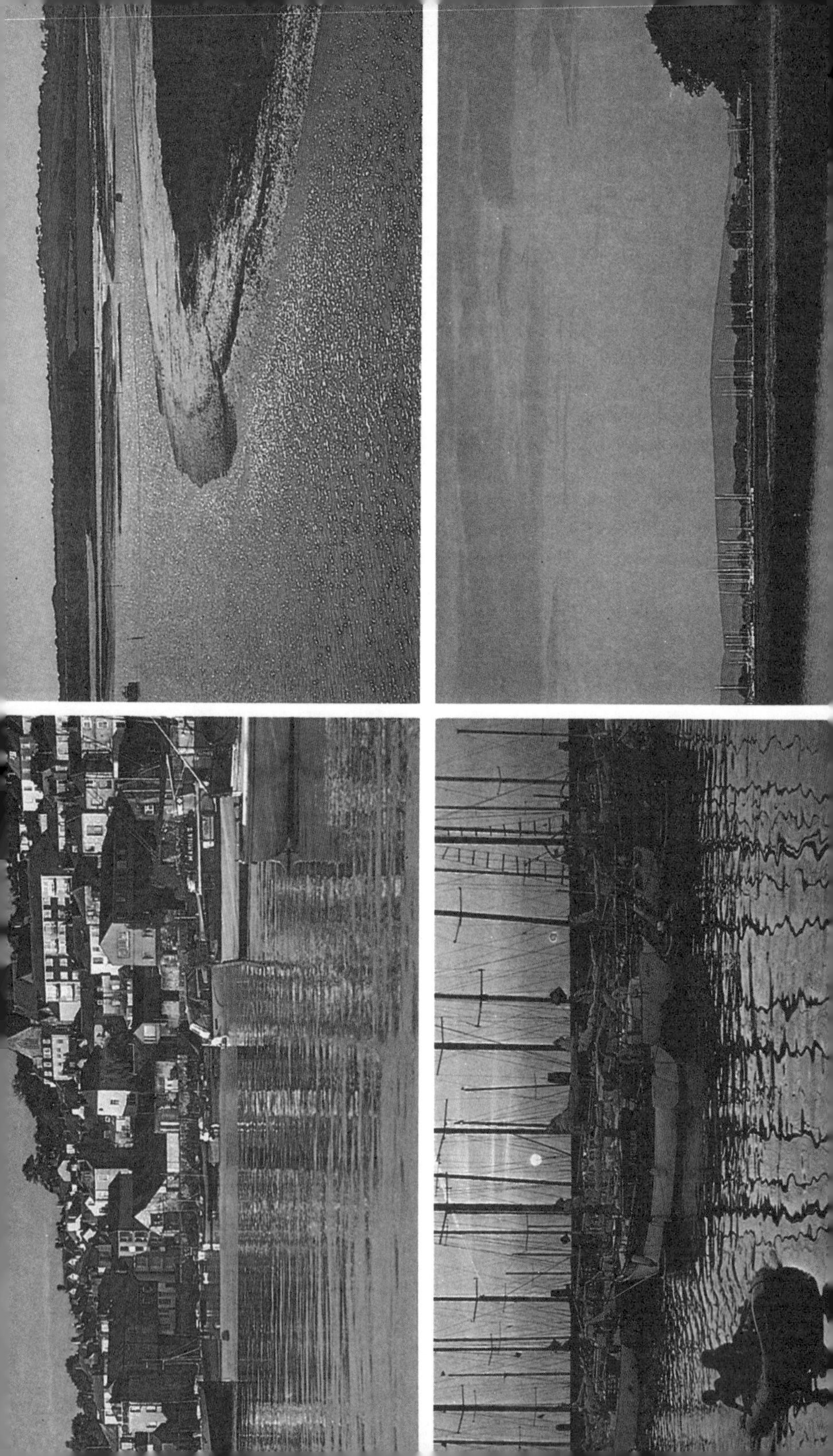

A.H. MOODY & SON. LTD.
BOAT BUILDERS
RENNER
SOUTHAMPTON
ENGLAND

EN ESTA PLAYA ENTRO LA CARABELA PINTA
A SU REGRESO DE DESCUBRIR LAS AMERICAS
CAPITANEADA POR MARTIN ALONSO PINZON
EL DIA 5 DE MARZO DE 1493
BAYONA FUE EL PRIMER PUERTO DEL VIEJO
CONTINENTE EN CONOCER ESTE GLORIOSO HECHO
RUTA DE PINZON
RUTA DE COLON

and coat the surface with epoxy paint. And other odd things can happen: at one yard we saw an employee working on the stem of a recently completed clipper-bow hull where the waterline would be, and on being asked what the trouble was, he said that the area had generated a lot of heat, so he had to cut it out and now was patching up the hole. We met that yacht later; her bobstay fitting had pulled out of the stem just where the patching job had been done, and it was only through a stroke of luck that she did not lose her mast. Then there appeared in the American magazine, *Sail*, an article about the polyestermite, a creature which lives on GRP. Naturally, many of us had hoped such a creature would evolve to dispose of the discarded hulls which otherwise would eventually line the shores of rivers and harbours, an indestructible form of pollution. The appearance of this article caused some consternation among the owners of GRP yachts, and it was not until a letter appeared shortly after in the same magazine that they were able to relax. The writer said that he had been able to catch a few of the glass-eaters and had found they made excellent bait, *especially for suckers*.

Steel? We now consider that we know quite a lot about this, the strongest and most elastic of the boatbuilding materials. If the steel yacht is unfortunate enough to hit something and dent her hull, usually the dent can be hammered out from inside without weakening the plating, provided it is accessible, but because of lockers, ceiling, and the like, it is probably not. Then again, how easy it is, they say, to alter or repair, for a skilful operator with a cutting torch and welding equipment can do it all so quickly. And so he can, but the heat from the appliances will destroy the paint over a wide area on both sides of the plate being worked on, as I know very well, having spent some time inside lockers or down in bilges beating out the flames when the interior paint blistered and then ignited due to the heat from a welding job being done outside; and if any insulation, ceiling, or electric wiring is near, that may also be damaged or destroyed. But perhaps these are minor

---

9 *Left* At Moody's, *Wanderer* was plucked gently from the water by Rennerlift to have her paint attended to. *Right* The pests we grew to dread most—a few goose-barnacles in way of the propeller.

10 *To view A* and *B Top left and right* The east and west harbours at Puerto Rico on Gran Canaria. *C Bottom left* Yachts lie anchored fore-and-aft at Santa Cruz de la Palma. *D Bottom right* The chart on stone commemorating the arrival of *Pinta* at Bayona in 1493.

matters, for few of us want to make drastic alterations or big additions to our yachts, and most of us do not try to bounce them over coral reefs. If one's standards are reasonably high, however, maintenance is the big trouble. I feel sure that no matter what care is taken in preparation, or what wonderful new products are used, paint is not a permanent protection for steel; if it were, gangs would not for ever be hard at work painting the Forth and the Sydney Harbour bridges, nor would nearly every merchant and naval ship we see in port have stagings hanging overside with people on them using paint rollers. Sooner or later salt water will get in behind the paint, rust will form, expand, and throw the paint off; then the only way of doing a respectable job will be to scrape or chip the old paint and the rust-scale off, and with a wire brush or other means, such as grinding, or sandblasting or shot-blasting, clean the steel perfectly and coat it at once. An alternative is to follow merchant navy practice; when rust appears slap on another coat of thick paint. In theory this is wrong, but it may have something to recommend it, for it is well known that ships new from their builders readily spew rust, while old ships with thick layers of paint built up over the years look fairly smart—at least from a distance. The plain fact is that steel does not like salt water. Other well-known disadvantages are that it is subject to electrolysis, though with adequate sacrificial zincs correctly placed this should not be troublesome, and the magnetic compass will be subject to abnormal and possibly changing deviation; also certain types of radio direction-finding equipment cannot be used. Cupranickel (seventy per cent copper and thirty per cent nickel) would appear to be the ideal metal for yacht construction were its cost not so high (probably nearly twice that of steel). It is strong, almost inert, and it is reported of the fifty-two-footer (sixteen-metre) *Asperida*, built of it in 1968, that she never had any paint on her bottom nor ever needed any because of itself the metal had antifouling properties, and the slight fouling that formed when she was in port could easily be wiped off.

Of ferrocement as a boatbuilding material I have little knowledge, though I know it suffers from some of the paint, rust, and magnetic troubles associated with steel; but I have gained the impression that because it is cheaper than other forms of construction, people are inclined to build yachts that are much too big, forgetting that the hull accounts for a comparatively small proportion of the total cost. The material has had much bad publicity because of some shocking amateur designs that have been built to in it, and the very poor workmanship that went into them, whereas it is not possible to tell a well-built 'stone' boat just by looking at her. Being a heavy material, strength for strength with others, many a ferrocement yacht at her launching either floated below her designed waterline, or was crank through having insufficient ballast, yet both of these are faults that could have been avoided at the design stage.

In my view the best and most trustworthy boatbuilding material is wood, provided it can be had of sufficiently good quality and is properly knit together. With bottom paint undamaged there is little or no risk of attack by gribble or teredo; if the wood is well seasoned and the hull properly ventilated and is free from fresh-water leaks, there should be no dry-rot; painting is straightforward, lasts well and, apart from the underwater body, is needed more for appearance than protection, and—to me this is important—if I want to make a hole in a wood boat I can do it, and if after all I find I do not need it I can bung it up again. But construction in wood, except in a few places like Hong Kong and Taiwan, is expensive, and woodworking shipwrights are scarce. Multiple-skin construction may overcome this, but I have recently heard of one yard building in the traditional manner with copper-fastened planks caulked and payed and, although labour costs were high, it was thought they would be outweighed by the fact that no expensive glue was needed. If oil products continue to rise in price, perhaps wood will resume its proper place as a first-class material for the construction of yachts.

At Lymington our socialities were considerable and, when they became too much for us, we retreated to the Beaulieu River where we could not too easily be reached. In early days I used to keep my boat lying to her own anchors just off Gins Farm, parking my motor cycle in the farm's pigsty, and mooring my dinghy off the quay, to which an occasional spritsail barge came to load farm produce. But for some time it had not been possible to anchor anywhere near Gins which, with its mellow, tiled roof and twisted chimneys, seemed to have sunk a little lower into the saltings, because there were so many moorings; however, a little further upstream in what we called 'millionaire's reach' there was a mooring to which we had access, for it belonged to the Old Carthusian Yacht Club, of which Susan happened to be an honorary life member; the mooring lay right off Clobb Copse, the lovely home of the Ehrmans, whom we were fortunate enough to know, so we could land at their pontoon and make our way through their garden to Buckler's Hard to buy bread and post our mail. With the distant island downs peeping over the marshes (Plate 8 D) we spent peaceful days there, and after dark listened to the nightingale, and at dawn watched the soft mist lift from the river to herald yet another glorious summer's day. But we noticed that the river had widened a little and grown shoaler, and that the marsh grass had receded from its edges, and we wondered if this might have been due to the vessels which travelled at too high a speed and made too much wash: ferries bringing holidaymakers from Southsea, and the yachts which, under power, were determined to reach the Master Builder's before the bar closed.

Time for us was running out. The work Moody's had done for us, and the many things we had bought there, had been exempted from tax because we were not resident in or staying on in the country; but for this exemption to hold good we must leave not later than September, which, indeed, we wanted to do so as to avoid the risk of meeting an autumn gale in the Western Approaches or the Bay of Biscay. With many a sad backward glance at the familiar waters in which both of us had learned to sail, and in which we had enjoyed much happiness, we sailed down past Yarmouth, where the thicket of masts told us that the 'harbour full' flag would soon be flying, and so passed out through the Needles Channel bound once more for Falmouth, which was to be our port of departure.

There we made our preparations and did our final provisioning. Although we had done it many times before we still found this business as fascinating and exciting as ever. One by one the items on the long lists of things to obtain, do or arrange got crossed off, then new lists were compiled, and no matter how early we started, as the date set for departure approached it seemed that we would never be ready in time. On this occasion not many things eluded us in the end, but we never did manage to obtain any of the old-fashioned, black, sticky insulating tape for which I have a passion, and we failed to find a flat toaster to use on the cooking stove; so I said I would make one from a large biscuit tin, but seemingly biscuits no longer came in tins. There were a few minor irritations, and one of these concerned our stores out of bond. Of the few brands of duty-free Scotch available from the chandler, we chose one, the round bottles of which we knew neatly fitted the ready-use rack; but when later at sea we broke the seal and opened a case, we discovered that one of those little men whose job in life is to alter the shape of things without good reason had been busy: the bottles were flat and thin instead of round, as though intended to travel at high speed, unable to fit in any normal stowage space and almost incapable of standing up on their own. Fortunately we had kept an old, empty, round bottle, and decanted into that.

PART III

ENGLAND TO PANAMA

WITH SOME THOUGHTS ON

Harness and guardrails—Ethics of anchoring—Floating objects—Midocean meetings—Chafe—Port officials—Theft—Alarm systems—Poet and artist—Longshore robbers

HAVING topped up with fuel and water at Mylor one lovely blue day in late August, when combine harvesters were leaving geometric patterns on the hillsides, we slipped out of Falmouth harbour. We had set the working sails and were hanking on the genoa to make the most of the light east breeze, when Susan, who was working beside me on the foredeck, tumbled heavily.

'Are you hurt?'

'I've broken my wrist,' she replied in a matter-of-fact tone.

She at once went to the wheel, switched off the autopilot, and with her good hand turned the ship back towards the harbour while I handed the sails, started the engine, and prepared to re-anchor. We were fortunate in finding Frank Edwards, the harbourmaster, out in his launch. He took Susan ashore, calling the port doctor by radio as they went, and then when Dr Develin said Susan must go to Truro hospital to have her wrist X-rayed and set, Frank took her there in his car. Such quick, kind help was touching. That evening Susan returned in the club launch with the information that her arm must remain in plaster for five weeks, and must be X-rayed again at the end of the first week. How fortunate it was that the accident happened when it did and not when we were far from medical aid.

Of course, our enforced delay was an anticlimax, but I put it to some use learning a bit about cooking, washing up, bunk making and laundrying for, like many a spoiled husband, I had done little to help with those time-consuming chores in the thirty-five years of my married life. I also experimented to find out what I could and could not do as a single-hander—a role I had not played since before the war—and it seemed that provided I was content with a modest spread of sail I might manage without too much difficulty, but one thing I could not do alone without risk of damage to the varnished topgallant rail, on which Susan had lavished much care, was to hoist the dinghy inboard or launch her.

The day after Susan's final X-ray, West Country Chandlers, who had been helpful in many ways, found a diver who, for ten pounds, was prepared, on his day off from being an income-tax inspector, to come and give our bottom a rub over, for it was growing slimy. It was good for our morale, to say nothing of our progress, to leave after only one week's delay with a clean bottom. The weather was kind, giving Susan a chance to become accustomed to steadying herself—below and in the cockpit only, for there was to be no scrambling about on deck—with one hand, and so little wind was there that we did a lot of motoring before nearing Ushant. But then the wind came from ahead, and the reef which I had with prudence (or was it cowardice?) put in the mizzen, and the small jib which I was determined not to change, made our total sail area too small for efficient windward work; in twenty-four hours of beating we made good only forty-seven miles, and we passed Ushant at a distance of nearly fifty miles, which was well outside the main shipping lane to Finisterre. The vane gear, of course, did the steering, but we had to keep a lookout, and for this foul-weather clothes were needed. To keep her plaster dry Susan wore her arm in a plastic bag, and I had to learn a new drill, how to zip and button her into her oilskin, and how to tie the laces of her shoes—all back to front of course. In turn we used the same berth in the saloon for sleeping (that saved some bed making) and our meals were *very* simple.

For years we had carried safety harnesses with us, but our attempts to use them had been half-hearted and sporadic. I now felt I ought to wear mine when working on deck, for if I were to tumble overboard Susan would be in a bit of a fix. With this in mind, I had rigged lines from boom-gallows to mast to bowsprit-end, so that I could clip myself on before leaving the cockpit. But what a business it was, first to get the harness on over my oilskin, and then to keep its line clear of obstructions as I moved about, and again and again it held me either too close to my work or out of reach of it, and the attachment then had to be shifted. I also found, as I had on earlier attempts to use a harness, that in a short-handed vessel, and we were certainly short-handed now, when a job on deck needed doing it was usually urgent, and to put a harness on caused delay. So, after a couple of days, I abandoned it and relied, as I had always done, on my arms and legs and balance to keep me inside the guardrails, which were well secured and thirty inches (seventy-six centimetres) high, and it was a relief to be able to move freely once more. It should, however, not be thought that I do not approve of harnesses; indeed, in the unlikely event that we had someone sailing with us, I would, largely for my own peace of mind, ask him or her always to wear a harness and remain clipped on while on deck. I have been aboard many yachts, including modern ocean racers, where the upper guardrail was only twenty-four inches (sixty-one centimetres) above the deck instead of thirty inches (seventy-six centimetres), which I regard as the minimum height; perhaps that is one reason why harnesses are considered to be so essential.

Fishing vessels, of which there were plenty, presented the usual problems. I never have found it easy in the dark to tell what a fishing vessel is doing, for she usually has such a blaze of working lights that her navigation lights, if she is showing any, are hard to make out. Taking bearings or watching her in relation to a low star is not much help, for, when her movement has been determined, she will as likely as not suddenly alter course or extinguish all her lights. Another thing we found perplexing was something that looked like a trident, with each of its three prongs festooned with lights so bright and numerous that, like those of a town, their loom in the sky could be seen for hours after they had dropped below the horizon. We thought this might be an oil-rig under tow, but we saw no sign of a tug.

After we had worked our way laboriously a little south of the latitude of Ushant the wind freed, allowing us to sail easily on our course for Finisterre; this was as well for, during one of my fishing-vessel-avoiding actions, my left elbow had, as a New Zealander might say, 'gone crook', and it was painful to use that arm even for light work—what a pair of old crocks we had become! However, it was good to be progressing in the right direction, and a relief to be now outside the 100-fathom line where the sea was easier and more regular. But the BBC shipping forecast, which now we could receive only in the afternoon, and faintly, predicted gales for most areas including ours; the sun had a halo, and the north-west swell was building up.

Our fourth day at sea was spent either rushing along in hard squalls or slatting in calm patches, but we made a run of 139 miles, and, at noon, Cabo de Villano, our intended landfall on the north-west corner of Spain, lay only seventy-five miles distant. We lifted the light, the loom of which we had seen for an hour or more, above the horizon at midnight; but the wind then backed so that we could do no better than head at the light, and, therefore, were crossing the shipping lane, outside which we had until then managed to remain. There were many ships, and they, unlike the fishermen of which there were also a lot, behaved well. Two hours later we tacked offshore, but soon had to put about again to avoid getting involved with more fishermen, and then the night, which was already dark, became darker still as rain enveloped us, obscuring the lights of all the vessels which had been in sight. That seemed to us in our weak state not a good place to be, so once again we tacked and stood well away from the land. By then the wind was up to thirty-five knots, and I reduced our already snug rig by rolling a reef in the mainsail. The sea was rising, and the swell, when the first faint greyness of dawn revealed it, looked enormous. At about that time we had a near encounter with a container ship. Through the rain I sighted her off our starboard beam heading directly at us, but while I was in the act of putting our helm up, for I thought it wiser to bear away and gather more speed in an attempt to dodge her rather than tack, I saw with relief her masts slowly separate as she swung to a new course; I felt grateful to her alert lookout as she passed silently under our stern.

At breakfast time we hove-to to wait for an improvement which was not long in coming, for soon the sky cleared and the wind veered and fell light, leaving us to slam about in what looked and felt like Portland race superimposed on the swell; apparently we were not to have the forecast gale after all. Cabo Finisterre was visible in the sunlight and, as none of our sails would draw because of the wild motion, we started the Ford and headed for it. We rounded the famous headland in the afternoon, and the remarkable thing was that, instead of building up and breaking on the several shoals which lie a mile or so offshore, the great swell subsided as we neared the land, and, except at the feet of the cliffs, there was not a breaker to be seen.

That evening we brought up in the Ria de Corcubion, which lies five miles east-nor'east of Finisterre and is well sheltered from all but south winds. It may be recalled that in 1925 Claud Worth rode out a southerly gale there in *Tern IV* with seventy fathoms of cable out in a depth of 6 fathoms, while two steamships were blown ashore and lost. The only vessels we found at the anchorage were a couple of coasters, and the 100-foot (thirty-metre) Swedish ketch, *Nitro*, which had lain there for the past three months. Her owners kindly took us ashore in their dinghy to do our shopping, thus saving us the difficult task of launching ours, and we spent a pleasant evening with them in their big steel ship; she was fifty years old and they had themselves converted her from an oil-carrier to a floating home and workshop.

During our second day at Corcubion the wind blew straight in, raising a steep little sea and causing us to feel uneasy. *Nitro* let go a second anchor, and we moved into the small bay on the west side just north of Punta Quenje, where I believe one might safely ride out a southerly gale; but there is not much room, and kelp may foul the anchor.

We had first visited this corner of Spain some twenty years before when a yacht was a rare sight, and the people were so curious that all day and often through part of the night they, in their big rough boats, hung on to us watching our every action; but now so many yachts cruise the coast that little interest is shown in them, and at Corcubion we were not visited even by the port officials.

Passing to seaward of the several unmarked reefs, we managed in quiet weather and in daylight to reach Bayona, which lies near the mouth of Ria de Vigo sixty miles to the south. There we noticed changes since our last visit, when only fishermen and the occasional overseas yacht used the place, and one could anchor in perfect shelter close to the sand beach at the feet of the magnificent ramparts of the fortress, Monte Real. Now we found a government-sponsored yacht club with an embryo marina, an hotel topping the battlements, and the best part of the harbour occupied by apparently little-used Spanish yachts and powerboats on moorings; so the visitor, unless prepared to jostle for a berth at the club, had to lie further out where the shelter was not so good and weed rendered the holding ground treacherous. Nevertheless, I still regard this as the best harbour between Finisterre and Gibraltar, and it was here that Columbus's consort, *Pinta*, put in at the end of the voyage to the New World in 1493, and near the club is a fine chart on stone commemorating the event (Plate 10 D). In the narrow streets of the older part of the town, where one tracked down the bakery by the delicious smell, pools of dazzling sunlight lay among the inky shadows.

It has sometimes happened that we have fallen in with another yacht with which we have immediately become friendly, and, if our paths lay in the same direction, we remained in company perhaps for several weeks; we referred to such a yacht as our 'buddy ship'. At Bayona our near neighbour was the thirty-eight foot (11·5-metre) Nicholson ketch, *Grockle*, with a crew of three Englishmen; she became our buddy ship, and as she, too, was bound towards New Zealand we hoped we would see more of her along the way. Unfortunately, the yacht club, with its restaurant, and bar, its panelled rooms and oil paintings, had at the time no water supply, so, as we wished to top up our tanks we had to go to the town quay among the fishing vessels lying there. The three from *Grockle*, Nick Lowes (part-owner), David and Andrew, came with us, and never had we enjoyed such cheerful and efficient help—I did not have to do a thing except pay for the water. Each day *Grockle* provided us with the shipping forecast, which we were then no longer able to get on our receiver, and often did our shopping for us; we had an excellent dinner aboard her, all of it carefully planned so that Susan could eat it with a fork, and on one occasion we had the pleasure of Andrew's company for the night when it blew so hard that he could not safely row back to his ship, for the weather was boisterous and we had a succession of hard gales from the south; indeed, so bad was the weather then that there were twenty-five large fishing vessels sheltering in the harbour, and nearly as many yachts, and among the latter there was some drama. Several dragged, one repeatedly, which did not surprise us as she had no chain; yet she had veered a lot of line, as we discovered one night when the gale suddenly stopped blowing, and although her anchor must have been a long way from us, she managed to wrap herself and her dinghy round us. When I hailed her people, a delightful American couple who next day rowed over to say how sorry they were, to come up and help unravel the tangle, the wife was first on deck. She gave one glance at the situation and shouted to her husband:

'On deck, on deck, and at the double.'

So often on this and other voyages and cruises had we seen demonstrations of indifferent anchoring technique, that I sometimes wondered if the people concerned had much idea of the anxiety or even damage they might cause to their neighbours; so, at the risk of being accused of trying to teach my grandmother how to suck eggs, I propose to express here the ethics of anchoring as I see them, as well as a little of the practical side.

Anchors depend not so much on their weight as on their shape to dig into the seabed and hold, but for any anchor to do this the pull on it needs to be in a horizontal direction, that is, parallel to the seabed. As the pull must come on the correct part of the anchor, at the ring or shackle, the cable must not be allowed to fall on top of the anchor when letting go, or a bight of it may foul some part of the anchor and cause it to drag. For this reason cable should only be veered while the vessel is moving over the ground; though it is best if the movement is in an astern direction that is not always convenient, especially when bringing up under sail, when it may be better to let go with headway, and then give the vessel a sheer one way or the other so that, as she falls back under the influence of the wind, the cable will make a wide sweep clear of the anchor. I use the word 'cable' as this is defined in the *Concise Oxford Dictionary*, the *American Heritage Dictionary*, and in the two nautical dictionaries I happen to have on board, as 'the chain or rope to which an anchor is secured'. The term 'rode', which today is often used by yachtsmen, particularly in America, does not appear in this context in any of the above books.

Seeing that the pull on the anchor must be in a horizontal direction, obviously one must veer a lot more cable than is needed just to let the anchor reach the seabed; but no matter how much cable is veered, if it is of rope the pull will not be in a horizontal direction, for the rope will make a straight line between the vessel and her anchor and tend to lift the latter from its proper efficient attitude. It is here that one of the advantages of chain as opposed to rope becomes apparent. Because of its weight the chain cable will hang in a curve (catenary) so that the part of the cable nearest the anchor will not lift from the seabed except perhaps momentarily in a very strong wind; also, if there is any sea running at the anchorage the catenary will act as a spring to stop snubbing, damping out the jerks the vessel might otherwise subject her anchor to. When using chain cable, it is customary to veer not less than three times the depth of water at high tide though, as many of us have discovered, the ratio needs to be increased in shallow water but in deep water it may be decreased; in strong winds or on poor holding ground more cable should be veered—chain in the locker never did anybody any good. When using rope cable, at least six times the depth at high tide ought to be veered, and, of course, the greater the length the more nearly horizontal will the pull be on the anchor; a travelling weight let part way down the cable will, if heavy enough, improve the angle of pull, but it is an added complication and may cause chafe. When using rope cable, however, it is usual to have some chain at the anchor end of it; not only will this improve the angle of pull, but will reduce the risk of the rope part of the cable being damaged by chafe on the seabed or on any sharp object that may lie there. Often this length of chain is too short, and I believe that five fathoms should be regarded as the absolute minimum. The advantages of rope are its light weight, lower original cost, great strength, and elasticity that may take the place of a chain's catenary in preventing snubbing. Some people claim that it is easier to handle, but I do not find it so; when wet it is difficult to get a grip of; if a windlass is being used someone will have to tail on to keep tension on the barrel, and the cable must either be coiled down or wound on a reel, and if it goes below deck a lot of water will go with it if it is of the plaited or braided variety. In contrast, chain will feed itself round the windlass gipsy unattended and take itself below, where with some planning and a bit of luck it will stow itself and do so in a remarkably small space. It was unfortunate that an editorial in the fine, old-established American magazine, *Yachting*, stated that all yachts should use rope for their anchor 'rodes'; probably more yachts have been damaged or lost by following that advice than through any other cause.

Of the anchors commonly used by yachts, I prefer the CQR ('secure'), the sophisticated plough type invented and perfected by Professor Taylor. Its only disadvantage is that if on letting go it is not immediately given plenty of cable so that it may at once turn over and dig in, it may drag, and while doing so may pick up a bunch of weed or a tin or jar on its point, and then it will not be able to dig in no matter how much cable it is given. A similar remark applies in some degree to the Danforth anchor, which is perhaps more commonly used in America than it is in Britain, and, so far as holding power is concerned, there seems to be little difference between it and the CQR. Incidentally, should the CQR anchor foul some obstruction on the seabed, such as a rock or chain, it is sometimes possible to free it by veering plenty of cable and then sailing or motoring up-wind of the anchor. While we were lying at Falmouth I suggested this to a couple who had for some time been trying to free their fouled anchor, and it came up at the first attempt—I think they regarded me as some sort of a magician.

In an anchorage where there is no tidal stream, all normal yachts lie head to wind, though they will sheer about from side to side as puffs of wind catch them on one bow or the other. Those with chain cables will lie more steadily than those with rope cables, partly because of the friction created when the yacht on sheering tries to drag a bight of chain over the seabed, and partly because she will have only half the scope that the yacht lying to rope will have out. Therefore, when Susan and I come into a crowded anchorage, we look round to see which yachts are lying to rope and which to chain; avoiding the former, we let go near the latter with the comforting knowledge that we and our neighbours will all behave much alike. Conversely, it is sensible for the man who uses rope to choose an anchorage near other rope users, and not foul up with his wild gyrations the area where the diehard chain-users are lying steadily. Both they and we avoid if we possibly can anchoring anywhere near multihulls, for they with their great windage and slight grip on the water do sometimes behave in the oddest manner.

A yacht with good ground tackle, by which I mean a proper anchor of the correct weight and plenty of cable, preferably of chain, will, if there is no tidal stream and little sea, ride out almost anything, perhaps even a hurricane, to a single anchor if the holding ground is good; but, if in wild weather she needs a second anchor, that will normally be laid out in much the same direction as the first. In a gale, however, it may be impossible to take a second anchor away; it will then have to be dropped under foot and cable veered on both. If the wind is expected to shift to the right, as it should in the southern half of an east-going depression in the northern hemisphere, the first anchor to be let go will normally be the one on the port bow; then as the wind shifts, the vessel as she swings to it will ride with open hawse, that is, her cables will not cross, and the cable of the first anchor will not be able to foul the second anchor.

Many anchorages have tidal streams flowing through them, and then unless the yacht has a large area entirely to herself, she and her neighbours will need two anchors if they are to lie clear of one another. These should be laid up and down stream, so that on the flood she lies to one and on the ebb to the other. I feel it is wrong, except in the special circumstance mentioned below, to secure one cable at the bow and the other at the stern (anchoring fore-and-aft) because the yacht might obstruct the passage of other craft, and if wind or tide were to come strongly on the beam she would place a heavy swigging strain on both anchors. The seamanlike procedure is, having got the cables as straight and tight as possible, to secure one to the other outside the stemhead roller (usually this is done with a rolling hitch), and then veer cable a little until the point of attachment of the cables is well below the keel. Moored like that the yacht will not obstruct the passage of other craft, and will remain in one place, though she will be able at the change of tide and/or wind to swing round, but in only a small circle. I believe that anchoring fore-and-aft should only be resorted to in an uneasy anchorage with no tidal stream, when one wishes to keep one's vessel end-on to the swell to ease or stop her rolling.

Perhaps because they are accustomed to living and working in a crowd, and searching for parking spaces for their cars, many sailing people appear to be of a gregarious nature. Most of those of us who prefer some degree of solitude have had the experience of anchoring in a spot well away from other yachts only to be almost overlaid by the next yacht to arrive, which brings up so close that there is risk of collision, and one can hear her crockery being washed and her heads being pumped. I would suggest that those who like being in a crowd might go and find themselves a crowd (that should present no problem except in high latitudes) and leave the yacht lying alone on her own, for she probably values her peace and privacy. But having found a crowd, some discretion in picking a berth ought still to be exercised, and it is important that this be not so close to any other vessel as to give her a foul berth, that is, with any risk of touching her in any conditions of wind or tide. If one cannot be sure about this one should bring up outside and to leeward of the fleet, even though that may be inconveniently far from the shore—the first to arrive have naturally picked the best berths and are entitled to them. It is particularly bad seamanship to anchor close to windward of another vessel so that when cable has been veered one lies only a few feet from her; although the newcomer may feel confident his anchor has a good hold, the people in the other vessel cannot know this, and may spend anxious hours awaiting a collision, or in self-defence may even be driven to shifting berth, especially if the people from the newcomer have gone ashore leaving their vessel unattended.

* * *

In the bad weather at Bayona the mortality among dinghies (mostly inflatables) was high; some flipped, if that is the correct un-nautical term to use when they become airborne and fall on their faces; some vanished without trace, and others in flipping spilt their oars overboard and lost them. One night, a rather run-down Swedish yacht had a fire on board; it warped her plastic ports and melted her echo sounder and radio set, shocked the crew, and burned the owner who came to us for medical attention. The two young owners of *Winetta* borrowed our grease gun to free their windlass which had rusted up; they got it working, and, while enthusiastically trying it, lost all their chain and the anchor to which they had been lying. *Grockle* went to their aid with her spare anchor and chain, and *Winetta* recovered hers next day by diving for it.

So life in our floating village was far from dull, but we were all disturbed a bit by the news that tropical storm Fay, north of the Azores, was moving fast towards us, and that we were to expect storm-force winds. The wind certainly was freshening, but there were still lulls in which we could hear the deep rumble of heavy surf on the seaward side of protecting Monte Real. Like some others we veered a lot of cable and prepared a second anchor; then we waited.

Night had fallen before Fay arrived, and the first violent blasts of wind came while we were clearing the supper things away. A few minutes later a hail, faint and thin above the roar of wind and rattle of rain, had me out, and I found Nick from *Grockle* on our foredeck attempting to tame his airborne inflatable dinghy. He had come to warn us that *Winetta*, which had been lying ahead, was dragging down towards us, and to offer any help we might need; he secured his dinghy alongside our port bow to act as a fender. I at once started our engine with the idea of making *Wanderer* sheer one way or the other to avoid or soften the collision; but this proved to be unnecessary, for *Winetta*, moving steadily although her anchor was still down, only needed fending off with our long boathook as she drove past. I was about to heave her a line in the hope that our own anchor might hold the pair of us, when to my great relief I heard her engine start, and in the glare of the harbour lights watched as she got her anchor up and punched her way slowly up-wind and let go again; that time her anchor held.

Nick's kind and thoughtful act was a courageous one, for had he failed to reach us and been swept past in his dinghy, he would almost certainly have been blown out of the harbour; that or a capsize could have been fatal. He now wanted to return to *Grockle* and somehow transfer her spare anchor and cable to *Winetta*; but we were able to dissuade him from such a risky and almost impossible enterprise, and, although he must have been worried about his own ship lying a short distance to windward, when he saw that *Winetta*'s anchor was continuing to hold he allowed himself to be persuaded to remain with us. So we got him to stand on deck while we shone our Aldis lamp on him so that his crew might know that he was with us and safe; then we provided him with dry clothes, and one of my pipes and some tobacco.

We were glad to have Nick's quiet but cheerful company throughout that violent night. He and I took turns going into the rain-lashed cockpit at each violent squall to see if all was still well with us and our neighbours. It was during one of these sorties that I saw a red flare burning aboard one of the smaller yachts inshore. I knew there was nothing we could do in such conditions—the wind by then had reached its peak of about sixty-five knots—and I did not believe the couple aboard her could come to any personal harm even if their yacht, then dragging fast, finished up on the breakwater as seemed likely, for there they could scramble ashore. So I did not mention the flare to Susan or Nick at the time. In the event the couple aboard managed to grab a vacant mooring as they dragged through the crowd of uninhabited small craft, and next day were a little embarrassed about the flare. Through the long wild night we smoked and talked and from time to time drank coffee, and it was not until well after breakfast that the gale moderated enough for *Winetta*'s hard dinghy with a good outboard motor to come over and ferry Nick back to his *Grockle*.

A few days after the weather had returned to normal a large new ketch arrived in port. She was on her way to the Genoa boat show, and the young Dutchman who was delivering her kindly invited us aboard and showed us round. She was flush-decked, probably seventy feet (twenty-one metres) or more in length, and, with her pretty, black hull, clipper bow, and stern windows, was to my eye very attractive. But we were astonished at what we saw below. In the deckhouse above the throbbing engine-room—she was running a generator because cooking, like most other things on board, was done by electricity—was the dining area with chairs and an L-shaped settee round a polished table, and one could look through large windows; but, if the diners did not care for what they saw without, or grew tired of being looked at, a switch could be pressed and the whole dining area together with the people in it was gently lowered a few feet. Below there were many cabins beautifully fitted in teak or mahogany, but as each was lighted only by a port in the topsides they seemed to us a little gloomy, and they smelt of diesel exhaust. But the pièce de résistance was in the great cabin aft, a lovely spacious place where light reflected from the sea slanted up through the gracefully raked windows in the stern to make water patterns on the white deckhead. Most of the space was occupied by an enormous circular bed. Again electrics were in evidence, and on a switch being turned, the bed silently split into two, and up popped a pair of identical boudoirs, complete with drawers, make-up lights and mirrors.

'This isn't a ship,' whispered Susan, 'it's a floating sex-pad.'

A little while after we met one of the delivery crew, an Englishman, and asked him how the vessel performed under sail.

'We don't really know,' he told us. 'We've only once tried to set the mainsail and its boom didn't clear the top of the deckhouse.'

How an owner arranges the accommodation of his yacht is, of course, his own affair, but often one is asked to comment, as I was once when aboard a new and very lovely New Zealand cutter. I was much taken with all I saw, and said so, but on being pressed to make a criticism I remarked that the galley was not on the traditional port side. When I was asked why the port side should be preferable to the starboard side, I went through the old rigmarole and explained that a galley is safer and more convenient to work in if it is to leeward, for then anything that carries away does not fall on the cook. So when heaving-to in bad weather, or for some other reason, it is best if there is any choice in the matter to do so on the starboard tack; I added that this has the advantage that a vessel hove-to on that tack has the right of way over all other craft except a vessel not under control, a vessel laying cables, and a lightvessel.

'Ah,' said the other with a perfectly straight face, 'but we don't have any lightvessels in New Zealand.'

So far as we were concerned, there was only one other incident before we left Bayona in early October. The time had come for the plaster to be removed from Susan's arm. I had been instructed how to do this, and, in anticipation, had sharpened the bread-knife and fitted a new blade to the hacksaw. But I need not have bothered, for there were no fewer than five doctors in yachts at Bayona all apparently keen to do the job, and, in the end, the plaster was removed with a pair of rusty metal-cutting snips by the two doctors who were aboard the big American-owned ketch, *Astral*, when we were invited to dine aboard by her skipper, our old New Zealand friend Dick McIlvride, and his wife Pat, who was acting as supercargo. Susan's naked arm looked a frail stick and it pained her a lot, and many weeks were to pass before it filled out and became once more a serviceable, seagoing limb.

We sailed in company with *Grockle*, not by design, for we do not care to be in close company with another yacht when at sea because of the constant lookout needed, but by chance, for she was bound for Madeira and we for Lanzarote, the easternmost of the Canary Islands; but, as Susan and I wished to get well away from the land and outside the shipping lane as soon as possible, we and *Grockle* steered the same course for a day or two; as a result we were within sight of one another for the first twenty-four hours. Under full sail the Nicholson thirty-eight was a fine sight, lifting and dropping on the swell which often hid most of her, but she had the legs of us, partly perhaps, because in our weak state, we could not boom out a running sail. There was but little wind, however, and we both used our engines from time to time. It was on this occasion that we had a good chance to see how efficient the modern tricolour masthead light is, for *Grockle* was fitted with one.

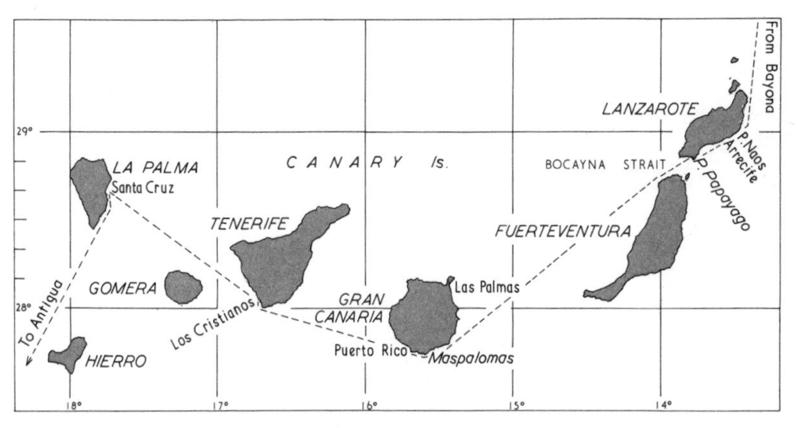

Canary Islands

The 880-mile passage to the Canaries took us nine days, and even though we went many miles offshore before turning south we did not manage to get away from the shipping, and much of the time one or more vessels were in sight to keep us on the alert. Otherwise, until the final three days when the wind freshened, it was a dull passage, for the Portuguese trade, which on earlier trips we had found to be fresh or strong, was scarcely in evidence. As we drew near the African coast we were visited by a number of land creatures which we thought must have been lifted by a thermal current and then blown out to sea; there were flies, two moths, a butterfly and a couple of tiny birds, one of which decided to remain with us. We put out water and ground-up nuts and left the door of the sleeping cabin open so that the bird could shelter there. Next day we missed the tiny fluttering creature and presumed it had taken off, but a little later when we were at anchor and sleeping in the proper place I noticed a strange smell in my bunk, and there Susan discovered the bird's decomposing remains under my pillow.

Rumours and scraps of information about places tend to spread and swell like grapes on the vine of the ocean voyaging fraternity, but some of this, based perhaps on a one-day visit, can be misleading, and, although there had been plenty of rumours, reliable information on changes and new harbours among the Canaries had not been available in England. Our intention was to investigate some of the rumours, and avoid the oily agony of berthing at Las Palmas or Santa Cruz de Tenerife, which filthy commercial ports were until recently the only places sheltered from all winds, including the violent southerly which occasionally and without warning sweeps over the archipelago.

The first of the 'grape-vine' harbours was Puerto Naos on the south-east side of Lanzarote, and this was our immediate objective. We had been there before, but only when the harbour was indifferently protected by an islet and a reef; now, we had been told, a breakwater had been built making a snug and perfectly protected anchorage. We arrived too early while it was still dark, so when the shore lights drew near we hove-to until daylight and then went on in. The harbour was long and narrow, its shore side occupied by a fish-canning plant and other major works in progress, and the place was packed with fishing vessels; also it contained a number of old hulks either at anchor or on moorings, along with several wrecks which were awash when we made our cautious entry at low water. We could find no vacant berth, so we turned and came out again, crossing the place off our list, and rightly so, as we learned later that yachts were not permitted to anchor there even if they could find room. Only a mile away and off the town of Arrecife was another harbour which did have a few yachts lying in it; I suppose we should have tried it, but there seemed so little room, and we had been told that the harbour-master insisted that part of a yacht's crew must remain aboard in case the wind should blow from the south, to which direction the harbour is open.

This was not a promising or very enterprising beginning; but the day was still young, so we ran on along the island's south coast to an anchorage we had used in the past in Bocayna Strait and just round Punta Papayago, anchored in clear water off an empty sand beach and spent two lovely quiet nights there, confident of being able to leave in the dark if the need arose, for there were two lighthouses in sight. While sailing along the Lanzarote coast that day we had noticed much new building and, when we left our pleasant anchorage, we saw on the island's western tip a huge hotel, and there were two more on Fuerteventura with a third one a-building; it seemed that the Canaries were on the crest of a tourist boom, and this was to be confirmed a little later.

Having heard of a new yacht harbour at Puerto Rico on the south coast of Gran Canaria, and another at Los Cristianos on the south-west coast of Tenerife, we decided to have a look at both of them, and if they failed us there was always Santa Cruz de la Palma, which we intended to visit in any event, for we knew La Palma to be the least spoilt of the islands and a good place from which to start an Atlantic crossing.

The distance from our anchorage to the southern tip of Gran Canaria was 120 miles; expecting the wind to be light (which it was) we started in the early morning and took twenty-four hours over the crossing. In the night we sighted the lights of one of those seagoing mysteries which were becoming so common. This one, which appeared to be of great length, exhibited at its eastern end two white lights vertically disposed; at its western end stood row upon row of orange lights like those on the promenade decks of an old-fashioned passenger liner; in the wide gap between glared a single brilliant green light. We thought at first this must be a tug towing something big (why else the two white lights?) but, if so, then the green light should have been a red one. We gave it up and slowly sailed clear, and a little later met a large passenger ship lit up like a Christmas tree; she passed us port side to, and we wondered why she displayed a green light immediately under her red one. On arrival at Puerto Rico our near neighbour was a fishing vessel which had her red light on her starboard side and her green one to port; if we had met her at sea by night we really would have been puzzled.

We soon saw the loom of the lights at Las Palmas glowing in the sky and, as we drew nearer to the island, a blaze of lights lifted above the horizon, many of them in undulating strings climbing up the mountainsides; among them flashed the headlights of cars. But this glittering array did not concern us as we were heading for the island's southern end where, at Maspalomas, was a twenty-seven-mile occulting light; this, however, was almost eclipsed by the great gathering of lights round it shining out to sea and up into the sky. We realized there must be a new town there of which we had heard nothing, and I wondered, as I had so often done in the past, why man, if he is so frightened of the dark that he must surround himself with a million lights, does not put shades or reflectors on them so that they illuminate only what he wants to see instead of shining uselessly elsewhere; then they would not dazzle or mislead the sea or air navigator, and would give twice as much light for the same consumption of electricity. In this connection it may be of interest to note that later, when we were sailing to La Palma, and while still forty-five miles from that island, we could clearly make out the street lamps of some high-up village.

At daybreak, as we approached the tall and slender lighthouse tower at Maspalomas we saw that, in its neighbourhood, and crowding along the inshore edge of the wind-blown sand beach, was a complex of big hotels and apartment blocks. Apparently these were of recent construction, for all that the chart marked in the area, apart from the lighthouse, was 'Cave', 'White rock, conspic.', and 'Huts'. We did not know about it then, but there was a new yacht harbour about a mile north-west of the lighthouse. However, we were bound for Puerto Rico, which we had been told lay between two points that were not named on the chart or mentioned in the sailing directions, so that the information was not of much help. It felt strange to be looking for a town and harbour not shown on the chart (they tell me the road maps for this area are much to be preferred) and we continued for several miles along the coast until we spotted a town built on both sides of a valley. Apart from the many high-rise buildings, the most conspicuous objects were three white flagpoles at the water's edge; but, as we approached, we noticed that they were on the move, and presently they proved to be the masts of a schooner, which came out from behind a wall, indicating where the harbour entrance lay. It turned out that there were two harbours (Plates 10 A and B) separated by the dry bed of a river, and we chose the western one from which the schooner had emerged. We found the harbour complete with marina berths (all full), fuel pumps, a sand bathing beach packed with people, a roar of speedboat exhausts, and a blare of amplified music. It had no appeal for us, and so crowded was it that we turned ourselves round only with difficulty, and poked our enquiring bowsprit into the eastern harbour. That was much more to our taste, quiet and clean and containing about a dozen overseas yachts. The owner of one indicated where we should drop our anchor and he kindly took our stern-lines to the wall.

This was the sort of safe, friendly and comfortable harbour we had been hoping for, and we remained there for eight days, much enjoying the company of the other voyagers, British, American, Canadian, German, Swiss, and Swedish, most of them from the Mediterranean, and nearly all Atlantic candidates for the first time. A pleasant German engaged in the building business brought along a copy of the German edition of one of my books to be autographed, and was most helpful. He and his lovely French wife took us in their Jaguar on a big shopping expedition in Las Palmas, where all manner of good stores, both British and American, could be had at very reasonable cost; they drove us up into the harsh, grey, stony wilderness of the mountains for lunch at a restaurant where, as guests settled at each table, a family with musical instruments came to play and sing in welcome; we had an excellent meal, but oh the flies! The town of Puerto Rico, like Maspalomas, was tourist-oriented; in hotels and apartments along the island's south coast there were beds for 40 000 visitors, mostly Germans and Swedes, and it was said that not a bed was empty. The roar of diesels and the staccato rattle of pneumatic drills working in clouds of dust continued daily, excavating more sites among the barren hills for more and more accommodation for the seemingly endless torrent of holiday-makers, and the commonest object on the skyline was a contractor's crane.

Los Cristianos on Tenerife was only sixty miles away and we made an overnight trip of it, motoring out from the lee of Gran Canaria and then sailing; the lee sides of all these high islands make sailing slow and difficult, for the wind-shadow extends thirty miles or more offshore. We found a good outer harbour protected by a 1000-foot (300-metre) breakwater, and within it, a small fishing boat and yacht harbour; as this was too crowded for us to get into we anchored in the outer harbour, but were soon told by a port official that we must not remain there after dark as the Gomera ferry would want all the space for manoeuvring in. So, after a rest, we set off in the evening for Santa Cruz de la Palma, motoring in a calm through the notoriously windy passage between Tenerife and Gomera, then picked up a good breeze and reached our destination in the morning. There again we found congestion, for it was a busy little place loud with the comings and goings of inter-island ships, and yachts had to anchor fore-and-aft on the western side close to the towering cliffs (Plate 10 C), where much of the room was already taken by fishing vessels and run-abouts on moorings. With kind help from John Clark, owner of *Keryl* out from the Hamble, we got ourselves nicely arranged, but soon had to move elsewhere as our Swiss neighbour, who apparently had cast out five anchors but had not tightened up on any of them, bumped into us in a faint evening breeze and complained bitterly of the bad holding ground. We visitors were all much in the way of the local fishermen, but they, when manoeuvring among us, always did so with smiles and waves, and showed a rare regard for our topside paint. The Real Club Nautico, which had two swimming pools and a bar, offered all of us the use of its facilities, and the port officials, like the other inhabitants, were courteous and helpful.

There was more surge than usual in the harbour on the morning of the last day in October when I put Susan ashore for her final shopping in the jolly little town, while I took off a load of water from the club; then John kindly got our kedge for us and helped with the dinghy, and before lunchtime we were away bound towards Antigua in the West Indies on our fifth Atlantic west-bound crossing.

* * *

We soon picked up a strong north-east wind—perhaps this had been the cause of the unusual surge at Santa Cruz—lost it again for a time and motored through the island's lee, then came out into it once more and steered in a south-westerly direction more or less towards latitude twenty-five degrees north in longitude twenty-five degrees west, which we called Point A, with the wind aft and not so strong now. Averaging 110 miles a day, we passed a degree south of Point A on our fourth day at sea, and made an approximate alteration of course more westerly for eighteen degrees north in forty degrees west, which we called Point B; but, on a long passage such as this, we were more concerned that the ship should sail on the most advantageous course as regards speed and comfort, rather than on a precise compass course.

Life was easy, for the weather was fine and the vane gear did the steering; but, as I lay in my bunk at night with the ship pressing on through the darkness, I did sometimes wonder, as I had on other occasions, about the risk of collision, not with a big ship, for we were well away from any recognized shipping lane, but with some other smaller object, such as an oildrum awash or a balk of timber, for sometimes ships do lose such things overboard. Occasionally, they put them there intentionally; for example, the New Zealand navy found, in the autumn of 1977, an unlit buoy measuring twenty feet by five feet (six metres by 1·5 metres) anchored twenty-five miles off Banks Peninsula. It was thought to have been placed there by one of the numerous foreign fishing vessels working in the area, and it would have been a kindness if the navy had picked it up or sunk it instead of leaving it where it was and mentioning it in *Notices to Mariners*. However, one is not likely to meet that sort of hazard outside the 100-fathom line unless it has broken adrift.

There was, I supposed, a slight risk of being in collision with one of the fleet of more than fifty yachts that had gathered in the Canaries to prepare for the crossing, but at least all of them would be going the same way as ourselves, so presumably a collision would result in only a glancing blow. It was not as though we would be meeting head-on a fleet of yachts being raced single-handed from Plymouth to Newport, RI, with among them, perhaps, Alan Colas's 236-foot (seventy-two-metre) four-masted schooner, *Club Méditerranée*, a risk some yachts have had to face when crossing from west to east; it is a slight relief to know that in future a fifty-six-footer (seventeen-metre) will be the largest yacht allowed to take part in that race. However, we could collide with an unmanned yacht; though this is a very remote risk it does exist, as may be shown by the following incidents.

While in Australia some years ago, we met the owner of a fine Laurent Giles-designed yacht. He told us that while crossing Bass Strait she lost her mast, so he sent up distress signals, and he and his crew were taken off by a passing ship. The yacht was left adrift without lights in those busy waters, and after some days was found undamaged by a fishing vessel out, I think, of Eden and was towed into port. Apparently, the owner made no attempt to sail her in under jury rig.

The second incident concerns the big trimaran, *Gulf Streamer*. While on her way from Key West to Plymouth to take part in the single-handed transatlantic race, and while still in the Gulf Stream, she was capsized by a double-headed rogue sea judged to be forty feet (twelve metres) high. Philip Weld and his shipmate lived aboard the capsized vessel for five days—a remarkable feat of courage, endurance and ingenuity—until they were taken off by a container ship. For more than three months the trimaran then drifted, first south-east, then east, then north-east, a total distance of about 1200 miles, all of them in waters frequented by yachts; at least four times her position was reported by ships to the United States coastguard, and eventually she was picked up in a rather battered state by a Russian freighter and taken to Odessa.

I know it would be hard before abandoning one's ship at sea to ensure that she would sink and not remain on the surface to be a danger to others, for one would like to hope she might yet live to sail again. Nevertheless, failure to do so seems to me unethical. I believe an orthodox, ballasted yacht will slowly sink if a sea-cock is opened and the pipe it serves is severed; so the dismasted yacht in Bass Strait could have been disposed of in that manner, though it is likely that the insurance claim, if any, would have been lost. But the trimaran was another matter; being of foam-sandwich construction, having neither ballast nor engine, and possessing great reserve buoyancy in her outriggers, she was almost unsinkable. Opening a cock or cutting a hole would not have sunk her; indeed, her crew did cut holes in her main hull so that they could get in and out and obtain stores from an otherwise inaccessible compartment. But had the container ship rammed the craft, presumably she would have been broken up into smaller and less lethal pieces.

Points A and B, though not named as such, are referred to in *Ocean Passages for the World*, and the sailing route 'by the way of the trades' shown on the American pilot charts passes near them. It seemed to us that this recommendation, based as it is on thousands of observations and reports from sailing and other vessels spread over many years, was the logical one to follow. Some people contend, however, that, on leaving the Canaries, one should steer a more southerly course until near the Cape Verde Islands before turning west, to benefit from stronger winds. We began to think those antitraditionalists might have a point, for with us the wind fell lighter and lighter.

We were running under mainsail and boomed-out staysail, a total of only 530 square feet (forty-nine square metres), which was not nearly enough, but we knew from past experience that it would not help to set the 200-square-foot (18·5-square-metre) mizzen, for it would partly blanket the main and make that sail even more restless than it already was. That is one of the major drawbacks of the ketch rig. The alternative would have been to tack to leeward, when the mizzen would not have interfered with the main, but what we might then have gained in speed would have been more than lost by the increased distance we would have had to sail. What we needed was a really big, light spinnaker, but we have never felt ourselves to be a sufficiently strong crew to deal with such a sail safely.

Light fair winds are harder on the sails than are any other conditions, for, although our boom was held steady by sheet and foreguy, each time we lifted on the swell the main filled and emptied itself with such a crash that if one happened to be touching any part of it the effect was similar to that of an electric shock.

Since the advent of synthetic materials, the damage caused by chafe is not so serious as it used to be when sails and ropes were made from vegetable fibres. Nevertheless, the seams of a terylene sail are vulnerable, for the cloth is harder than cotton so the stitches do not sink into it to gain protection; for this reason, the seams of our working sails had three rows of stitches instead of the more usual two. It might be thought that three rows will be just as easily chafed as two, but that is not so, for the centre row is better protected than are those near the edges of the cloths. Nevertheless, I continued to be astonished that sails could withstand for so long the harsh treatment that ours had been subjected to—at that time the mainsail had been in use for about 20 000 miles—and that they did so said much for the integrity of the workmanship put into them by the sailmakers in Cranfield's loft at Burnham-on-Crouch.

We did our best to protect the sails in one way or another. If a headsail would not draw we took it in and bagged it, for sunlight is probably terylene's worst enemy, and, when main and mizzen were not in use we coated them. With sheets eased, both those sails bore heavily on the shrouds; I believed that did not matter much provided the sails did not rub up and down, and, to reduce such movement to a minimum, we used a tightly set-up boom guy. Presumably a kicking strap, which I prefer to call a martingale, would have done the job just as well, but as we had roller-reefing for the main this was not convenient. Yet, in spite of this precaution, there always was a little movement, especially against the lower after shrouds and, to stop the chafing of the sail there, we made use of a quantity of baggywrinkle, the soft, antichafe device made from old rope, and used by generations of seamen. No doubt the use of baggywrinkle can be overdone, and sometimes one sees a yacht festooned with it and looking rather a figure of fun; but placed at strategic points where experience has shown it to be desirable—with us where the ratlines were seized to the after lower shrouds, and where the lee running-backstay when released lay against the crosstrees—we considered it to be the best and cheapest chafing gear ever devised. Due to this care, we never had to put more than an occasional stitch in any of the sails, but we did have to replace slides now and then, for being of plastic they became fatigued by exposure to the sun. Originally all were of white plastic, possibly nylon, but on our sailmaker's recommendation we changed to slides of black plastic which did appear to have a slightly longer life; but, unlike many other sailing people, we never once had a slide attachment break or work loose.

The method of attachment was like this: a closely woven terylene tape, half-an-inch (1·2 centimetres) wide and about twelve inches (thirty centimetres) long, was passed through the slide and sewn to itself; the rest of it was then passed through the eyelet and back through the slide several times until all of the tape was used up. It was not put on tightly, because sufficient space between slide and sail had to be left so that the tape could be sewn to itself there with terylene thread to hold the whole in place. When a slide had to be replaced we found we could not force a sail needle through so many thicknesses of tape without first punching a hole with a bradawl. We did not have slides on the lower third of the luff, that is, from tack to lower crosstrees, but used a rope lacing there (Plate 11 *left*); this greatly reduced the number of slides, making the sail easier to stow and simpler to reef and unreef.

In the light winds we were then experiencing the boomed-out staysail also backed and filled as we rose and dropped on the swell, but it did not do itself much harm as there was nothing for it to slam against, and it was an old sail which we used for that purpose only.

All the standing rigging was of one by nineteen stainless wire with swaged terminal fittings, and I often wondered how many jolts and snatches the latter could withstand without suffering from fatigue. Occasionally I searched the terminal fittings for hair cracks and never found any, but, if I had, I could have done nothing about them until we reached a port where wire and terminals could be replaced. I came to the conclusion that a yacht making a long voyage should not be so dependent on outside help, and I might have felt happier with seven by seven wire which I could have spliced round thimbles myself. We gave up using wire for halyards many years ago and changed to Marlow three-strand pre-stretched terylene rope, which we found had a much longer life than wire, was pleasant to handle, required only simple open-barrel winches, and was easy to splice or turn end for end. In seven years we replaced all halyards and topping-lifts once (the latter were of nylon), but the original sheets of braided terylene were still in use at the end of this voyage, and although they had worn a little smooth where they worked over the sheaves of the blocks, appeared still to have many years of life in them.

While there is no appreciable electrolysis between stainless steel and bronze, there is a considerable difference in the hardness of these metals, stainless being the harder. We, therefore, found that the stainless shackles of the main topping-lift and of the upper mainsheet block had, due to small but constant movement, bitten deeply into the eye and the bail of the bronze swivel fitting at the end of the boom. I tried to protect the bronze by building it up with a hard surfacer such as Marinetex, but this cracked and chipped and usually had to be renewed at the end of each long passage. A similar trouble, though of lesser importance, occurred at the outboard end of the boom with which the staysail was boomed out when running. The eyes on the boom were of stainless steel and, in a surprisingly short time, they ate through the bronze snap-shackles securing the fore and after braces although we lubricated them. Also the bronze hanks, which held the luffs of staysail and jibs to the stainless forestay and topmast stay, wore through and had to be replaced. Such problems aboard the deep-sea yachts are not easily overcome, but at least the makers of bronze hardware could ensure that the eyes, bails, bolts and pins were of larger scantling so that the wear on them of stainless attachments would not seriously weaken them so quickly.

The modern yacht block is a handsome and expensive item of equipment, but I do not know that it has much, except little need for maintenance, to recommend it for cruising over the old-fashioned ash or elm block with galvanized pin and sheave; some of these were made with a score in which the owner could fit a rope strop of his own making to suit his particular requirements. Such blocks offered a cheap and seamanlike solution to many rigging problems, but they are not now readily available. One used to be able to buy them fitted with what were known as 'patent' sheaves, that is, sheaves fitted with roller bearings; these much reduced friction and, when under load, made a delightful clacking noise instead of squealing. I see that a modern block with roller bearings is being advertised, however, the inference being that this is something new and almost as wonderful as the price being asked.

As we headed for Point B the light wind became lighter still, and, in place of the heavy working sails, we ran on under our two lightest sails, the mizzen-staysail of 400 square feet (thirty-seven square metres) of three-ounce (105-gram) terylene, and the genoa of 500 square feet (forty-six square metres) of six-ounce (210-gram) (Plate 11 *right*). But eventually even they would not remain asleep, so we took them in and bagged them. By the following morning even the faint airs had died away, so we spread the big harbour awning, rigged the cockpit table, and got to work on various jobs just as though we were in port.

We felt sure we must get some wind soon, for there we were on 11 November in nineteen degrees north, thirty-three degrees west, on the old, stained, eastern sheet of the North Atlantic chart, all among a hatching of crosses in inks of different colours showing our noon positions on earlier trips, and in a five-degree square on the pilot chart where there were nice long arrows flying from between east and northeast, each with four feathers on it, and only two per cent of calm was indicated. Our old logbooks told us that on earlier crossings in this same area, and at the same time of year, we had been hurrying along, sometimes with too much wind. But now the sun beat hotly down from a partly clouded and hazy sky—there was no real blue to be seen—the saloon temperature rose to 88 °F (31 °C) and there was not a ripple on the shiny surface of the sea in which the featureless clouds were reflected. The calm lasted for nearly a week, and although an occasional air enabled us to make good a mile or two under genoa and/or mizzen-staysail it never lasted for long and, on three consecutive days, our noon positions lay on top of one another on the chart, showing that there had not even been a drain of current to help us along.

You may wonder why we did not move on under power in an attempt to escape from the calm area. The trouble was that we did not know how much fuel remained in the tank, which had not been topped up since leaving England. Although the dip-stick said the tank was a little less than half full, I did not believe it, as I had just noticed that the ten-litre marks put on the stick by the builder were all equidistant, as indeed they should have been if the tank was rectangular; but, of course, it was not rectangular, for its sides and bottom were formed by the skin plating of the hull making the tank vee-shaped in section. So, knowing that we might well need some fuel for reaching an anchorage later, and for charging the batteries, we remained where we were to wait for wind, and peacefully shared our small circle of the ocean with its other quiet inhabitants. A school of glamorous fish with bright-yellow tails drifted about beneath us, apparently enjoying the shade our hull cast; a solitary storm petrel fluttered round repeatedly but never stopped; a pair of squawking bosun birds called on us briefly at breakfast-time each day; and once we had the close company of some small, black whales, pilot whales perhaps, though we saw no white patch on their under sides; occasionally, one stood upright in the water as though to have a better look at us. That was all the wildlife we saw during that long drawn-out calm. The sunrises and the sunsets told us nothing; the clouds remained shapeless and of no specific type, and the barograph continued to make its normal diurnal movements.

In time, of course, the trade wind blew again, but there was little heart in it, and for much of the time it was not strong enough to keep our sails asleep, for there was always some movement of the sea to make us roll and to indicate that there must be plenty of wind not far away; later we learned that was so, and many of the other yachts on passage at the time had been enjoying fair progress.

During the week following the calm we covered only 560 miles, and one afternoon as we lay again becalmed we were overtaken by the ketch, *Queen Mab*, of Boston, whose people we had got to know and like while we were together in Gran Canaria. They stopped their engine, which they said had already run for 100 hours since leaving the islands, and they thought they had enough fuel for ninety hours more. We had a pleasant and relaxed mid-ocean talk about the weather, which we all thought peculiar, and discussed our mutual friends. After twenty minutes or so they started up again, and soon *Queen Mab* was only a speck on the horizon ahead.

A few days later when we were running slowly under main and staysail we were again overtaken, this time by the ocean racer *Tantara* of Wilmington. She had her mainsail set but was under power, and she cut much too close across our stern before ranging up alongside so near that if her main had gybed, and it might easily have done so as it was not guyed, the boom would have tangled with ours. 'You worry me coming so close,' I said, for we could not ourselves alter course without having the staysail taken aback. There were seven people on deck, and one of them replied that he had already told the helmsman to keep away. Had they stopped their engine we could have talked comfortably, just as we had with *Queen Mab*, but with it running no doubt they had to come close to hear us. When the yacht had gone we noticed that our patent log was not spinning properly, and on hauling in the rotator we found that three of its four blades were badly bent, no doubt by *Tantara*'s keel or propeller.

The very next day at about sunset we were again overtaken, this time by the large motor yacht, *Passage II*. She approached from astern, and as she showed us in turn a little first of one of her sides and then of the other, we presumed she was being steered by autopilot, and were relieved to see figures in her wheelhouse as she came nearer. Carrying her way with engines stopped, it looked to us as though she was going to come rather close, so we

---

11 *Left* A lacing instead of slides on the lower part of the luff made reefing and stowing the mainsail easier. *Right* We ran on under our two lightest sails, the 400-square-foot (thirty-seven-square-metre) mizzen-staysail and the 500-square-foot (forty-six-square-metre) genoa.

REGENTAG

gestured her away, meaning only that she should keep a respectable distance, for we still had our visitor of the day before vividly in mind. Unfortunately, *Passage II* misinterpreted our gestures as signifying a desire to be left alone; a puff of smoke issued from her exhaust, and without a word or a wave she gathered way and hurried on; this upset us, for we feared we might have given the impression that we, like some other sailing people, did not hold with those who cruise in big motor yachts, and that is not so. To my eye a well-designed and built, and properly maintained motor yacht is a thing of grace as well as of purpose; she need not be a gin palace nor need her people misbehave—these are common suppositions but are rarely true—and we have usually found such vessels to be quiet and pleasant neighbours in an anchorage.

We had known Peter Cornes for many years (we first met him behind the counter in a Port Moresby laundry), part-owner of the big and handsome motor yacht, *Sirdar*, and skipper of her on her maiden voyage from Europe, where she had been built, to New Zealand. *Sirdar* had everything a proper motor yacht should have: twin Gardners, stabilizers, luxurious but practical accommodation, deep-pile carpets, hi-fi music, and apparently inexhaustible supplies of food and drink. So when Peter invited us to join him for a day in the Hauraki Gulf we needed no persuasion, though we did wonder if we might perhaps grow a little bored. But the day proved to be enjoyable and instructive: from chairs on the boat-deck, or when it became too windy there, from the comfort of the saloon with its big windows, we could watch the familiar scene slip effortlessly by; there was a rendezvous with another yacht at an island for lunch, all arranged by radio telephone, and there was some sophisticated navigational equipment to be investigated and visits to be paid to the immaculate, pulsing engine-room. On the way back in the evening, there was the rescue of a small boy in an outboard dinghy which had run out of fuel; he had been rowing for hours, but with little success as he had omitted to tilt the propeller out of the water. Picking him up in a choppy little sea from so large a vessel, and towing his dinghy to where his anxious father was waiting in a shallow and congested corner of the harbour, involved a display of unhurried and competent seamanship, and I recall that while *Sirdar* was turning in a

---

12 *Top* The snug, mangrove-hedged inner part of English Harbour; a telephoto shot from Shirley Heights. *Bottom* An artist's ship: Hundertwasser's ex-salt-carrier, *Regentag*.

restricted place with one engine running ahead and the other astern, Peter found time to leave the wheel and consult the tide-tables.

We did a little better in our fourth week at sea, managing to average 100 miles a day; that was nothing much, but was probably the best the ship could do, for goose barnacles were growing along her waterline, where they made a strange, watery sighing as they were repeatedly lifted out and re-immersed. It seems strange that these creatures (Plate 9 *right*), which manufacture and use a glue so good that scientists are trying to find out more about it, inhabit only the deep oceans where there are so few objects to which they can adhere—they even thrive on a fast-rotating log-line. Also to help retard our progress, the beam swell from north-west (the prevailing direction in the North Atlantic) kept us rolling, and often flung us over so far that our rubbing strakes slammed down hard on the sea and jets of water shot up through the 'secret' scuppers to flood the side decks; then *Wanderer* with, as it were, a shrug of the shoulders, sluiced the whole lot aft and across the stern locker's flush-fitting hatch. That hatch had given us a lot of trouble over the years for, in spite of our efforts and those of some friends, it was not entirely watertight. Only a little water could enter at a time, but a few cupfuls were sufficient to sluice up the curved sides of the locker as we rolled, and it could then reach one of the steering gear's ball races. Therefore, a little later when a less rolly day offered the opportunity, we removed the ropes, fenders and cans of paraffin from the stern locker, and I, like a contortionist, got in and inserted myself beneath the moving parts of the steering linkage, with my head against the skin plating where the noise of goose barnacles was loud and clear, and with a sponge removed the water from the little well under the rudder-stock stuffing-box.

Slowly we crept on across the ocean and the chart, only to be becalmed again when within 300 miles of our destination. By then we were growing impatient and were anxious to be done with this long drawn-out passage; had that been our first trade wind trip I believe Susan and I might have agreed that ocean voyaging was not for us, and would have taken an interest in some less frustrating occupation. We had long since finished the good citrus fruit from La Palma along with most of the wine, and now the only fresh foods left were potatoes, onions and eggs, some of which were growing a little tired.

* * *

A landfall on Antigua should be easy and straightforward as there are no offlying dangers but, as the Antilles are approached, one can expect the current—of which, incidentally, we had experienced very little—to gather momentum and possibly change direction; so the navigator is grateful for any check on this. But the day before we expected to make our landfall the sky became overcast, as it so often does when one is approaching the land, and no sights were possible. However, Desiradé, an outlier of Guadeloupe, appeared next morning where it should be on the port bow, and in the afternoon, lowish Antigua lifted out of the sea ahead but was too far off to be reached before nightfall; so, as English Harbour on the island's southern side, for which we were bound, was not lighted, we hove-to for the night, went in after breakfast, and were quickly and courteously entered by a smiling young Antiguan policeman—we were lucky, because the other policeman there did not like yachts and took no pains to hide the fact.

This was our fifth visit, and the harbour was more crowded with yachts than ever. Many lay out in Freeman Bay, where the water was clean and clear for bathing, and there were beaches to stroll or sit on. The famous dockyard with its fine old buildings, including the charming house in which it was thought Nelson may have lived on the rare occasions when he ventured ashore from HMS *Boreas*, had not changed, but round it, like the spokes of a wheel, a gathering of yachts, mostly engaged in the charter business, lay stern-to. Some were enormous, and one, registered in the Cayman Islands, actually had a helicopter squatting on her specially designed stern—no doubt a 'chopper' makes an excellent dinghy—and other attractions, for, as she came stern-first into her berth, her crew of bikini-clad honeys stood by the fenders. There was a burble of generator exhausts, and diesel fumes hung in the hot air.

The inner part of the harbour, above the dockyard, was the snuggest anchorage one could wish for in two fathoms on mud, and was neatly hedged by luxurious mangroves (Plate 12 *top*). That was where we chose to lie among a fine gathering of voyagers several of whom were old friends, and, although most of them had made reasonably good crossings, it was a slight consolation to us to know that the lovely and efficient old *Keryl* had taken exactly the same time as ourselves for the same distance from the same Canary island, a tiresome thirty-four days. Another yacht took forty-four days and ran out of food and low on water, and the big ketch, *Nitro*, which we had met in Spain, took thirty-three days and had her engine running all the time.

Life in our small floating village was full of interest and entertainment. We had always found the majority of ocean-voyaging people to be friendly, kind and helpful, assisting one another with tools, materials and skills and, in an anchorage such as that, there were few problems which could not be solved by some near neighbour; most were busy refitting, maintaining, altering or improving, and only in one or two new GRP yachts did we see the owners sitting during the day in their cockpits with nothing much to do. Over Christmas there was a great round of parties; Mount Gay rum at sixteen dollars a case flowed freely, and under the brilliant stars, often to the thrilling music of a steel band at the Admiral's Inn, there were drink and/or dining engagements aboard one yacht or another until well into the new year. The Nicholsons were in residence at the Powder Magazine and still held their big Sunday evening parties. Since we had last met, Emmie Nicholson had developed trouble with her throat so that she could not swallow and could barely speak, and Vernon had to feed her with liquids by way of a plastic tube in one nostril. Yet in spite of this terrible disability, she stood at the door slim and erect, and welcomed every guest with an air of assurance and grace that might have been the envy of any governor's lady. How proud we were to have known her for so many years.

Although most of us keep fit on long voyages and any kind of illness is rare, I did find my legs a bit weak and unsteady after a month at sea. Accommodating English Harbour offered a convenient cure for this. A few yards to windward of us lay a clean, unused, stone quay at which at first light I could land and leave the dinghy snug among the mangroves while I walked up past Clarence House, in which the duke of that name lived in 1786 before he became William IV, and where balls were held in Nelson's day. Past the mounting block and along the drive beneath the shade trees, I made my way to the road which, engineered by the British, rose steadily. Up past the ruins of old Government House it went among the cactus and the thorn, and, after half-an-hour's breathless climb, I found myself on the 500-foot (150-metre) summit of Shirley Heights, with all round me the remains of the forts which used to defend the harbour against the French, and the remarkable ruins of some once-splendid buildings, one with a patio of thirteen perfectly preserved arches, which must have been either barracks or officers' quarters. From my point of vantage, the whole of English Harbour lay spread out like a beautifully coloured relief map in front of me, while behind me, in lines of foaming white, the long-running swell of the North Atlantic met its roaring death at the feet of the cliffs which made my promenade. Sometimes on the way back, and just as the sun was rising, I met one of the strange wild men who had taken to living on windy Shirley Heights; as he strode along beside me, barefoot and ragged, he proclaimed in a loud clear voice that the day of judgment was at hand, and he spoke of 'death and the wounded spirit'. I felt full of good fresh air and virtue when I got back aboard at seven o'clock, to find Susan hard at work on some project, probably rubbing down the brightwork in preparation for another coat of varnish. Sometimes Susan accompanied me on my early morning jaunts, but more often she took her exercise later in the day, rowing, for she found that was good therapy for her damaged, but now fast-mending arm, which she was determined to have in seagoing trim before we left.

Early in the new year in ones and twos, and mercifully without the blare of foghorns with which some people are inclined to 'farewell' their sailing friends, the voyaging fleet dispersed, some bound back for Britain, others for the United States, and a few, which we hoped to meet again, headed for Panama and the wide spaces of the Pacific. Before we left, we hauled out at Antigua Slipway for a bottom scrub and paint. Overnight we secured all-fours between piles which straddled the slip, and, in the morning, the cradle was run down under us, our lines were shifted to the arms of the cradle, and within a few minutes and without any of the shouting which sometimes accompanies a haul-out (and usually speaks of inefficiency) we were high and dry. As the yard wanted to do the work we let it, and we felt rather idle, though not too wealthy owners, as we watched the bottom being attended to instead of doing the job ourselves. Unfortunately, there was no fresh water available for rinsing off the bottom before painting (that had always been a common feature of life in English Harbour) and later we wondered if it might have been the reason for the poor service we had from that coat of paint. By mid-afternoon we were back at our anchorage.

It was necessary to clear and enter when sailing between islands of the West Indies, even between those of the same nationality, and the police sergeant at English Harbour had just made a new rule that a yacht must leave within two hours of obtaining her clearance. This was inconvenient for yachts bound south, as we were, for usually they wished to leave first thing in the morning so as to reach an anchorage before nightfall. We, therefore, got our clearance and moved to Freeman Bay for the night, hoping the sergeant would not notice us there, and departed in the morning.

Sailing south along the chain of islands in that area is usually easier than sailing north, for the wind is more likely to be abaft the beam. And so it was that day, and fresh too; with our tan sails stiff in power-filled curves, a spraybow in the bow-wave, and a broad lacy wake streaming out astern, as we moved at seven knots across the unimpeded ocean swell in the forty-mile-wide gap between Antigua and Guadeloupe, we had the kind of sailing that charterers pay a mint of money to enjoy. With a bit of luck, most of the interisland passages should be like that, a rollicking sail to remember, which is one reason why the Caribbean is such a popular cruising ground; but the islands, through the lee of which we would have to pass on our way south, were high islands with peaks of 4000 feet (1200 metres) or more, and we knew from earlier cruises we had made in those waters that enjoyable sailing cannot be expected there. It is said that if you keep really close to the shore (within a couple of pistol shots) you may get a little wind, otherwise you may have to go twenty miles or more offshore to find it. So after a night in Deshayes Bay near the north end of Guadeloupe, we motored right through that island's lee and did not find any wind until we neared its southern end; from there, we were able to sail to an anchorage at the Saintes, a group of small and attractive French islands with a largely white population. But they had become something of a Guadeloupe suburb, and all day and part of the night, ferries with high-speed unsilenced engines destroyed the peace.

We put in at Prince Rupert Bay in Dominica to buy the best and cheapest grapefruit in the world, but we did not have to go ashore for them as boys came out to take our order and our money, and within an hour were back with the fruit. We then moved on to Fort de France on Martinique where we found the paper work much easier. At the root of the pier where we landed was a shack housing the health, immigration and customs officer, all embodied in one man affectionately known as '007'. He greeted us with a smile, gave us free entry and clearance at the same time to save us further bother, and offered any help or information we might need.

Such friendly and courteous officials used to be common, but today unfortunately they are rare, for in many places a visiting yacht is no longer treated as a welcome guest, but is looked upon with suspicion and is got rid of as quickly as possible. Some people say that yachts have brought this on themselves, but I doubt it, for, although there are certainly criminals among us—those who behave badly ashore or afloat, smuggle, or peddle drugs—they are I believe a tiny minority; the majority of voyagers are quiet, simple people, often married couples, who behave impeccably and are no risk or bother to anyone, except that there are so many of them that they overload the amenities (if any) and cause a little more work for the officials. When a yacht arrives in port at the end of a long passage, the minds of her people are likely to be empty and ready to absorb greedily the first impressions of the land. If the officials are friendly, as '007' was, an immediate good impression of that country is formed; as this is good for international relations, and the voyager usually makes a good ambassador, it would seem sensible when selecting officials to act as boarding officers for health, immigration and customs, to choose those who have natural good manners or have been trained to be courteous. A little intelligent thought might be applied to easing the rules a trifle, so that the visitor could be saved the tiresome business of having to go round a strange town on the first day there in search of scattered offices where papers of one sort or another have to be stamped or signed. Someone high up the bureaucratic ladder could so easily see to it that the yacht is treated better than she usually is. Of course she, like any ship, must be entered and finally cleared from the country; of course her people must produce their passports for checking, and changes of crew be reported; but some of the absurdities could so easily be removed by a word from the right quarter. What, for example, is the point of an owner having to list with their values and serial numbers his radio equipment, tape-players or recorders, binoculars, cameras, and so on, if the items are not going to be checked against the list immediately before sailing? If the maximum permitted stop-over period is, say, six months, why does the owner have to visit immigration every second week? Why must a firearm be held by police while the owner is in port?—that is probably the only time he or she is likely to have need of it to discourage the characters who may creep aboard by night with theft in mind. Why has the vessel to be searched unless the authorities have a strong suspicion that she is carrying undeclared or unlawful goods? If a search is made (in twenty-six years of voyaging this has happened to us only twice, both on this voyage) why is the search not properly carried out? It would appear that these searches are made not with much hope of finding something incriminating, but just to show that the petty officials do have the power to search. It is not a pleasant experience to have a pair of strange hands rummage through one's personal belongings—a yacht is not a suitcase—neither is it reassuring to know that when the official leaves, he has a good idea where valuable items are stowed. Usually, it is the newly independent countries which treat the yacht with suspicion or dislike, yet they are the countries most likely to benefit from the money the visitor spends, and even the poorest of us spends something.

The risk of a yacht being burgled is now considerable in many places, but, short of remaining on board all the time, there is little that can be done about it. Once, when we were at Suva, John Harrison and his wife Bette came off for a drink. As they were leaving John said he would much like us to dine ashore with them, then added:

'But I don't think you should.'

'Why,' I asked, 'has Bette lost the art of cooking? She used to be very good.'

'No, it's not that. Bette's still very good, but if you leave your ship after dark she is likely to get burgled.'

We thought that a bit alarmist, nevertheless as John was Director of Marine and had lived in Fiji for a long time, he was in a good position to know, so we did not go ashore after dark. During our final night there, having taken the dinghy aboard in readiness for an early start in the morning, we turned in. I was awakened an hour later by a noise, and from the sleeping cabin switched the floodlights on to surprise a couple of Indians in the act of boarding us from a canoe; no doubt they supposed we were ashore as they saw no dinghy lying astern.

A yacht is vulnerable, for even when she is locked up not much skill with a knife, screwdriver or chisel is required to force an entry, and, provided he does not make too much noise over it, the thief does not care what damage he may do. There are, of course, alarm systems which can be arranged to do one or more of several things, such as ringing a bell or switching on a siren if there is an escape of gas, an accumulation of carbon monoxide, a fire, or an increase of water level in the bilge, and some can be so rigged as to make a noise if a hatch, door, or skylight is opened. We have shared marinas with yachts so equipped, and not uncommonly did a bell ring or a siren scream, but we never saw anybody take the slightest interest. Recently, a near-neighbour's alarm sounded, so we went to have a look, but she was locked and nobody was on board; fearing that the siren might be warning of an escape of gas, and that the owner when he next paid a visit might light a cigarette or start the engine and cause an explosion, we reported the matter to the custodian.

'Oh, *Waspy II*,' he said, 'not to worry, she often sounds her alarm.' And she did, twice more while we were there.

So, as an alarm does not seem to be the solution, I wondered whether we might convert our guardrails into an electric fence such as is used by farmers, then anyone touching it, and it would be difficult to get aboard without doing so, would receive a salutary shock. But with a steel ship I felt the chance of an electric leak and consequent damage would be too big a risk; also, I remembered about the padre in Fiji who, with an electric fence, tried to stop the local boys from raiding his orchard, and had the misfortune to electrocute one of them; I concluded, therefore, that a dog would be better. While we lay at an anchorage with a great reputation for theft, the outermost yacht did have a dog which barked vigorously when anyone went near, so we all felt safe. But eventually that yacht departed, and the next night the British yacht, *K. G. Jester*, was broken into while her people were ashore, and was robbed of the presents they had just bought to take to their daughter in Australia, as well as all their spirits; when they reported their loss, the customs charged them duty on it. So a dog might be the best guard, though quarantine regulations make life for seagoing animals and their owners very difficult; and one must have the right kind of dog, perhaps a small, black schipperke or 'barge dog', for, as I had discovered on my early morning walks, some dogs only bark when their owners are up and about—when their owners are away or asleep the dogs sleep too.

* * *

We had come to Fort de France to buy wine, and we found a lot of other good but expensive things in that bustling town. We then sailed for St Lucia with a strong sou'easter, an overcast sky, and visibility about five miles—not at all typical Caribbean weather. We had a grand sail, but only I was able to enjoy the satisfaction of overhauling another yacht of about our own size, for Susan was below making a St Lucia courtesy ensign, and it was a question whether we would arrive before her needlework was finished. We spoke of putting in for the night at the anchorage in the lee of Pigeon Island near the north end of St Lucia, but, as that would have involved making a tack, whereas we could just lay for the entrance to Castries (capital and port of entry) we held on, and in the late afternoon anchored there off Vigie Cove. In the morning we went by dinghy across to the town to enter. The immigration officer dealt with us quickly, charged ten dollars for entry and asked if we had a flag.

'We have lots of flags,' I replied, 'which one do you mean?' though I knew well enough.

He opened the plastic case in which I had supposed he kept his papers, and it was stuffed with St Lucia flags.

'Twenty-five dollar,' he said, holding one up, but I shook my head.

'We already have one and it's flying at the crosstree.'

We moved over to the customs officer at the next desk, but he would not attend to us. 'You must wait,' he said. We asked why this should be, for we only required his stamp on our papers and then would be free to go and buy what we wanted in the town.

'I have to rummage a yacht,' he replied with some importance, and that was what he proceeded to do, for it turned out that an American yacht with six charter guests aboard had done exactly what we had talked of doing: she had anchored for the night off Pigeon Island, but as she flew flag 'Q' and nobody landed it was thought that no offence was being committed; however, she was found there by a police launch, was escorted to Castries, laid alongside the wharf and was rummaged for two hours while we watched and kicked our heels impatiently.

Such incidents do not endear a place to one, but we would not again wish to visit St Lucia because of the problems of theft; it had a bad reputation when we first went there twenty years before, and many of our sailing friends had been robbed; but now we learned that down at Marigot, that lovely little harbour hidden by a palm-covered spit where Rodney concealed his fleet, theft from yachts had become a local industry. So reluctantly we passed

Marigot by, and, not stopping at St Vincent, we went straight through to the small and pleasant island of Bequia. It was there that many of the interisland schooners had been built, and in the past the men of Bequia had been highly prized as seamen by merchantmen and whalers. The islanders still did build a few small craft on the wide foreshore under the trees, and on the beach the big ketch, *Diligent* (she looked like an ex-Brixham trawler), was having some major repairs done. But the chief occupation appeared to be in connection with the many yachts that called there and, as there were never less than fifty at the anchorage during our ten-day stay, and with a constant coming and going, the islanders were probably doing well enough.

'Hey, skip! Want me to do your varnish?'

'Hey, skip! Got any laundry?'

'Hey, skip! You want limes? bananas? my sister?'

'Hey, skip! Hey, skip!' And each evening boatloads of youngsters went round the fleet importuning each yacht in turn with songs or steel bands.

There are some very remarkable men who continue to voyage in small vessels in spite of advancing age: Humphry Barton, for instance, founder of the Ocean Cruising Club. In his Laurent Giles-designed *Rose Rambler* he had, in spite of failing sight and other disabilities, made so many crossings of the North Atlantic, most of them with his wife, that even those of us who know him have long since lost count. Then there was Frank Casper, a quiet and gentle American in his seventies. His *Elsie* was a Colin Archer-type thirty-foot (nine-metre) cutter, and, since the death of his wife in 1963, Frank had been living aboard and sailing single-handed. He made a very fine three-year circumnavigation, and since then had crossed and recrossed the Atlantic repeatedly. *Elsie* was of sturdy wood construction, but now and then she had her little troubles, and whenever she needed a cracked frame strengthened, or a new mast-step or keel-bolt fitted, Frank sailed her over to Mashford's, his favourite boatyard near Plymouth, to get the job done. A great seaman and accomplished navigator, he rarely talked about himself but always showed great interest in the other voyagers as they came sailing into wherever he might be lying; and if he had ever met one before he would probably enquire how some fitting or piece of gear one was talking about installing at the last meeting had stood up to work afloat; he usually brought with him some little welcoming gift. We had not seen Frank for several years, but there he was at Bequia rowing over to us in his curious square-ended dinghy; he had a smile and a pineapple for us, and, unlike so many others that one meets, he wanted to know what *we* had been doing. Recently we had one of his brief, rare letters, and we learned that since we met at Bequia just over a year ago he had popped across once more to Plymouth, where work on *Elsie* so delayed her departure that she did not get away from the Scillies until towards the end of September, and then endured three weeks of gales on her way to La Palma. No doubt she is by now safely back in the West Indies preparing for another trip.

On many occasions when cruising in the Caribbean, we had met Morris Nicholson, an Englishman who skippered the American ketch, *Eleuthera II*, and while we lay at Bequia, that smart blue yacht came in and anchored near. Her owners, Gustav and Jane Korvens, treated Morris more like a son than a paid skipper, and most of his evenings he spent at Hope House, their lovely, hillside winter residence on the island. Knowing that we were friends of Morris, the Korvens kindly invited us to dinner, and it was there in the candlelight that we met Richard Morris Dey whose poems about the Caribbean had graced some of America's leading magazines. He gave us copies of several of them, and after our return on board that warm, black-velvety night, I put my feet up, lit a pipe, and in the slightly bemused mood a fine dinner and an evening spent in such good company and glamorous surroundings can engender, read all of them. I discovered many thoughts and phrases to delight me: 'The hilltop windmill blades the trade wind's cheek'; '. . . sailing the Carib Sea across the brow of Venezuela, free'; 'the deathless, diamond trades'. But there was much I did not understand, and some facts I queried in my pedantic way, though I did not say as much to Dey next time we met, for it is so easy unintentionally to antagonize, to hurt, or to be misunderstood, as I was when I said of Frank Eyre's anthology of verse that in his selection he had put too much emphasis on death, whereas life is for living.

It was also at Bequia that we met the Austrian artist, Hundertwasser, of whom I regret to say Susan and I had not heard. He had bought an old wooden Mediterranean salt-carrier, had her cut in half and lengthened and given a new eliptical stern, christened her *Regentag* (rainy day) and now, with his business manager, secretary, and professional crew, was making the voyage in her from Venice to New Zealand, where he owned property. With his entourage he came to call, and presented us with two books printed on thick black paper; one, a tantalizing display of photographs on which paintings had been superimposed, was about himself—often nude, which seemed out of character, but for which perhaps his manager was responsible—and *Regentag*; the other, a smaller volume, showed in miniature a selection of his paintings beautifully reproduced in colour. He had already autographed the books, and one bore the delightful inscription: 'To Hiscock heartily'. We much enjoyed his visit, but felt embarrassed at being unable to make any intelligent comment on his paintings. They in their colouring were remarkably vivid and clear-cut, and much use had been made of metallic paints, which with a scintillating sheen of gold, silver and copper almost leapt off the black pages; but the paintings were all 'modern' and we were able to understand few of them. That did not seem to matter, however, for Hundertwasser had not come to talk about himself or his work, but to discuss boats and routes. When we reached New Zealand and made enquiries, we learned that he was well known there, and had been guest of the City of Auckland in 1973–4 when the art gallery staged an exhibition of his work. It was said that he was that very rare person, a living artist who was making a financial success of his art, and that his paintings were particularly appreciated by the younger generation. We were told he owned 900 acres (364 hectares), but did not know where they lay until one day, when we happened to be at anchor in the Waikare River, he came alongside to invite us to visit his ship and his farm, which it appeared lay only a mile or two upstream.

Regentag, with her comparatively shoal draught, was lying in a bay which was too shallow for us, so we went by outboard dinghy. Her red, green and blue paint and the gold of varnished hull and stumpy masts lent a welcoming splash of Mediterranean colour to the predominantly dark-green scene (Plate 12 *bottom*). Down below she had the air of a small farmhouse, with lots of bare wood, mellow with age, straight-back chairs of the sort one sees outside a Greek café, a book-lined great cabin, and a studio with a table on runners so that it could be moved about at the artist's whim, and beside it a huge square opening port from some dead ship let in a flood of light and air. A particularly pleasing feature was an oblong port low down in the topside so that looking out through it one's eye was almost at sea-level, just as it is in that canal-side restaurant in Amsterdam, or as when swimming, and one almost expected to get a mouthful of salt water.

But we could not stay long if we were to see the property, for it was nearing the time of high water, and the channel would not be navigable even by dinghy two hours after that. Hundertwasser led the way in his outboard dinghy, and we in ours followed close astern, first up to the head of the bay and then in through a winding and ever-narrowing channel among dense mangroves—for us a surprising, though not unusual, feature in New Zealand's rural scene. The final quarter of a mile or so was partly artificial, for a grab had recently deepened it and made low embankments on either side so that one had the sensation of being in a canal a little above the level of the water elsewhere. Rounding a final sharp turn we came to an area of grass spreading to the water's edge, where we landed before the old timber house with its red roof and tall, sash windows.

Perhaps it was because he knew we were English, but Fred, as we were now to call him, insisted on giving us tea, the brewing of which was, I think, unaccustomed to him. There were a few of his unmistakable paintings scattered about (he courteously refrained from mentioning them), a wood box of artist's colours, and there were raindrops painted on all the windows. He showed us round and took us to the heads to see his latest import from Sweden on which, he told us indignantly, customs had charged him 100 dollars duty. It was a big affair; one had to mount a sort of platform to use it, so presumably the works were underneath.

'All done by electricity,' he told us proudly. 'Heat removes the humidity, see,' and he withdrew a drawer from beneath it to display its brown, powdery contents.

'My shit,' he explained as he slipped it back. 'Humus for the garden, so the more I use it the richer I become.'

On his property he had planted many trees, and his intention was to encourage the water frontage to remain in its natural state as a mangrove swamp, for Fred was an ecologist and well understood the value of the mangrove and the mud. He took us to see his Jersey cow and tried to draw some milk from her, but others had been there before him including a calf, so instead of milk he gave us one of the excellent loaves he had baked that morning.

'Come again, any time,' he shouted as we started the outboard, 'spend the night,' and then the mangroves hid his tall, lean, bearded, barefoot figure. Next day he flew to Vienna where some of his paintings were on exhibition.

We felt we knew him better then, a highly successful sensitive artist, but also a kindly, gentle and perhaps a rather lonely man.

* * *

On 15 February we sailed for Panama, where we had a date to keep with *Grockle*, whose people had offered to come as our line-handlers through the canal. We were barely clear of Admiralty Bay when a tremendous downpour of rain spread over us, and when it had passed only a faint grey smudge showed where Hey Skip Island lay astern. It proved to be a lovely trip, for the winter trade was now fully established, and at a steady twenty-five to thirty knots blew us swiftly on our way, '. . . sailing the Carib Sea across the brow of Venezuela, free', though we saw nothing of that country. The current also was in our favour, but always had a tendency to set us towards the shore of South America. In the afternoon of our third day out we passed well to seaward of Curaçao, and that evening checked the compass with an amplitude of a somewhat unusual nature, for we were in the area where there was no magnetic variation (thereafter, it would be east instead of west) and our course chanced to be exactly the same as the sun's true bearing at setting.

Next day off the Peninsula de Guajira, where Henri Charrière (Papillon) lived with the Indians after his first escape from prison in French Guiana, we altered course more to the south-west to keep parallel with the coast. It was pleasantly cool as we slipped along at six knots, and over our evening drink in the cockpit we discussed whether or not to put in at Cartagena for a short stop as we were well ahead of time. The Colombian coast then had such a bad reputation for piracy that some insurance companies would not cover yachts cruising there (that did not much concern us as our ship was not insured), and the naval officer in charge at Martinique had reported that in the past year thirty yachts had been hi-jacked in the Caribbean (the figure has much increased since then), some of them in Colombian waters, and that not many of their people had survived. It was said that some had been caught in the following manner: a rubber craft was sighted with three men in it, and, of course, the yacht stopped to pick them up; the three then drew revolvers and covered the yacht's crew until their mother ship, which had remained hull-down but with her radar working, closed in for the kill; however, there appear to be some weak points in this plot. We did not suppose there could be any risk to voyaging people at the big city of Cartagena, but in the event we did not put in there because the wind was so strong and visibility so poor, and seven days out from Bequia, with 1100 miles astern of us, we made a night landfall on Manzanillo light thirty miles from Cristobal, which lies at the north end of the Panama Canal.

It was still blowing hard, and right onshore, and having twice before entered Cristobal Harbour in the dark we had no wish to do so again, so we handed the mainsail and ran on under head-sails only. But even so the loom of the port rapidly grew brighter in the sky, and individual lights began to pop up momentarily above the black horizon when we lifted on the swell; it was clear that we would arrive too early if we went on like that, so we took in the remaining sails, put the helm down, and lay a-hull for the rest of the night. We timed and identified each of the navigational lights as it appeared. The brightest was the thirty-miler at Toro Point two miles west of the harbour entrance, and this had been the innocent cause of the recent loss of two yachts that did not carry or failed to consult the *List of Lights*; believing that the great light must stand at the harbour entrance they steered for it, and drove ashore on the fangs of the low rock breakwater; each was a total loss but their people were saved.

We entered at dawn in company with a Greek freighter, and when we saw the crowd of ships lying within the harbour we were glad that caution had counselled a daylight entry. We made our way across to the Flats at the eastern side and anchored near some other yachts. The boarding officer, a pleasant young man who had been born in the Zone and loved it there, was soon with us to do the paper work and tell us what our procedure should be, and he handed us a copy of a booklet which had been prepared specially for yachts wishing to make a transit of the canal. Nothing much seemed to have changed since our last visit seven years before: one still had to row (the use of outboards being strictly forbidden) half-a-mile to windward to Pier 9 and land through a sea of oil, visit customs to get permission to walk to the yacht club to ask for a berth there, and then go to another office to get permission to move to it. As the dinghy trip entailed crossing the tracks of big ships going to and from the fuelling berth, an outboard motor would have made it less hazardous. I could not believe that this and other restrictive measures had been imposed because the Americans who ran the port and the canal particularly disliked yachts, though these must have been something of a nuisance, but because of the pressure put on them by the Panamanians who were so keen to take over the canal.

Next day we shifted to an alongside berth at the dear old Panama Canal Yacht Club, which was just as we had remembered it, a bit seedy looking but very helpful in an offhand kind of way, and most convenient with its showers and washing machines, its bar which was open twenty-four hours a day, and its inexpensive restaurant, in which we could sit at our ease looking at *Wanderer* and the other yachts only a few feet away, while eating combi-sandwiches or chow mein. The clatter from the kitchen and the drone from the air-conditioner, on which I found I was still liable to hit my head in the dark passage leading to the office, the whine of a sander being used on a yacht on one of the nearby-slips, and the never-ending deluge of distorted Spanish music screaming from a radio turned up too high for the benefit of the staff—all these sounds were nostalgic to our ears.

There was no difficulty about arranging to transit the canal—I hope the use of a noun as a verb will be forgiven, but this is common American and seems sensible to me, like much else in that language. The people in the terminals building were friendly and helpful, and in one office, they gave us rich pastries to eat while the paper work was being done. As *Wanderer* had been through before she did not have to be measured, so we chose a day, paid our dues—still only seventy cents a ton—and it was arranged that a pilot would board us at 6 a.m. on Sunday. But there were other matters to be sorted out. With so many yachts transiting (an average of one a day at that time of year) there was a waiting list for the limited number of moorings off the Balboa Yacht Club at the other end of the canal; we, therefore, decided to get everything we needed at the Cristobal end and not to stop at Balboa, and thus incidentally saved ourselves the time- and shoe-leather-consuming bother of having to enter and clear there. Our three earlier transits had convinced us that, because of the great inrush of water in the up-locks at Gatun, the safest way to go through was 'centre chamber', that is, to be held in the middle of each lock by four stout lines. Nobody objected to this, indeed, they recommended it, but the rule was that there must then be a separate 'line-handler' for each line, plus an 'operator', that is, a helmsman. Unfortunately, *Grockle* had been delayed with engine trouble at Grenada, but Paul Broadbent, a United States Army doctor stationed in the Zone, said he would like to come with us and bring his wife Marilyn and a young Englishman known as Mango. The Broadbents were sailing people and had already made several transits of the canal; Mango had not, but would be a useful hand as he had been a member of the expedition looking for Drake's remains, not as I had supposed in Nombre de Dios Bay but at Porto Bello.

We had a busy five days (the longest period one might remain at the club) for this would be our last opportunity to buy much in the way of stores until we reached Tahiti in perhaps two to three months' time. Potatoes, onions and fruit had to be picked over for bad ones and cockroaches and stowed away; eight dozen eggs had to be greased to preserve them, fresh butter had to be salted down in sterilized jars, and there was some work to be done on deck and aloft. Often our saloon was filled with visitors, for Cristobal is a great staging point for voyagers—each a little apprehensive about the forthcoming transit, not only because of the stories they had heard, but because for most owners this would be the first occasion that their yachts were not under their own control—and much interest was shown in them by people living in the Zone. On one occasion, three doctors were on board having a consultation about Susan's ear, the drum of which had become perforated while she was diving at Bequia, and a remarkable scene it was, for one doctor was in smart army uniform, another in tee-shirt and slacks, and the third, owner of the Swiss yacht, *Sarah la Noire*, wore only the briefest of bathing pants.

I needed some bromide paper on which to make the illustrations for a story I had written, and was told it could be obtained in the free zone of Colon, the Panamanian town adjoining American Cristobal. So one afternoon we walked there and back through the teeming, sleazy streets, and, when our American friends heard of our expedition, they told us sternly it was a foolish thing to have done, for Colon had always been a hunting ground of pickpockets, but now it seemed they no longer picked one's pocket but with a knife or razor cut the pocket clean out of one's shirt or trousers together sometimes with a hunk of flesh. We could hardly believe such stories, but the next day the French owner of a yacht lying close to us was robbed, and stabbed in the arm; as this incident occurred not in Colon but just outside the yacht club in the American Zone, which until then had been considered to be well policed and quite safe, everyone was a bit alarmed.

We had met at English Harbour and become friendly with a delightful Canadian family, Jim and Erica Leach with their newly married daughter and her husband, aboard the cutter, *White Water*; I do not know if there was insufficient room below or lack of privacy, but the honeymoon couple slept in a huddle on the foredeck; frequent sounds of mirth came drifting across the water from them, so we came to know them as the laughing Canadians. Jim and Erica had an unpleasant experience in Colon: while walking along one of the streets in that town, two youths who looked like students crossed over to them, and one from behind threw a stick on a lanyard between Jim's legs, tripping him, while the other made a dive for his wallet. But quick-witted Jim rolled over on his back, clamped a hand on his wallet, and kicked and yelled while Erica screamed for help. All this happened in the middle of the morning in a busy street with people walking and traffic flowing, and the Leaches were rapidly coming to the conclusion that nobody was going to help them when there was a sudden loud roar from a powerful-looking man standing in an office doorway; the youths left and sauntered away, and the man asked Jim if he had been *tiffed* (from the Jamaican 'thieved'), to which he replied that he had not for he still had his wallet. He and Erica then continued towards the yacht club, and were feeling none too happy about it for the street they found themselves in seemed to be closing in on them, when a Panamanian police car drew up. Through a bystander, who spoke a little English, the policeman asked where they were going and, on being told, said it was not safe and that he would drive them, but as he was short of petrol he needed some money; this, contrary to Erica's whispered wishes, Jim produced and it was quickly and expertly palmed, but no stop was made at any filling station.

The trouble was that people from yachts were too obvious, for no other European would think of walking, and if one of them came out of a bank it would be clear what he had been there for. The city of Panama seemed to be just as dangerous as Colon. The Wommelsdorfs, a German couple in *Mona Lisa II*, had been to cash travellers' cheques at a bank in the city. Ingeborg had the money in her shoulder bag, and, as they left the bank, a man grabbed the bag, breaking the strap, and ran off with it; Werner was not going to put up with that and gave chase, but he was wearing sandals and tripped in a gutter breaking a bone in his foot to become a hospital case, and the money was never recovered. More examples of similar incidents came to light as we met other voyaging people who had come through Panama, so it seemed it was not the up-locks at Gatun or the risk of a drunken pilot that presented the hazard, but the piratical habits of some of the people, and the only safe way to get about was by car or taxi. When we bought stores at the Tagaropolus supermarket the manager said he would send an employee with the goods on a barrow to accompany us to the club, but when the barrow-boy saw what we had bought he reckoned such a trip would be unsafe, and we had to take our purchases by taxi.

* * *

Confusion over times, or failure to keep promises, appeared to be not uncommon in the Marine Traffic Control office, and several of our neighbours failed to get away on time or even on the agreed day. On the Saturday evening, as instructed, I 'phoned Traffic Control to say that we were ready and to confirm that our pilot would arrive at 6 a.m. as agreed, but was told that he would now not come until 9.30 a.m.; the Broadbents were in the club, so I informed them about the change of time. It was, therefore, with some surprise that we were woken by a pilot knocking on the side at 6 a.m.; I at once tried to get in touch with the Broadbents and with Mango, but could not contact them, so the pilot, who was apparently quite accustomed to having to get out of bed at 4 a.m. to take a yacht which had no line-handlers, went home, and another arrived at 10.30, by which time Mango and the Broadbents had joined us. The pilot was a reserved man, but we soon realized that he was competent—he knew a bit about small craft as he had once crewed in a Bermuda race—and throughout the day, which was a long one, he never relaxed his vigilance for a moment. This was in sharp contrast to some of the pilots about whom we were told later. The pilot handling *Grockle* ran her aground twice, and in getting off damaged her clutch; another left *Solent Dove* somewhere in Gatun Lake, saying that he had done his stint, and that poor little yacht did not get through until early the following day; *Quinquereme*'s pilot ordered her to overtake a big ship about to enter one of the down-locks, and to pass through a rapidly narrowing channel between her and the stone wall, and to save his yacht the owner had to disregard the order and go hard astern; *Pendragon* had her forward guardrails carried away through mismanagement; and Traffic Control spotted by the way he spoke on his walkie-talkie radio that *White Water*'s pilot was drunk, and had him relieved.

We got under way immediately, but had to jill about for more than an hour waiting for the container ship, *Oakland*, with which we were to share the locks, to get her anchor and move into the first lock ahead of us. We followed her in with Susan at the helm, as she was to be throughout the day whenever any tricky manoeuvring had to be done; Captain Nathaniel Gladding II, our pilot, sat beside her giving sensible orders in a quiet voice.

'Heads up,' he warned, and four monkeys' fists on heaving-lines came whistling down from the high sides of the lock to thud on our deck; to each of them we made fast a 100-foot (thirty-metre) line to be hauled ashore and its bowline dropped over a bollard. We hove them taut, the great gates silently closed astern of us, and the water started to boil and swirl as it rushed in through the eight-foot (2·4-metre) diameter culverts in the floor of the lock. Quickly, we rose, hauling in the slack of the lines when we could, Mango and I working forward and Paul and Marilyn aft—we could not have wished for a more efficient or seamanlike crew.

Within eight minutes the lock was full, the next pair of gates opened, and *Oakland* gave a kick ahead with her propeller to help the mules (electric locomotives on rails) move her into the next chamber. We were prepared for the backwash, which was considerable, and kept all our lines taut until it subsided, for if one of them had been slack just then we could have been in trouble. Twice more the whole routine was repeated, and then with sighs of relief that the most awkward part of the transit was over, we came out upon the broad waters of twenty-three-mile-long Gatun Lake eighty-five feet (twenty-six metres) above the sea, and spread the awning.

We had laid in a stock of fresh food with which to feed our hungry party, for we could not afford to use up ship's stores as there would now be no chance to replenish them for about 5000 miles. In turn, our friends steered while Susan prepared a sandwich lunch, and I got the Coke, the rum and the beer out of the icebox which the Broadbents had thoughtfully brought with them. At our best cruising speed under power of six-and-a-half knots we made our way through Banana Cut, thereby saving a mile or two, and on across the lake by way of the buoyed channel between the upstanding trunks and branches of the trees that had been drowned when the forest was submerged to make the lake, and then through Gaillard Cut, the narrowest part at the continental divide, where a dredger was at work on one of the frequently occurring landslides. With such delightful companions it was, for Susan and me, a memorable and enjoyable occasion. But our speed was not quite good enough to keep up with *Oakland*'s seven knots, so on arrival at Pedro Miguel, first of the three down-locks, we had to wait for the next south-bound ship, *Pacific Exporter*, to catch up with us, for a yacht never has a lock all to herself. There was no small craft such as a tug or a banana boat alongside which we could have lain, so once again heaving-lines were thrown—I came to dread those hard and heavy monkeys' fists for I could not see them coming and felt as though under fire. There was only one awkward moment when a monkey's fist went foul of the rigging above the crosstrees, but fortunately it did not take a round turn and somehow disentangled itself; that left only one heaving-line that side, but Paul was quick in bringing his quarter line forward to my bow line so that both could be hauled ashore together. *Pacific Exporter* crept in astern of us, filling the rest of the lock, her great flaring bows growing broader and taller as she approached; the gates closed and down we dropped together, paying out our lines as we did so.

Night had fallen before we were spilt out of the final lock on a strong current into the seven-mile-long dredged channel leading to the Pacific. As we approached the great curved span of what we still called the Bridge of the Americas, though its name had been changed unromantically to Thatcher Ferry Bridge, *Pacific Exporter* was overhauling us to port and an incoming ship was approaching on our starboard bow. Nat, who had been speaking quietly on his walkie-talkie, said to Susan:

'Turn to port a little and stop,' and to our friends: 'A launch will take you off in a few moments.'

Quickly they collected their belongings, though I could give them no more light than was shed by the red lamp over the chart table for fear of dazzling Nat or Susan. The black hulk of *Exporter* was slipping by across our bows now, and at Nat's request I switched on the floodlights. A big fast launch superbly handled swept alongside in a milky froth of her own screw-race but did not touch us, and there was barely time to say thank you to Paul, Marilyn and Mango, though Marilyn found time to give me a charming kiss, before they made a jump for it and instantly were rushed away into the darkness.

'Starboard a little and full ahead.' The bridge passed high above our masts, and Susan was glad to have Nat beside her, for the bright lights of Balboa were confusing and ships were on the move. Down the long straight channel we went between the red and white lights of the buoys, and to seaward right across our bows was spread another thick row of lights where thirty ships lay at anchor awaiting transits. As we neared the first of them we turned to port and anchored in the lee of Flamenco Island, the hump of which was silhouetted black against the distant city lights of Panama. We had barely straightened out our cable when a pilot launch ranged up alongside, and as Nat stepped aboard her he said:

'You'll be all right here; I've told the boarding officers not to bother you. Good luck.' And he was gone.

PART IV

PANAMA TO NEW ZEALAND

WITH SOME THOUGHTS ON

Very high altitude sights—Killer whales—Making bread—Provisions—Cockroaches—'Flopper-stoppers'—Darkroom work—Mail—Making a landfall—The safety syndrome—Gas versus paraffin—The abyss—Time and the date-line—Calibration of instruments—Charts—The green flash—Wildlife

IN the past year or so many yachts had applied for permits to visit the Galápagos Islands, but only a few, notably those which were able to claim they carried scientific expeditions or tourists, obtained them, and Ecuador, to which country the islands belong, made it clear that not many more would be issued; Susan and I did not consider it wise to go there without a permit, and when we again met the Wommelsdorfs in *Mona Lisa II* and they told us what had happened to them, we were glad we did not. After Werner's foot had mended they went without permission to the Galápagos and visited Tower and two other islands before reaching Floreana, where they were discovered by a gunboat and ordered to go to Wreck Bay. They made the mistake of trying to escape under cover of darkness, were pursued, captured, and taken to Wreck Bay where Werner was put in prison for ten days; in addition, the naval commandant demanded a heavy fine, but Ingeborg, who had a legal background, managed to talk him out of that; meanwhile, she looked after the yacht and took food to her husband. I understand, however, that Werner was treated fairly well and spent much of his time drinking with the policemen. After his release they made a fast passage to the Marquesas.

We had been fortunate enough to visit the Galápagos on an earlier voyage before the islands became a tourist attraction, and to enjoy undisturbed the remarkable wildlife that abounds there. Nevertheless, we would have been glad to put in on this occasion for a rest and refreshment, for the islands lie about 1000 miles from Panama on the route to the Marquesas; but we felt it would be more sensible to sail direct for the Marquesas, though in our view a non-stop passage of 4000 miles was too long to be enjoyable. However, we were well prepared, provisioned and watered, and we left busy Panama Bay and saw our last ships on 2 March, that is, before the rainy season was due to set in.

So far as winds are concerned, that is as good a time as any, and better than some, for a sailing vessel to get out of the Gulf of Panama and down into the region of the south-east trade wind, though it is a difficult trip at any time of year, for the winds tend to be light, calms extensive, and the currents strong. The Humboldt, a cold current which is thought to be responsible for penguins living on the equatorial Galápagos, sweeps north up the west coast of South America, and to avoid it one should not go too near the land; but, if a sailing vessel gets too far to the west too soon, the beginning of the south equatorial current, which can run at twenty to thirty miles a day, may carry her away to the north or north-west and into the counter current, which would sweep her back towards the coast. We, therefore, attempted to steer a middle course where the current, an overflow from the Gulf of Panama, should be in our favour. But, unfortunately, we did not know to what extent we were succeeding, for our old patent log, which for more than 120 000 miles had faithfully recorded the distance we sailed through the water in this and our earlier *Wanderer*s, and had recently been back to its makers for an overhaul, was not working correctly due to a too-tight ball race about which we could do nothing except let it spin and hope it would ease itself in time, which, with liberal doses of paraffin instead of lubricating oil, it eventually did. But currents there certainly were, and again and again we passed through swirls, overfalls, and ripplings, a strange sensation when one knows that the depth is at least 1000 fathoms; the overfalls were particularly widespread and angry in the vicinity of Malpelo Island, a barren rock which serves as a signpost 300 miles along the way. An odd thing was that although at some point we must have crossed the Humboldt, at no time did we experience a drop in temperature; the sea remained at 81 °F (27 °C), and in the middle of the day the temperature on deck was 100 °F (38 °C), in the saloon 87 °F (31 °C), and in the engine-room when the engine was running only 95 °F (35 °C), but after the engine had been stopped it rose for a time well above that, the reason being that when the engine was running it drew a plentiful supply of fresh air in through the ventilators, a stream which stopped when the engine was stopped.

We started off with quite a flourish. A fresh, fair wind—a continuation of the north-east trade blowing across the isthmus—pushed us quickly out of Panama Bay, which abounded in fish and bird life; terns crying and fluttering in their fussy manner, pelicans silent and graceful until they made their astonishing crash landings, surrounded us, and gulls marked every bit of flotsam, notably waterlogged tree trunks and empty, rusting oil-drums. The good wind gave us a day's run of 133 miles, but thereafter so light was the wind that throughout the whole long passage, we equalled or exceeded that run only on three occasions.

The wind fell light next day; the sky was a pale misty blue, and the sea was barely rippled except by the meetings of the currents; but from then on there was often enough swell to knock the wind out of the mainsail, so, for much of the time, we went along under genoa and mizzen-staysail and/or a running-sail (some might call this a spinnaker, but it was cut with very little belly), and sometimes under the latter and the mizzen only, for, although this was of cloth as heavy as that of the mainsail (ten ounce (350 gram)) it remained asleep remarkably well. We worked hard to make the most of every puff, and sometimes made five sail changes in as many miles. The mainsail was stowed and coated, uncoated and reset on nineteen occasions for, as Miles Smeeton had remarked when in those same waters: 'The noise of the main emptying and filling was an agony not to be borne'. When the wind died completely, as it did too often, we motored, and did so for a total of fifty-seven hours; after that we saved our fuel for more important things. But on that first difficult stretch we did not do too badly, for on the tenth day out we reached a position 120 miles south of Hood Island, the south-easternmost of the Galápagos, so the current must have been in our favour a good deal of the way.

At about that time, an interesting navigational situation arose. We were still making some southing and the sun was coming north to meet us and to pass overhead at noon. It is difficult, indeed, it may be impossible if there is much sea or swell, to obtain an observation of a body when its altitude exceeds about eighty-eight degrees and, as in such circumstances the body's azimuth (true bearing) will be east all the forenoon and west all the afternoon, morning and afternoon position lines cannot cross to provide a fix. Michael Richey, *Jester*'s owner and Director of the Royal Institute of Navigation, had kindly told me how to overcome this in the following neat and easy way, which is described by Lecky and Burton and is known as 'very high altitude sights'. Although one may rarely have occasion to use it, perhaps brief instructions might be of interest.

Work out in advance the time of ship's noon; if you know your longitude within fifteen miles you cannot be more than one minute in error, and that is accurate enough for the purpose. Take a timed observation of the sun shortly before and shortly after local noon—I have found that five to six minutes each side of noon is convenient (see below). Mark on the chart or plotting diagram the sun's geographical position at the time of each observation—the sun's declination is its latitude and the sun's Greenwich hour angle is its longitude, and both are obtained from *The Nautical Almanac*. With these points as centres, and with radii equal to each of the zenith distances (altitude deducted from ninety degrees) sweep arcs; where the arcs intersect is your noon position. The only thing to be careful about here is that, as the arcs cut in two places, it is essential to know whether the sun passed north or south of you at noon. If the observations are taken at more than about six minutes each side of noon, the resulting zenith distances may be too great to be drawn conveniently on the chart or plotting diagram. I need hardly add that a third observation, which may usefully be the meridian altitude if this is possible, forms a valuable check. This is the simplest, quickest and most satisfying method known of obtaining a fix as opposed to a single position line, and so far as I know is the only way that a fix can be had from a single body. The only other time during this circumnavigation that I was able to use 'very high altitude sights' was when we, sailing north up the Atlantic, overtook the sun going the same way.

Having reached a position south of the Galápagos, we had to work through a five-degree square in which, the pilot chart informed us, no wind averaged more than six knots, and thirteen per cent of calm could be expected. To get across, it took a considerable time, and when we could move, we tried to move more south than west because the next five-degree square in that direction showed stronger winds and fewer calms, but it also showed the favourable current to be weaker. This part of the trip wearied us, but I must not weary you, so let me tell of a few of the outstanding things that happened in the long succession of days and nights when we tried so hard to make some progress, always hoping for an improvement in the wind, an improvement that did not come.

One fine morning when the sun was just lifting above the horizon and the ship was slipping along at about three knots, Susan was in the cockpit straightening her hair and I was below scrambling Panamanian eggs for breakfast—my only contribution to the domestic economy was getting breakfast—when she called me to come up and have a look. I emerged to find we were surrounded by a party of about thirty of what I at first took to be very large porpoises or perhaps pilot whales. I made my way out to the end of the bowsprit to watch them perform round the forefoot, as I had so often done on other occasions, and then I realized that these big black creatures with white undersides were much larger and heavier than any porpoise or dolphin I had ever seen; their heads were blunt, their bodies thick-set. Then Susan drew my attention to the ill-defined saddle of pale colour on each back abaft the dorsal fin, as though a muddy hand had been daubed there.

'Killer whales?' she suggested almost in a whisper.

While I was still up forward digesting her remark and thinking of the Robertsons' *Lucette*, which was sunk, it was claimed, by a concerted and unprovoked killer whale attack not far from where we were, Susan watched with awe one character which swam abreast the cockpit, but so far under the turn of the bilge that only its outboard side was visible; now and then it turned away a few yards to blow, then at once charged back as though to ram us, but at the very last moment swung round into its original position. The creatures varied much in size, possibly indicating that there were females among them, for the female is only half the length of the male; the largest in the party was perhaps twenty-five feet (7·6 metres) long. Our escort remained with us for about half an hour then turned aside and, much to our relief, vanished. The genuine killer whale, not the smaller and apparently harmless false killer, has a bad, though probably exaggerated, reputation; it is said to be cunning enough to break up or capsize an ice-floe if penguins, seals or men are seen to be on it, but its chief prey is the harmless whalebone whale that is defenceless when attacked by killers which, on such occasions, behave like a pack of wolves.

On another morning similar to the above, except that we were going so slowly that the vane gear was barely able to steer, Susan was kneading dough on the galley bench while I worked out the forenoon sight, when a metallic clang from aft brought us both on deck in a hurry to discover a turtle rubbing itself on the servo-blade of the vane gear, the safety latch of which had been released by the blow. Clearly that hard, heavy reptile, lifting and falling on the slight sea that was running, was doing the blade no good, so we hinged the latter up out of danger. The turtle had on its carapace a growth of goose-barnacles and, as it was within close reach and apparently unafraid, Susan got out the long-handled broom and gave it a good scrub. This seemed to be appreciated, and once or twice the reptile took the broom gently in its mouth. But after the clean-up it still persisted in bumping and rubbing the ship's bottom and rudder, and we thought it might knock off too much paint; we had said we would not again use the engine until we made a landfall, but we did start it up then and ran it for half an hour to outdistance our tame turtle. I do not know much about these slow creatures which, although they seem to be of poor design for seagoing, may be found far from land in all the oceans, and presumably rely solely on their armour plating for defence; but I do know that in the South Atlantic the female turtle makes the long voyage all the way from Brazil to the small island of Ascension to lay her eggs, up to 200 of them, in a pit she digs in the sand, leaves them on their own to hatch, and then swims back to Brazil—not only a remarkable voyage but a fine feat of navigation.

One quiet, star-filled night through which we, as usual, were both sleeping while the vane gear steered and the riding-light on the boom-gallows kept watch, Susan chanced to wake in the early hours and went on deck to cool off and have a look round. To her astonishment, she saw not far off the starboard beam a yacht with a big ghostly headsail partly illuminated by a light low down; there was no figure to be seen on deck or in the cockpit. Susan watched as the yacht overhauled us and slowly crossed our bows, for she was steering a more southerly course than were we and was probably tacking to leeward. Susan returned to her bunk a little thoughtfully, wondering how many other near misses there had been while we slept, and told me of it in the morning. We both had the idea that the yacht could have been *Running Wild*, one of the sleek and swift Moody 44s, which our New Zealand friends Doug and Rosie Johnstone had bought in England and were sailing home; we had both been at Cristobal together, and we knew that when at sea they, like ourselves, showed an all-round white light below the sails while they slept at night. It was ten months later that we next met the Johnstones, and at once asked them where they were on 22 March. Doug got out his chart of the Pacific on which, like us, he had marked his noon positions, and then there was no doubt about it, for *Running Wild*'s noon position that day was almost identical with ours. At the time, the nearest specks of land were: the Galápagos about 750 miles astern, Clipperton Island 1000 miles to starboard, Easter Island 1300 miles to port, and the Marquesas 2000 miles ahead. Probably what had brought the two yachts so close together in that lonely area of ocean was that both had on the previous day avoided a little dotted circle on the chart marked: 'Breakers & disc[d] water rept[d] 1906', by passing north of it.

Day followed almost identical day; there was no squall nor even a shower of rain to cool the deck or break the monotony; there were no gaily coloured sunrises or sunsets, and not once did we have to gybe, for the feeble wind, which could barely raise a white cap, remained always on the port quarter. The days added up to make weeks, and still there was no strength in the trade, the wind which had brought so many sailing vessels in the past at high speed across that part of the ocean. After we had been at sea four weeks the starboard topside had on it a growth of slime and weed, and when we were below we could hear the wet soughing noise of the pests we had grown to dread most: goose-barnacles on the hull being lifted out of the water and re-immersed as we rolled.

Half of the lemons bought in Colon had gone bad a long time ago and the rest had all been finished, but the grapefruit lasted well, which was a good thing as all we fancied for our supper those hot, humid evenings as we rolled with slamming sails was a mug of soup and half a grapefruit. As on the Atlantic crossing, we had our best meals in the middle of the day, and for these, hot Cornish pasties were what we looked forward to most; next in popularity came a fresh-baked crusty loaf with corned beef, sardines or jam. The close-knit cabbages from Colon lasted four weeks, and with cold potatoes, onions, a hard-boiled egg, and a can of peas, made an excellent coleslaw. Our best stand-by when palates were really jaded was one of those excellent Molly O'Rourke fruit cakes from Dublin with a wee drop of the hard stuff in it; fortunately we had bought a generous supply of these.

Among voyaging people the making of bread is a much discussed and controversial subject, and there are recipes galore, each sailing cook apparently having his or her own. Over the years Susan had experimented with several, and some of her earlier efforts produced loaves so hard and heavy they might almost have been made of cement; but by the time we had reached this stage of the voyage her bread making and baking operations were so consistently successful that, although they are in no way likely to influence expert bakers, they might be of interest to those neophytes who may be going through the early run of failures, and this is what she told me:

'The two greatest variables in making bread are ambient temperature and the age and activity of the yeast. After experimenting with different recipes I came to use the following: 500 grams (eighteen ounces) of white flour, one teaspoonful of raw sugar, salt, and one level teaspoon of yeast pellets. I melt the sugar in half a cup of warm water and add the yeast, leaving it to stand for fifteen minutes. I have the flour ready in a bowl and add to it the yeast mixture plus about another cup of warm water. The dough needs to be wet and manageable only by very floury hands, otherwise the finished product will be tight and heavy. I knead it for five minutes, stretching its elasticity, and then let it rise for (perhaps) forty minutes. Then I knead again and place in a well-greased baking tin [the inside measurements of mine are twenty-three by thirteen by six centimetres (nine by five by 2·3 inches)] and let it rise before baking. Mary Livingstone told me the dodge of putting the dough (in its bowl or tin) in a plastic bag in the sunshine to keep the temperature up and hasten rising ("kind of fuggy", she said), and on cool days I use a hot-water bottle to help; on rough days I let the rising be done on the gimballed cooker otherwise the motion tends to keep on kneading. All the flour I bought "in the islands" contained creatures, but I have had clean flour on board for more than a year without deterioration.'

I have mentioned here and there the salting down of butter, and this is how we did it. We placed the containers, usually glass jam-jars, in a large pan of salt water and brought it to the boil. When the jars were cool, fresh butter was packed into them, the aim being to leave no air spaces; the top of each was then given a thin layer of salt and the lid screwed on. We found this more satisfactory and much cheaper than buying canned butter, and often the latter had become tainted before we opened it, for the life of even the best quality canned butter is limited.

When Susan knew the brands and believed them to be good, she gave preference to meat when buying canned foods; she did not buy 'mixtures' such as meat loaf or stew, but went in for corned beef, ham [only cans of less than two pounds (0·9 kilo) would keep unrefrigerated], tongue, steak-and-kidney pudding, and stewed steak; fresh onions and other vegetables were cooked before being added to the already cooked canned meat to make a more pleasantly flavoured and wholesome meal than ready mixed stews. With the exception of ham and bacon, canned meat generally stayed good for years or until the cans gave way from rust; on discovering a swollen can (usually ham) we threw it away without investigating the gas, and we did not carry crab or lobster because we believed there could be a risk of food poisoning from those exotic and expensive items. Portuguese and Spanish sardines, though cheap and popular in their countries of origin, sold at delicatessen prices throughout the Pacific.

Although we had the occasional cockroach on board we never had an infestation. Perhaps this was just luck, but we did take a lot of trouble when in the tropics. Every potato and onion was laid out on deck and checked before being handed into its stowage bag; egg boxes, which as Susan said make excellent cradles for baby 'roaches, were carefully examined; cardboard cartons were not often allowed on board, and stems of bananas were first immersed in the sea for several minutes. Nevertheless, we were fortunate in that we never shipped a clutch of cockroach eggs.

On that long passage I had plenty of time to look round and enjoy the many pleasing features of our ship, and to take pride in some of the little things we had done to improve or beautify her; I found that those which gave me the greatest satisfaction were usually the simpler things that we had made on board ourselves instead of buying or having made professionally: a shelf here, a rack or fiddle there, the removable bar arranged to stop the cook from being thrown against the galley stove; the little paper shades for our reading lights cut from *National Geographic* envelopes, stuck on with contact glue, and embellished with bits of tortoiseshell or postage stamps from remote places; the red nylon bag with elastic in its hem to slip over the chart-table lamp when we needed to retain our night vision; a rattle-proof stowage for the mizzen sheet

---

13 *Top* Pacific calm. *Bottom* As a spectacle we had seen nothing quite the equal of this for a long time: Hanavave Bay, Fatu Hiva.

winch-handle, and extra handholds hewn out of hunks of teak and fastened in strategic places on the coachroofs. Some of these things had been done in a hurry when the ship was new and we were preparing her for her first long trip, and they had never been properly finished, for I found that if a thing did the job for which it had been made, no matter how clumsy it might look it would be left like that while more urgent matters were attended to. Now, as I looked about me, I could see how many little tidying-up improvements could be done, and still more comforts and conveniences added, and I promised myself that one day soon, when there was nothing more important to do, I would attend to them. I used to think that a trade-wind passage with a vane-gear steering would provide countless opportunities for maintenance and improvement, but I soon discovered that the continuous rolling was not conducive to doing anything that required two hands; so, unless a job was of immediate importance, affecting the efficiency or safety of the ship, or the wellbeing of her people, it was neglected. Therefore, instead of making proper use of this long stretch away from the land, I often sat and read and, among many other books, I particularly enjoyed Hailey's *The Final Diagnosis*, Glemser's *The Fly Girls*, Hemingway's *Islands in the Stream*, and Villiers's *Captain Cook, the Seaman's Seaman*, which helped to make enjoyable many an hour, as did our stereo tape-player.

The fourth week passed and then the fifth and, although there was then a trifle more weight in the wind, we seemed to move with it no faster. The soughing of the goose-barnacles was becoming a nightmare dirge, and we began to understand how, in the past, sailing vessels on long, slow passages had sometimes become unmanageable due to their foul bottoms; our ship had no life in her, but crept only slowly along. The ocean, too, seemed lifeless; there were no birds, only an occasional flying fish or squid, and never a porpoise to be seen or heard—even a school of killer whales might have been welcome then. The remotely distant stars, many of them old friends on which Susan spied with her sextant at twilight, wheeled across the sky: the Southern Cross to port, the Plough to starboard, Orion on our latitude—and the moon began again to grow.

* * *

---

14 *Left* Down staysail as we head up Cook Bay towards Moorea's Tiger's Tooth. *Right* In Robinson Cove we took a line to a tree and hauled our stern to within a few feet of the beach.

The Seven Seas Cruising Association, to which Susan and I had belonged from time to time since it was started in California in 1952, is a unique body of men and women who live permanently aboard their sailing yachts; many of them cruise or make long voyages. The monthly *Bulletin*, to which anyone may now subscribe, comprises letters written by members and subscribers scattered all over the world. Although some of the letters are verbose, from many of them can be obtained valuable items of information on coasts, anchorages, provisions, port officials, and so on—a wealth of fascinating, local knowledge which is not available from any other source and, although some of it inevitably becomes dated, fresh information continues to flow in.

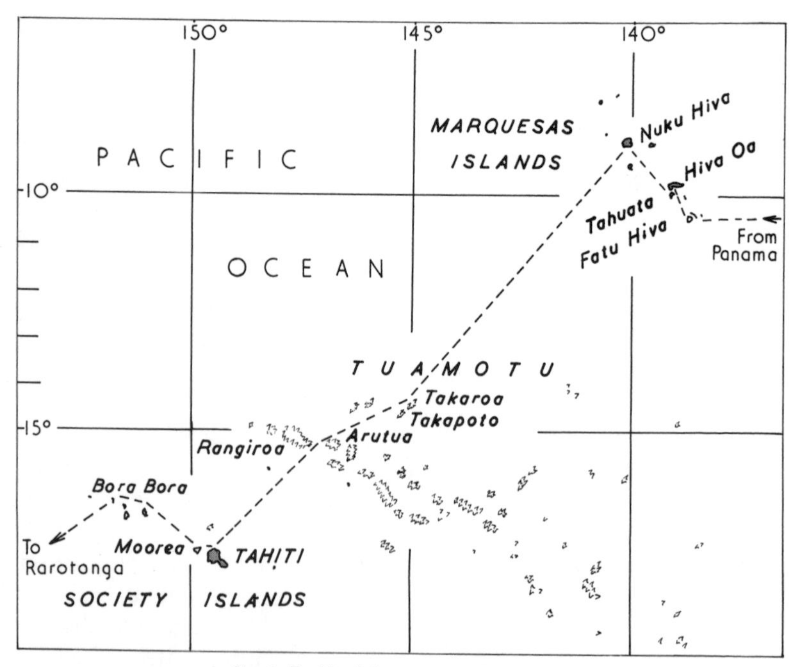

South Pacific, Marquesas to Bora Bora

The Marquesas used to have only one port of entry, at Taiohae Bay in the western group, so that a visit to the eastern group usually entailed a long, hard beat back against the trade wind. But we had learned from recent issues of the *Bulletin* that there was now a port of entry in the eastern group at the village of

Atuona on the island of Hiva Oa; but to reach the anchorage there, we would have had to sail into Traitor's Bay, all of which is a lee shore when the trade wind blows. Feeling that this would be a risk with our ship in her badly fouled state, sluggish through the water and slow on the helm, we decided to find some other anchorage easier of access, and where we might dive and scrape some of the barnacles from her bottom. Fatu Hiva, the south-easternmost island of the group, appeared to offer what we needed, so we steered for where it should lie and, in the forenoon of our thirty-eighth day out of sight of land, its misty peaks grew out of the sea ahead. We were up with the seven-mile-long island in the afternoon, and crept along in its lee to an anchorage in Hanavave Bay. As a spectacle we had seen nothing quite the equal of this for a very long time (Plate 13 *bottom*). The bay was about one cable wide and thrust into the land for two cables, its sides of sheer black rock topped by steep tree- and bush-clad slopes. At the head of the bay, the swell broke white and loudly on a beach of black boulders, inshore of which was a small area of flat land with a tiny village and some palms, and from it a valley with a stream probed inland. The flat area was flanked by pillars of rock, and was hemmed in by 3000-foot (900-metre) barren mountain peaks; down from these at frequent intervals, violent but short-lived squalls rushed upon us as though to drive us away. To seaward the sky was blue and flecked with small, fine-weather clouds, but our narrow vista of overhead sky between the cliffs and peaks of our bay was heavy with inky rain cloud.

The water, reflecting sky and cliffs, was dark and deep and a little sinister, but as soon as we were sure the anchor had a good hold, we dived overboard and, with goggles, could see why our poor ship had become so sluggish as to be almost unmanageable: her entire underwater body was thickly covered with a growth of blue-black goose-barnacles between one and three inches (2·5 and 7·5 centimetres) in length; never had we seen fouling as bad as that. With scrapers made of wood and sharpened with a plane, we set to work to remove the tough, rubbery creatures, beginning at the waterline and then going deeper and deeper, using a rope passed beneath the keel from rail to rail with which to haul ourselves down. As the scraper tore the barnacles away from the steel they slowly sank down into the blue void beneath, the white shells that they carried at the ends of their long necks flashing in the sunlight like snowflakes, and we wondered what creatures were watching and waiting in the depths for this stream of food from above, for, although our anchor was in seven fathoms, so steeply did the bottom slope that, when *Wanderer* had pulled back on her cable, there were fifteen fathoms beneath her; sting rays there certainly were for we saw some, and perhaps sharks came into the bay to clean up offal from the village. To clear a square foot several trips to the surface were required for fresh lung-fulls of air; some divers can hold their breath for two minutes, but scraping is hard work, and we could not stay down for half that time. It was a scaring job which we only risked when the sun was high, but at least some of it had to be done before we could safely move on.

Over four days we dived and scraped, and then sailed across to enter French Polynesia at the uneasy little cul-de-sac off Traitor's Bay on Hiva Oa. After landing at the head of the bay, we had a long, hot and dusty walk along the road the French were constructing round the inlet to the village of Atuona, where we had to explain to the gendarme why we had put in at Fatu Hiva (where, from another yacht in which he was having a holiday, he had seen us) instead of coming straight in to enter. Fortunately, we had not landed on that island, and he accepted our explanation, but then wanted to retain our passports. That was something about which we had strong feelings; any official who so wished might of course see our passports and copy particulars from them, but to hold them, especially in a little wooden shack which could catch fire or get robbed, was not reasonable; besides, we had no intention after cruising among the eastern islands, of returning to Atuona to collect our passports; indeed, if the weather was unsuitable that might not even be possible. The gendarme was firm about it, but Susan was firmer, and having picked the passports up off his desk she did not relinquish them. There were some Gallic gestures, but he was too courteous to argue with a woman, and he clearly wished to make our visit a pleasant one; so he shrugged his shoulders, looked at me with what I took to be commiseration, and drove us in his jeep back to where we had left the dinghy. We noticed with surprise that the new road was lined with concrete lamp standards, and that night we had our first demonstration of street lamps in paradise, glaring unshaded across the water so that it was hard to see the stars; the poor little lighthouse (there were only two in the whole group) was quite overpowered, for it too showed a fixed white light, but depended for its power on a paraffin-burning hurricane lamp.

We had often had occasion to remark on the help and kindness shown to one another by members of the voyaging community, and we had another excellent demonstration of it there. Several yachts lay at anchor with us, and we happened to mention to the owner of one of them when he came to call that we still had a lot more work to do on our bottom to get it clean. He organized a diving party, and the next afternoon one or more young men from each near-by yacht came swimming to us with goggles and flippers; quickly I made a few more wooden scrapers, and within about an hour those kind people had completed the job for us. Apparently it had been a good season for goose-barnacles; most of the yachts that had come across from Panama and Mexico had growths of them, particularly on the quarters, which is always a favoured spot, but none had acquired such a flourishing crop as we had. We were visited by Bill Woods, an ear, nose and throat specialist who, with his wife, had sailed from Panama in *La Mioche*. He kindly came to have a look at Susan's ear, about which our chief line-handler in the canal, Paul Broadbent, had told him by radio. Fortunately, Susan's perforated eardrum had mended, but Bill was able to help us medically in other ways, though it was he who became so ill a little later when sailing for Tahiti, that for several days his wife had to handle the yacht single-handed and do the navigation.

The Marquesas consist of six inhabited and several smaller uninhabited islands, and among them there is not one properly landlocked anchorage; so most of the time one rolls in the swell that sucks and breaks along the rocky shores, and runs high on the beaches to make landing awkward. Nevertheless, we much enjoyed our month among them at the end of our long trip from Panama, and this was partly because of the fine, settled weather in which the wind never shifted out of the easterly quarter to make us anxious, and partly because of the many delightful people we met in other yachts.

With our bottom now barnacle-free, we moved across to the nearby island of Tahuata, where the chart showed what looked like a fair anchorage on sand in Hana-moe-noa Bay. There were several bays close together on that part of the island and, as we were anxious to identify the right one, we took our pilotage seriously; but we need not have bothered, for, as we opened up that side of Tahuata, we saw a bunch of yachts at anchor in that bay, and we picked a berth among them. That proved to be our best stop among the Marquesas, for the swell was less than at any other anchorage; there was a steep sand beach at the head of the bay on which even we, who were not very clever at it, were able to land through the slight surf, and, perhaps because there was no fresh water, there were no natives. Some of our neighbours had been to Resolution Bay farther down the coast where there was a village, and had come to uninhabited Hana-moe-noa to get some peace for, although Polynesians are pleasant and friendly people they are inclined to come aboard in large parties and stay and stay; also, perhaps because of the large number of visiting yachts, they had become a little spoilt, and regarded the sailor in much the same light as they might regard the tourist. A gift of bananas or *pamplemousse* (something like an orange and a grapefruit mixed, but much bigger and better than either) was welcome, and might in earlier times have been repaid with a packet of cigarettes, an old shirt, or some fish-hooks; but now the donor would cast his eye round and choose something he wanted in return, which as likely as not turned out to be the mainsheet or the compass, and difficulties followed. It should not be thought that Polynesians behaved like that everywhere, but the less-endowed of the voyaging people needed to be on their guard among the Marquesas.

At Hana-moe-noa we met a wonderful crowd of voyagers wearing the flags of Britain, Australia, New Zealand, Canada, United States, Belgium, Germany, Austria and Switzerland. But it appeared that they did not know one another or make much attempt to mingle, and, as this seemed contrary to the usual behaviour of cruising people, we gave a number of afternoon coffee- or evening drink-parties for them; these seemed to be appreciated, they broke the ice, and thereafter we noticed a more frequent coming and going of dinghies among the fleet. It was fun, and we remained for ten days in that vivid yellow and green place, enjoying our new-made friends.

Although the swell was only slight, I found it was too much when I wanted to do some darkroom work, for it slopped the developer and hypo out of the dishes. So I constructed a roll-damper or 'flopper-stopper'. This consisted of a triangular piece of plywood measuring two feet (0·6 metre) along each side, and with one of its corners weighted with four pounds (1·8 kilos) of lead; a line from each corner was brought to a shackle to make a three-legged sling, and the whole affair was suspended a few feet beneath the surface of the sea from the end of the spinnaker boom.

The idea was that when the ship rolled towards the 'flopper-stopper' the strain came off the three-legged sling, and the lead weight caused the triangular plywood to dive; when the ship rolled the other way the ply on its sling resumed a horizontal posture, and offered strong resistance to being pulled up through the water, thus damping the roll. We soon saw that the lead weight was too great, so I cut it in half, and leaving one piece in its corner, secured the other in the middle of the triangle as ballast. Like that it worked better and made darkroom work possible, but it could well have been bigger in area, and ideally we should have had two such devices, one rigged out each side, like Canadian salmon-fishing vessels use; but we had only one spinnaker boom.

I feel that some apology should be made for the use of the word 'darkroom', for so many visitors had asked to be shown it, and, of course, it did not exist as such; but when we needed to make enlargements from black-and-white negatives, we turned the fo'c's'le temporarily into a darkroom by the simple expedient of covering the perspex hatch with oilskins to keep the light out, closing the door, and clipping an electric fan to the water-trap, light-tight vent. In the engine-room a small transformer of the type sometimes used in fishing vessels for increasing the current for ship/shore radio, stepped up our twenty-four-volt supply to 240 volts; a lead from this, separate from the rest of the wiring, went through to the fo'c's'le, where I plugged in a small home-made switchboard with leads to the enlarger and the darkroom and daylight lamps; thus, I could use normal mains equipment. There were two work-benches there: one served to hold the enlarger and paper, the other the dishes of chemicals. There was no way of controlling the temperature, though the fan kept the air stirring, and sometimes it became very hot in there, but this had little effect on the operation except to shorten the time of development. After developing and fixing, each print was put into a big basin of sea-water, and, when the batch was completed, it was washed in six changes of sea-water, using a relay of buckets on deck. Those who might wish to do this kind of thing on board, but who believe that much fresh water is needed, should take heart, for it is a fortunate fact that salt water will remove hypo from bromide paper and film more quickly and thoroughly than will fresh water, so the latter is needed only for dissolving the chemicals and for the final rinse. To dry and glaze the prints, we squeegeed them face down on a chromed-steel plate, fitted this on a simple box-type drier of my own construction, and placed the latter across the fiddles of the galley stove above a shielded burner; within a couple of minutes the prints cracked off dry and well glazed. For developing films, the darkroom was not needed, for we used a Rondinax daylight-loading tank, so the whole operation could be done in daylight; the washed film was hung on deck between two clips to dry. We found it advisable to develop black-and-white films, and have colour films processed, as soon as possible after exposure to avoid a loss of contrast or a colour change or fade, and in the interim we kept them stowed in sealed cans together with a tin of the desiccator silica gel—when the colour of this changed from blue to pink we gave it a new lease of life by heating it on the galley stove. We also kept the cameras stowed with a tin of silica gel as a guard against damp, and not only did it protect the films in them but prevented mildew or fungus from growing on the lenses.

I spent three mornings making enlargements, which Susan washed and dried, and so was able to clew up some articles I had written—it gave us satisfaction to have our own small self-contained factory on board. We were just about to sail back to Atuona and get them on the weekly mail plane for Tahiti, when a yacht arrived with the news that a heavy swell was running; two dinghies had been capsized while trying to reach the beach at Atuona, and two others had gone adrift and been lost; so we kept our mail on board and posted it later when we reached Nuku Hiva.

Such happenings were not uncommon, and at times we had posted mail with difficulty in some unlikely places, but I cannot recall that anything we posted in all our years of voyaging failed to reach its destination eventually. It was more often the business of receiving rather than sending mail that raised problems. I am sure one needs a permanent forwarding address, preferably in one's own home country; if this can be manned by a friend or relative who will sort the mail, dispose of the mass of advertising circulars, and send the rest by airmail to one's current address, the arrangement is almost ideal, except that individuals do become ill or go away on holiday. It might, therefore, be better to employ a firm of solicitors or a bank, and we used banks for both the forwarding and receipt of mail for many years with good results—some banks even have departments to look after customers' mail.

But we never succeeded in persuading our English bank to sort our mail and send letters by air and heavier things by surface, with the result that on some occasions a single forwarded magazine had between five and ten pounds' worth of stamps on it, for which, of course, we had to reimburse the bank. Nevertheless, banks have served us well in many lands by holding mail sent in their care. Consulates used to be equally good, but some consuls now do not like yachts and refuse to accept their mail; many post-offices will hold mail for only two weeks before returning it to the sender; yacht clubs do not usually sort mail but leave it in a pile for everyone to pick over, and we found them unreliable at forwarding, for, rather than re-address a letter, they would give it to the next yacht heading the same way. We never cared to send a circular letter to our friends, because we felt it lacked the personal touch, and were disappointed when we received one; but writing individual letters, though for us a pleasant occupation because it gave us a chance to think of each friend individually, did take a lot of time; on this voyage we wrote 660 letters.

We had heard great things of Hanamenu, a bay on the north coast of Hiva Oa, said to have a lovely white beach and a stream; so we sailed round there, identifying the bay by the remarkable, steep and massive 700-foot (213-metre) Grosse Tour which, like a fortress, splits the bay in two, and anchored off the beach—surely this could not have changed colour in a year or two, but it was not of white sand but of black. Landing on it was difficult because of the swell, and we shipped a lot of water in the dinghy, and then could hardly walk barefoot on the sand because it was so hot. But the stream was one of the most lovely we had ever seen, a torrent of cool, clean water from a mountain spring flowing swiftly over a pebble bottom; through the dark-green foliage overhanging it, shafts of sunlight speared through to dapple the water and pick out the scarlet blossoms of hibiscus and the white petals of frangipani. Susan did the laundry there, and we met Ozanne who was part French; he with his wife and family were the only inhabitants of that part of the island, and they made a little copra which the occasional interisland schooner collected. In that narrow, high-cliffed slot it would have been good if we could have imagined ourselves to be the first visitors for a long time, but Ozanne told us that forty yachts had put in there the previous year; he even had a little round, thatched 'yacht club' complete with bar, radio, visitors' book, and paper replicas of the flags of the yachts that had called there. Susan and an American off another yacht helped launch me through the breakers in the dinghy with the laundry and a load of water; I put the things aboard and then returned to pick up Susan, who swam out to meet me to save the dinghy another passage through the surf. Because of the high, near land each side of us, there was that evening a long, cool twilight, and we had the luxury of crisp, clean sheets on our bunks, but we rolled heavily when the wind died, and were not sorry in the morning to leave that narrow place with its rumbling surf and return for a day or two to delightful Hana-moe-noa; there, as soon as we had anchored in our old berth, it was on sail coats, up awning, out cockpit cushions, table and boarding-ladder, and welcome visitors.

We had an easy and pleasant overnight trip of eighty-three miles to Nuku Hiva, where at Taiohae Bay we anchored fore-and-aft in line with twelve other yachts all lying like that so as to be end-on to the swell. There again we found the village planted with naked street lamps, and we noticed that, instead of traditional thatch or more modern corrugated iron, most buildings were roofed with a plastic covering cleverly devised to look like weathered shingles.

The French, skilful civil engineers, had recently completed a narrow unsealed road in that hitherto roadless island, from Taiohae up and over the mountains to Typee Valley. One day we walked along it, starting in windless heat and humidity and a cloud of flies; but as we mounted, and the road rose steadily all the time with never a level or a dip, it grew cooler and a small breeze arose; the flies left us, the sweat began to evaporate, and below us the bay spread out enchantingly. Up and up we went, past an occasional garden hacked out of the mountainside, crossing streams that flowed over the road, in which we buried our faces and drank, and after two hours of climbing reached the summit, where, at about 2000 feet (610 metres), the road passed through a cleft in the mountain range and started to fall. We paused for a time there, luxuriating in the cool, sweet air, almost giddy with the magnificent view on all sides, and then retraced our steps. We found that descending was harder on our sea-weakened legs than climbing had been, and next day we could only totter about, especially when we had done some shopping and had bags of *pamplemousse* slung over our shoulders; but that had been one of our jolliest walks, for, although the island was rugged and steep and had some stupendous ramparts, it was small enough for us to make the expedition in half a day.

Throughout our stay, yachts came and went frequently, all but one of them under power, and for us it was a particularly stirring moment when we sighted a small white sloop with brown sails and green rubbing-strakes round the East Sentinel and come beating up the bay. At such a sight, the whole village used to turn out to watch and applaud as the best use was made of each vagrant puff of wind, for the arrival of a vessel was a rare and welcome event; but, alas, not today because of the widespread use of auxiliary power and the large number of yachts. We soon recognized the newcomer as *Wanderer III*, in which we had voyaged for seventeen years. Owned now by Gisel Ahlers, a German, who was sailing with his attractive French girlfriend (she delighted all male eyes in the anchorage when she exercised on deck beside the mast each morning), the little vessel was attempting a third circumnavigation; she looked immaculate except for her topsides, which displayed smeary patches of slime and weed to tell of her thirty-eight-day passage from Panama; but Gisel was soon out in the dinghy to scrub them off. It was of interest to us to recall that when *Wanderer III* first sailed into Taiohae Bay twenty-one years before with Susan and me aboard, she was the only yacht in the archipelago; on this occasion there were at least seventy-five yachts in the group, and we were told that fifty had lain at anchor in Taiohae Bay on Christmas Day.

* * *

As the new moon grew, excitement tinged with apprehension mounted among the fleet of yachts, for nearly all were bound for Tahiti, and spread across the direct route to that island lay the Tuamotu, or Dangerous Archipelago, a vast group of seventy-eight coral atolls. This maze of reefs and islands, which extends over fifteen degrees of longitude, has been the graveyard of many a fine ship, and today its reefs hold in addition the gaunt and bleached remains of many small vessels, among them some yachts from California; they, having left a safe area where there are few dangers but many aids to navigation, and a helpful and efficient coastguard service to assist in an emergency, had set out on their first ocean passages and made their landfalls on the easy Marquesas, which are high islands with no off-lying reefs and very few dangers; they then lightheartedly headed for what may well be one of the most difficult and dangerous island areas in the world. Although the French had spent millions of francs on their atomic explosions in the Tuamotu, they had done little for the navigator: apart from Ile Hao, where there was a military establishment, the *List of Lights* gave only four lights in the area, and in the 'remarks' column noted that one was 'unreliable' and the other three were 'intended'.

A few of the yachts wished to stop at one or more of the atolls, while others, including ourselves, planned to sail direct to Tahiti. A few days before the moon was to be full we set out, for although the palms on the atolls cannot be seen in daylight from more than about ten miles, the light from the moon may help one to avoid a danger before it is too late, and, by illuminating the horizon, perhaps enable star observations to be taken at night.

To me the making of a good landfall, that is, seeing the piece of land I wish to reach lift above the horizon ahead at the predicted time, or materialize out of mist, rain or fog, is the most satisfying moment of any passage no matter how long or short it may have been, for the landfall is the culmination of all that has gone before: the course steered and the allowance made for current and leeway from the last-known position obtained by observations of celestial bodies or by other means. But, as the time for making a landfall approaches, I always grow apprehensive, not because my landfalls in the past have been bad ones, but because I know that very often a large element of luck or guesswork may enter into it. Obviously, the only fix that matters then is the last one from which the final course must be steered, and if the sky clouds over, the run in may be a long one on which bad steering, an error of the compass, or a current of unknown strength and direction may have serious effects.

I am sure that everyone knows the old dodge of steering a little to windward of the correct course when about to make a landfall on a continuous coast, so that when the land appears and no feature of it can be identified, one has only to turn downwind until the headland, bay, or harbour one wishes to make, heaves into sight. But obviously, such a procedure cannot be followed when the landfall is to be a small island. In the days of sail before the advent of accurate timepieces, a ship seeking a small island endeavoured to get on the latitude of that island well up-wind of it, and stay on that parallel until the island was reached. But it was a chancy business because the opportunities for checking the latitude were few, probably the only effective method in the southern hemisphere being meridian altitude observations of the sun; but if the sun did not shine at noon what then? We are more fortunate today for we do know Greenwich Mean Time, so even if we are denied a noon sight we should be able to obtain position lines at some other time of day; and, if a position line can be had when the body is on the beam, so that the line obtained lies parallel to the course being steered, this can be of great value in showing whether the present course if persisted on will make the desired landfall or not.

I am sure that currents, or sometimes tidal streams, of unknown strength and direction are the most frequent causes of bad landfalls. Even out in the wide ocean where, by comparing the course and distance sailed through the water (as recorded by compass and patent log) with the course and distance made good between two fixes obtained from observations of celestial bodies, one can accurately determine the direction and speed of the current, it is often found to vary quite remarkably from one day to the next; but even when it is found to be of regular speed and direction it may quite often change its character as it nears the land. Although some information about currents can be had from pilot charts and sailing directions, it cannot be regarded as accurate, so, as I said earlier, guesswork and a bit of luck play their part.

Suppose we are intending to reach a low island and do not know our position until noon (a morning position line brought forward and crossed with a noon latitude), and it shows that the island cannot be reached before nightfall, what should we do, bearing in mind that a current could be setting us into danger? Some people go boldly on hoping to sight the island in the dark before they hit it, and this is one reason why the Tuamotu are sprinkled with wrecks as also are some parts of Fiji and the New Hebrides. In such circumstances I, being of a cautious nature, presume the current to be setting me into danger at a rate of at least one knot, and, either I stop a safe distance off, or steer a course to keep me well away from danger until daylight; so far I have been successful in such manoeuvres, but they have sometimes resulted in it taking a long time to recover the ground lost and to sight the island. But when we have made a landfall are we sure it is the right one? This often is where we can go astray, for we badly want that bit of land to be the one for which we hope we have been heading, so it is all too easy to believe that the hill, the headland, the bay, or even the lighthouse if we happen to sight it in daylight, is the one for which we are looking. Once that has been decided, our imagination gets to work, and all sorts of other features are made to fit into place, and if there are discrepancies we talk ourselves out of them: that cluster of buildings must have been erected since the chart was made; those rocks look much higher than the little pointed ones mentioned in the sailing directions, but perhaps the tide is low or we are closer than we think; there shouldn't be a gap in that line of mountains, but maybe there is mist or rain up there. It is so easy to delude ourselves. There used to be, on many charts, excellent sketches of certain portions of some coasts showing very well what the land looked like from the offing, but unfortunately for cruising people these are being removed from British charts as new editions are published; some are included in the *Pilots*, but too often the views there are from indifferent photographs which lack the perspective at which the early hydrographic artists were so good. Even so, I feel sure we should study any that apply to our situation, as well as the written description, and if any feature does not quite agree with what we see, we ought to consider other parts of the coast (or other islands) off which we could be lying.

But the Tuamotu are low islands; as we would be approaching them from north-east there could be no question of running along a parallel of latitude, or of making an up-wind landfall, and we had to bear in mind that, as the *Pilot* pointed out, all the atolls are similar in character and with great sameness of feature, each comprising a ring of coral enclosing a lagoon anything between one and forty miles in diameter, on the rim of which might stand one or many low islets called motus, most with bush and trees growing on them.

When we left Hiva Oa we headed for Takaroa. We chose that fifteen-mile-long atoll for several reasons: no dangers lay north of it, so in the event that we failed to find it before nightfall, we could stand away in any northerly direction without risk until we could make another attempt in daylight. Also, on the atoll's north-west side (which we planned to skirt) lay the hull of the sailing ship, *County of Roxburgh*, driven ashore there in the hurricane of 1906; that would be a useful identification mark should we be in doubt as to which atoll we had come to. But for us, the most important advantage of choosing Takaroa was that, having passed it and nearby Takapoto, there would be ninety miles of clear water to cross before we reached the next pair of atolls, Rangiroa and Arutua, between which we proposed to pass; so we could sail that stretch by night, and even if we did have a strong current in our favour—it is largely the variable currents that make this area such a nightmare for the navigator—there would be little risk of being set into danger before daylight.

Susan, like others on this trip, had a stomach upset which we put down to drinking the Taiohae water, and had to take steps to avoid dehydration, but apart from that all went well with us; the weather was fine, our progress good, and a clearly setting sun enabled us to check the compass with an amplitude. On our third day out, having made good 400 miles, Takaroa appeared ahead and we rounded its northern end at noon. It looked indeed a lovely thing, a brilliant gem, with its green scrub and leaning palms above a golden beach under the bright blue sky, and here and there as we sailed close in its lee, we had, through gaps in the vegetation, glimpses of the turquoise lagoon within. The old *County of Roxburgh* was still there, so high up the beach it seemed impossible the sea could have driven her there; her masts had gone and there were large holes in her iron hull, but there she lay, a landmark for the mariner. On that same beach we saw two more-recent wrecks, one a yacht, the other an interisland vessel, and on the atoll's far side lay the remains of a small yacht sailed by a single-hander only a few weeks before.

Coasting along, we looked in through the pass to the village and the wharf where a very large yacht lay tied up, but had little inclination to stop, for by then the afternoon had become overcast, a damp wind moaned in the rigging, breakers on the nearby reef boomed hollowly, and the sparkling gold, blue and green of noon had changed to a sullen grey with a sinister look about it; so we pressed on.

Takapoto dropped astern at dusk, and with that to fix our position, we needed no help from the stars, which was just as well for there were none to be seen, nor even a glimpse of the brimming moon. We expected rain, but only got drizzle as we sailed on at five-and-a-half knots, but towards dawn there were some patches of clear sky through one of which we managed to get an observation of Achernar; this showed us to be well south of our dead-reckoning position, and an hour later bunches of palm fronds stood out of the sea ahead and on the starboard bow where no land should have been. It soon became evident that we had made a landfall on the north-east instead of on the north-west corner of Arutua, the current having set us in the night ten miles to the east instead of, as expected, to the west. We then saw what a dangerous thing Arutua could be by night, for its motus were widely separated and one could easily have headed between two of them without seeing either, and so have crashed upon the reef which joined them.

Our difficulties were then over, however, for by noon we had passed between Arutua and Rangiroa, and could shape a course direct for Venus Point, where Cook observed the transit of the planet, on Tahiti. The following evening in fine weather we sighted the mountains of that lofty island, ghosted with light airs through the night, and soon after breakfast entered Papeete Pass, and were boarded by a cheerful but inefficient pilot, who berthed us crookedly in the long line of yachts lying stern-to at the waterfront.

Poor, beautiful Tahiti, Paradise Island of the would-be voyager's dream, had turned herself over almost entirely to the tourist trade. Huge hotels, some with rows of thatched cabins standing on stilts in the lagoon like Papuan villages, had sprung up, jets screamed in and out by day and by night, earth-moving trucks and a press of rush-hour cars roared along the four-lane highway a few yards from the yachts, and in clouds of dust, the characterful old buildings of the town were being torn down to make room for modern blocks of concrete and glass. No longer did bevies of laughing girls with sweet-scented flowers in their hair welcome each yacht as she berthed or go aboard to sing—the only place one was now likely to hear singing or see dancing would be at the floor show of one of the hotels—and Quinn's Bamboo Hut, the world-famous bar and nightclub, had vanished.

* * *

There were many fine yachts in port, the more gregarious of them gathered in a tight bunch at the eastern end of the waterfront with gangways to the shore, and from them emanated a hum of machinery and a fug of diesel exhaust fumes. The rest of us lay more spread out further to the west, where there were no power points and we used our dinghies to get ashore. Our near neighbour was the lovely centreboard ketch, *Affair*, whose owner and crew were kind and helpful though they had a serious difficulty of their own to resolve: *Affair*'s metal centreboard had become bent in the down position so that it could not be hauled up into its case, and with it hanging down the yacht could not be slipped to allow the board to be removed and straightened. The only thing to do was drive the pivot-pin out, and her crew spent many hours each day under water trying to do that, but the pin was a tight fit in the lead keel and they had not managed to shift it before we left.

For us the far-ranging yacht without an engine does possess a little extra glamour and for her people we have added respect and admiration, but it is rare today to find a cruising yacht without auxiliary power; there can be no doubt that the efficient and reliable marine diesel engine has made a great difference because it permits a yacht to poke into all manner of small, difficult and delightful places which without its help would probably be impossible except for very small craft; it also enables a yacht to make wider use of open anchorages from which a shift of wind might force a speedy departure, so that today auxiliary yachts call at islands which have no harbours or accessible lagoons, and which the earlier generations of voyagers dared not attempt to visit. The price paid for this amenity is naturally a lowering in standard of the sailor's skills.

There is a tendency for the modern cruising/voyaging yacht of forty feet (twelve metres) or more in length to carry with her all the comforts, conveniences and safety devices that can be crammed in. The almost inevitable result is that the owner and crew of such a vessel tend to regard her in much the same light as they might regard a car, that is, purely as a means of transport. She is likely to carry in her deep-freeze meat from her home port; her powerful engine with its bountiful supply of fuel enables her to motor through large areas of calm or even fresh headwinds. She probably has some sophisticated aids to navigation, such as radar and Loran, and without a doubt she carries radio equipment capable of summoning aid in her area should she or her crew get into any kind of difficulty, or the latter wish to speak to their friends ashore or in other yachts. In other words this floating-flat/conveyance is expected to transport her people from one glamour spot or tourist attraction to another with the least possible effort and with great emphasis placed on every aspect of safety, and I wonder if this is a good thing.

Why are the books by, for example, O'Brien, Robinson,

Smeeton, Tilman, Moitessier, such grand reading, not just once but over and over again? Why do the names of these men remain household words while others, perhaps with equally long voyages to their credit, make no mark and are soon forgotten? I am sure it is because of their attitude, which summed up briefly is 'men against the sea'. Not for them was the main attraction some beautiful place with 'warm' people, not for them the greatest speed over the longest distance, but just a simple pitting of their wits, courage and seamanship against the elements in their unsophisticated vessels in an endeavour to achieve a satisfactory conclusion, not to gain kudos, but so as to be able to think well of themselves; all of them successfully put across the axiom: 'It is better to travel hopefully than to arrive'. So in their accounts, these people carry us along with them, not to see far off and lovely places (though these do get their mention) but to enjoy the sometimes hard business of getting there. If something went wrong on a voyage of theirs, they did not switch on the radio and call for help—so far as I know they did not carry radio transmitters—they just got on with the job to the best of their ability, although in at least one instance the masts and rudder had gone and a hole gaped where the skylight should have been; then eventually, and without outside assistance, or indeed even any outside knowledge of what was happening, they quietly reached their ports.

There is here a certain similarity to the mountaineer. If he or she wishes to reach the summit for the pleasure of the view to be had from it, or the possibility of photographing the abominable snowman, presumably he could make his objective without effort or much danger, and in comfort, in an air-conditioned helicopter. But he prefers to use his feet and hands, a climbing rope and some pitons, and to pit his skill and cunning in a very simple manner against the mountain and the weather, and, unburdened by comforts or safety equipment, reaches the peak and so obtains his satisfaction.

Of course, it would be ridiculous to suggest that we should not carry radio, echo-sounder and the like, for we should live in our time and within reason take advantage of such aids as science may have placed at our disposal—even the climber now uses nylon rope. If ocean racing had started several centuries ago no doubt the diehards would have tried to ban the use of that new-fangled gadget, the magnetic compass. One cannot easily draw a line, but judging by the many voyaging people we had met in recent years, we concluded they could be divided into two distinct groups: those who carried in their fair-size yachts every possible item of equipment for comfort, convenience and safety, and those (usually) in smaller craft simply but efficiently equipped, and it seemed clear that the latter got much the greater pleasure through satisfaction. We had noticed that of the scores of overseas yachts that visited New Zealand each summer, only the smaller and simpler ones ventured south of Auckland; the rest remained in northern ports while their people hired cars in which to 'do' the South Island.

If a person wishes to sail in an unseaworthy vessel, or put to sea with little knowledge of seamanship or navigation, that I consider is entirely his or her own affair provided he does not harm or inconvenience others; I therefore do not understand why he should be advised, bullied or compelled to carry with him rescue and survival equipment. In the unlikely event that I were asked to legislate for yachts, the only rule I would make would be that, except for yachts taking part in a race for which some club or other organization felt responsible, no yacht should be permitted to carry ship/shore radio. We in yachts do not have to go to sea like the professional seaman does, we go because we want to, and therefore we have no right when in trouble to call on others, perhaps with risk to them, to get us out of a difficulty which, with a bit of planning and some common sense, we could probably have avoided. It is the 'mayday' calls that set off the air/sea searches which give all of us a bad public image. We are frequently told that the lifeboat, coastguard, or other services are almost overwhelmed by the large number of private craft that get into trouble and call for help—in 1973 in United States waters I understand there were 782 000 incidents in which people in boats needed rescue or assistance—and again and again there are government threats that because of this we shall all have to pass tests and our vessels be inspected; not only would that restrict our freedom but it would cost money to pay the bureaucrats who are so keen to protect us from ourselves. Such ideas need to be strongly opposed, for we must be allowed to go unrestricted on our suicidal way, otherwise our precious freedom, which already is being eroded by immigration laws, will be lost. In most walks of life there are little men who delight in controlling their fellows, and we must do all we can to keep their poking noses and prying fingers out of yacht cruising and voyaging, which at present are occupations open to any man or woman with a free spirit and an ability to rely on his or her own guts.

In one of his delightful 'Down the Hatch' features in *Yachting World*, W M (Winkie) Nixon put the real spirit of cruising in a nutshell when he wrote: 'Thus cruising aspires to be self-reliant, self-expressive and yet private. It should be the most harmless of activities as far as the rest of the world is concerned; a cruising yacht should go about her business without fuss or bother, giving trouble to no one, indeed it's hardly going too far to say that a real cruising person, in the unlikely event of getting into difficulties, would rather drown than cause the slightest inconvenience to potential rescuers.'

I sometimes wonder if some of the safety syndrome is not mixed up with the hard-hitting advertising business. I understand that all yachts using ship/shore radio (this is now compulsory in some countries) must change to single-sideband equipment, a highly expensive switch. Life-rafts also are costly, though if we should have to spend 117 days in one, like Maurice and Marilyn Bailey did, perhaps that does not matter. But these rather delicate rubber creations are supposed to be serviced every year, and although the cost of this is high, I think they need to be, for on upending ours the other day to paint beneath it, about a bucketful of water ran out. We are advised to carry flares (very wise, for we may need to alert a big ship on a collision course to our presence), parachute rockets and the like for use when in distress, but we are reminded that all such pyrotechnics must be buried at sea and replaced with new every three years. Incidentally, I wonder if the designers of these things have ever had to let one off from a sinking vessel in the dark; most of those we have aboard bear the firing instructions in small print on the coloured container, and as both ends are identical except for their colour, which one cannot see in the dark, a man unaccustomed to their use might take a long time to fire one, and he could let it off wrong end up with disastrous results. Fire-extinguishers are, of course, for defence, not rescue, but even they are supposed to be replaced from time to time.

With expenses like the above it is not surprising that the cost of yachting has risen so alarmingly. But there is at least one item of safety equipment that costs little and does not need replacing—the danbuoy. We are often told by those who are so keen to ensure our safety if we will not see to it ourselves, that one of these things attached to a lifebuoy should always be carried in a position from which it may instantly be tossed overboard if a member of the crew should happen to fall into the sea. I was so impressed with the arguments that I made one from a plastic mooring-buoy, and a twelve-foot (3·6-metre) bamboo with a lead weight to keep it more or less upright, and at its top a brilliant nylon flag. It was the kind of thing that every offshore racing yacht has to carry, and I took a lot of trouble over it, for one day I thought it might have to save a life, Susan's or mine. Just for fun we tried it out in a well-sheltered harbour with a moderate breeze blowing, only to discover that the danbuoy with the lifebuoy in tow blew away to leeward faster than either of us could swim; so we knew that unless our buoy could be let go up-wind of the man overboard, and he could manage to intercept it before it blew past, or it could be fitted with some form of not too complicated sea-anchor, such a thing is not only worthless but provides a false sense of security. It is far better to hold on tight than to fall overboard and rely on this or any other safety device.

We remained for only three days at Papeete, and then moved south along the well-beaconed channel inside the reef and past the airport to a quiet, clean and very pleasant anchorage off Maeva Beach, where we could land and leave the dinghy unmolested and when necessary go into town by *le truck*. That vehicle had not changed much over the years, and still comprised a truck chassis on which had been fitted a long, low, gaily painted bus body. They ran unscheduled and often had cargoes of beamy, smiling Tahitian ladies, and sometimes taped Polynesian music—*Mau Taria*, *Hoe Ana* or, appropriately enough, *Maeva*—turned up loud to drown the traffic noises. Roger Gowen, one of the Englishmen who had sailed out in the yacht, *Pambili*, ten years before, drove us round the island and showed us almost everything, even the green plastic carpet one of the hotels had spread over its garden terraces to simulate grass, and twice he and his Chinese wife gave us magnificent lunches in their restaurant perched right at the edge of a lagoon close to the Gauguin museum in the south part of the island. Roger and his friend, Bill Baker, had done well since they arrived in Tahiti as shipwrecked mariners from the Austral Islands, where they had, through no fault of their own and while doing a kindness for a friend, lost *Pambili*. Roger then started with a little market garden, selling its produce in Papeete's pre-dawn market; then went in for breeding rabbits, which the French on the island considered a delicacy, but was turned out by his neighbours who objected to the smell; after that he married and built the restaurant. Meanwhile Bill got into men's outfitting, and now had a first-class shop in the town. It was good to see these two hard-working men so well established on the island of their choice. Although Tahiti was a frighteningly expensive place for the visitor, it was not so bad for those who lived and worked there, for although all imports were heavily taxed there was no income tax.

In French Polynesia, our paraffin-burning refrigerator failed to operate; various experts came to have a look at it, including a man who had used such things in the African desert where he had served in the French Foreign Legion. He had never been aboard a yacht before—it was Roger's idea that he should come—and he was so taken with what he saw that he asked what we had paid for our ship, nodded his head and said he would get one, but bigger. It was not until we reached Fiji and tried the refrigerator on another brand of paraffin that it worked properly again; apparently it could not stomach the French fuel.

We also had trouble with the galley stove, which burnt paraffin (kerosene). In England the makers had provided us with a complete new burner assembly, but when the time came to fit it we found they had omitted to make provision for nipples under each burner, and without them the stove, which was fed from a remote tank, breathed so heavily that often it blew itself out. Since our arrival in the Marquesas all cooking had, therefore, been done on a single Primus, which I had fitted in the old cooker so that it was gimballed, and we continued with that primitive set-up until we reached New Zealand, where we decided to be up-to-date and change over to propane gas for cooking. We felt we were traitors about this, for ever since we had anything to do with boats Susan and I had used paraffin-burning pressure stoves, which we understood and liked, particularly the appetizing smell of the preheating spirit and the companionable hiss. We wished we could have got a proper seafaring model such as Taylor's made, but to have had one shipped out would have taken too long, so we bought an Australian cooker made for caravans, and as it had no gimbals or fiddles I had to make and fit them; we had no suitable stowage place for a twenty-pound (nine-kilogram) gas cylinder, so I built a locker in the cockpit, and then employed a plumber to run the pipe and put the fittings on it. To say 'we changed to gas' makes it sound so easy, but the whole operation took two weeks, and then we were not at all sure that we liked it. Certainly, the oven was more efficient, and the grill made excellent toast, but the cylinder had the normal habit of running dry while a meal was being cooked for guests, and, whereas paraffin was available at any little waterside store or filling station, to get a gas cylinder refilled sometimes entailed a journey of many miles. One cylinder of gas lasted us about five weeks, and we believed the cost was about twice that of cooking by paraffin. We were not too concerned about the risk of explosion, for the gas has a strong smell, the cylinder was out in the cockpit, and we made a point of closing its cock immediately after use. Nevertheless, we would have felt a little safer if we could have used compressed natural gas (CNG), for it is lighter than air and, therefore, cannot accumulate in the bilge if there should be a leak; but at the time of writing CNG is, I believe, available to yachts only in California.

From our anchorage at Maeva Beach we could look out across the reef towards the mountain spires of Moorea, Tahiti's sister island twelve miles away, and watch the sun go down in a blaze of colour behind them; our view was unobstructed and, we thought, very much better than that of the 100-dollar-a-night hotel guest. On the reef was a bathing platform belonging to an hotel, and speedboats used to take sun-worshippers out to it every few hours. One day we went there in our dinghy so as to enjoy a swim over the reef, but we found the raft in use by a mixed nudist colony, and the ladder up to it was slippery with sun-tan oil.

Moorea, we knew, had better things to offer, so when we had done all that we needed to do at Tahiti, we moved over to that island, and sailed into each of the two bays which, on the north coast, probe in among the mountains towards the remarkable Tiger's Tooth (Plate 14 *left*); we stopped in both, and in the western one (Papetoai Bay) anchored in Robinson Cove, and, taking a line to a tree, hauled our stern to within a few feet of the tiny, narrow beach (Plate 14 *right*). A short distance inland a 2000-foot (600-metre) cliff reared almost sheer; cool air dropped down it at night, when there was always a heavy dew and, as the cliff stood to the east of us, we enjoyed nearly four hours of morning shade before the sun topped it. We were fortunate to have that attractive and widely known berth in what we believe is the Bali Ha'i of *South Pacific* all to ourselves, but we were there during the arrival at Papeete of a double canoe from Hawaii which had retraced an old Polynesian sailing route, and nearly everyone else had gone to swell the welcoming crowd.

* * *

The six weeks we spent at Tahiti and Moorea had been remarkable on account of the fine, settled weather: there had been no rain and, at the Maeva Beach anchorage, there had been no wind, and our attempts to sail to other parts of Tahiti had failed on that account; but the channel between Tahiti and Moorea is often a windless area, and I recall that Alan Villiers in his square-rigged ship, *Joseph Conrad*, had lain becalmed there for two days, and was in danger of drifting upon the reef for the channel is too deep to anchor in. Unfortunately, the same calm conditions were still in force when we left on the passage to Bora Bora, one of the western Iles Sous le Vent, and to make any progress in the first eighteen hours we used the engine a lot. After that the wind got up and, by the time we were approaching Bora Bora, was blowing fresh. We went romping towards the pass; the swell, raised by some great storm in high latitudes, was big, thundering upon the reef each side of the pass with such violence it seemed impossible the reef could withstand the onslaught; but the coral polyp had built that massive breakwater to nature's design on a subterranean upheaval which rose almost sheer from a depth of 1000 fathoms and, except in a cyclone, the water within the reef remains smooth no matter how rough the sea may be outside, or how high the swell is running, for the tide in those waters has a range of no more than one foot (0·3 metre). So, once we had reached the lagoon, the water was quiet, and with Susan conning from aloft we made our way among the coral heads to a lovely anchorage in the lee of Toopua (Plate 15 *top*), the smaller, uninhabited island which shares the lagoon with highly populated Bora Bora. To leeward spread the wide expanse of the flat, sand-covered reef, over which there were only a few feet of water; when the sun shone, this was a glorious turquoise with, here and there, a patch of brown or mauve to indicate a coral head, and at its far seaward edge, perhaps a mile from where we lay, the swell broke in a line of dazzling white. We could hear its continuous rumble, but the dominant sound was the rustle of fronds as the palms on nearby Toopua nodded their heads in the offshore wind. Our only neighbour was the German yacht *Moritz B*, and we were careful not to bring up too close to her, for her owners had once very sensibly told us 'The smaller the boat, the further need she be from others'. There we enjoyed a snug feeling of security and content as we got on with the preparations for the next stage of the voyage.

Before starting on a passage I usually get Susan to haul me aloft so that I may see that all is well with the rigging, checking swages, shackles and clevis-pins, and the track screws. Each of the cross-trees (of wood as are the masts) was a tight, slightly tapered fit in a stainless-steel box, an arrangement I had always mistrusted because the boxes had no ventilation or drainage, and it was during one of my routine inspections aloft that I discovered the feet of three of the six crosstrees were rotten. As the masts would have to be unstepped for new crosstrees to be made and fitted, I decided that job would have to be left until we reached New Zealand, and to effect temporary repairs myself. So, with a piece of wood on top and another underneath, each with its inboard end butted hard up against the mast-band, I made a sandwich of each rotten crosstree, bolting the sandwich together, with the innermost bolt passing not only through the wood but through the steel box also. I discovered that even with the electric drill Rex Brink had rewound for me at Durban, drilling holes through stainless steel while sitting in a bosun's chair was a longer and harder job than I had anticipated, and it took me many hours; but it would have been difficult to have found a better place in which to do the job, for the lagoon was quite smooth, and the view out across the reef was breathtaking when seen from aloft. The ship and her gear stood up well throughout the voyage, and apart from the rot in the crosstrees, the only serious trouble we had was with water-pumps of the neoprene impeller type.

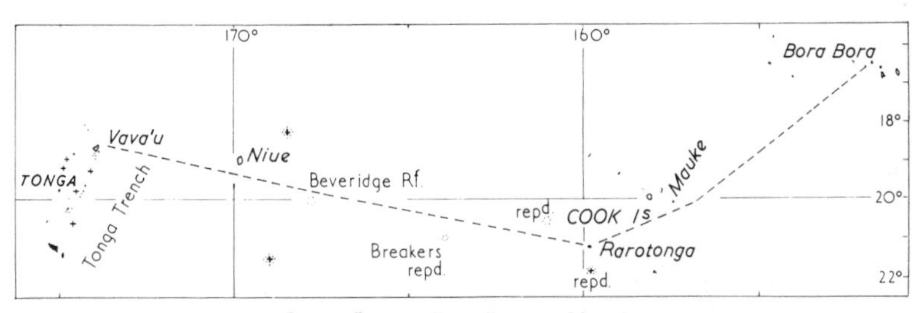

South Pacific, Bora Bora to Vava'u

When we were ready we sailed out of Bora Bora's lovely lagoon and headed for Rarotonga, which lay 560 miles away to the south-west. It is almost the southernmost of the widely scattered Cook Islands, which are administered by New Zealand, and was the only port of entry, something the officials were fussy about, and a visit first to any other island in the group was forbidden; an American couple we met later had sailed direct from Hawaii to Penrhyn (the northernmost Cook), a distance of about 2000 miles, and were ordered out into bad weather after a stop of only two hours.

Lying across the direct route from Bora Bora to Rarotonga stretched the chain of unlit Eastern Cooks, so we steered to pass south of Mauke, the south-eastern island of that chain, and planned to give it a wide berth because of the strong currents with which it is sometimes beset. On an earlier trip we had in the night been swept north of the island, on which more than one yacht had ended her voyage, and when we told Andy Thomson, the famous Rarotonga schooner captain, about this, he showed no surprise and said Mauke was the only island he knew which has so strong a current that 'it leaves a wake'. In an area where the trade wind should predominate, our plan ought to have been easy enough to carry out, but we were unfortunate with the weather, for after three days of light fair breezes the wind came ahead so that we could not lay the desired course, and overcast skies made celestial observations impossible; it was not until we had groped our way rather anxiously one black night south of where we thought Mauke should lie, that we were able to fix our position and discover that on this occasion there had not been any current at all. The light wind continued, and when eventually we sighted the mountains of Rarotonga dead to windward, we impatiently started the Ford and motored in.

From a distance the island looks not unlike Moorea and has a circumference of about sixteen miles, but it has no deep-water lagoon, for it is bounded by a fringing reef in which, on the northern coast, there are two small indentations, Avarua and Avatiu, one mile apart; they were the only harbours, though Avarua appeared no longer to be used. Avatiu had been 'improved' with shutter-piling and two wharves, but was open to the north. Several yachts were lying in it with their bows towards the entrance and sterns tied to the southern wharf, and with the help from one of them we inserted ourselves neatly in the row. But (we did not know this) as we had come from French Polynesia we would have to be fumigated against rhinoceros beetle, which destroys palms, and no sooner had we got ourselves nicely settled than along came the man from pest-control to tell us to move away to another berth as his fumes, he said, would be dangerous for our neighbours. So we reberthed alongside the eastern wharf, and one canister of spray was let off in the saloon and another in the sleeping cabin; but no attention was paid to places such as the hold or the cockpit lockers, where we would most likely have stowed fruit or vegetables if we had possessed any. Fumigation was supposed to continue for an hour, but the pest man was in a hurry to get away to a football match, so he did not give us the full treatment; nevertheless, for the next twelve hours the residue of the spray made our eyes prick and weep, and we were very grateful to the Roys in *Holokiki* for inviting us aboard for drinks and dinner while *Wanderer* ventilated herself.

But first we had to move once more and berth as directed by the harbourmaster stern to the eastern wharf and beam-on to the harbour entrance, and, a few days later, all the other yachts had to shift and lie with us, because the interisland ship, *Manuvai*, was expected. She came in early one calm morning to discharge copra, and had on her foredeck a party of out-islanders making splendid drum music, while two supple children dressed in white danced on her hatch, and, because no sound could be heard above the rattle of drums, she berthed without a word being spoken. We soon discovered that she was not only skippered by Don Silk, an old acquaintance of ours, but was also part-owned by him. Don, a New Zealander, had sailed to Rarotonga at about the time of our earlier visit; there he bought one of the several wrecks lying on the reef, rebuilt her, and traded with her for many years. But finally he lost her on that same reef while trying by night to bring a pregnant woman with severe haemorrhage to hospital; at that time the harbour had no leading lights, and the only aid was a street lamp masked by a milk-can with a slit in it, but unfortunately the slit was a bit too wide, and within its arc included the edge of the reef. He told us that since the shutter-piling had been installed the little harbour was more uncomfortable—even dangerous at times—for small craft when a norther blew than it had been before, as there was now nowhere for the sea to expend itself; that was something we were to see for ourselves very soon.

We have found that there is a direct relationship between the kindness and hospitality of the people on an island and the discomfort or danger of its harbour or anchorage, and Rarotonga was no exception. To get ashore was a squalid scramble up the crumbling, rusting piling, perhaps by way of a tractor-tyre fender, for there was not a ladder in the place, though our harbour dues for a couple of days could easily have paid for one. But once we were ashore we found everyone most helpful and friendly, and several people invited us to their homes and offered us drives round their attractive, fruit-growing island. At a dinner party in a house beautifully set among trees and lawns, we happened to meet the New Zealand Representative; he told us that, even though we were British, we would need visas on arrival in New Zealand if we were to be allowed to stay for more than thirty days, and he offered to provide them if we would call at his office. New Zealand, rightly in my view, was concerned about an increase in her population which she wished to keep below three million, yet Cook Islanders could come and go freely to and from that country, and many of them did. Our host and hostess at the dinner party proudly showed us photographs of their family of nine, all grown up, some married, and the lot established in New Zealand. If they were to follow their parents' example there could well have been eighty-one of that family in ten years' time, and just imagine how many there might be in, say, another thirty years. Yet New Zealand was making it very difficult for people wishing to go there in yachts. Few of these had any wish to remain permanently, but the majority did want to stay for six months or longer, partly to avoid the cyclone season in the south-west Pacific, partly to refit their vessels, and, of course, to see something of the wonderful country and her friendly people. But unless they arrived with visas they were not permitted to remain for more than thirty days. Normally when voyaging people get together they discuss the gales, the anchorages, the people, and the places, but now we had noticed that the main topic of conversation under the awning or round the cabin lamp was the latest New Zealand immigration regulation, a dull subject, but important to all of us. The radio hams had been busy about this, and all manner of rumours were rife. These worried us not a little for, before leaving New Zealand, we had obtained a re-entry permit, but the maximum length of time for which this was valid was eighteen months; ours had expired while we were crossing the

North Atlantic and was not renewable. The Representative gave us visas, but regretted that under the current ruling they could be only for a stay of three months, while Americans and Canadians in the same office were being given six-month visas. We could only hope that our three sponsors for citizenship, who had been working hard on our behalf, would be able to help, so that if we wished we could remain in the country of our choice; later we found that they had, and on arrival we were granted 'permanent resident status'; but even so there was a difficulty in that we would be permitted to leave the country temporarily only for a limited time, or we would sacrifice our status.

Another kind stranger invited us for a drive one evening to be followed by dinner at his home, but unfortunately on the chosen day the wind blew from the north straight into the harbour, and the sea running in caught us on the beam. We all laid out second anchors and doubled up our sternlines and, for thirty-six hours, we were anxious, for so much did we roll, and so closely had the harbourmaster berthed us, that our masts were in danger of entangling; indeed, one yacht did lose her masthead anemometer when it was struck by her neighbour's mast. We did not feel inclined to leave our ship, yet we could not send a message to our would-be host because we did not know his name; when he arrived at the appointed time he seemed to appreciate the situation, but we doubted if his wife, who we knew had prepared a special dinner and had invited other guests, would ever forgive us. How tantalizing it is to lie close to a friendly and hospitable island yet be unable with an easy mind to avail oneself of its pleasures, only those who have experienced such a situation can fully understand. Therefore, we had our regrets, but were not entirely sorry to leave when the wind shifted to the south, and to get away without damage from that awkward little harbour.

Although at that time of year (July) the southern limit of the trade wind belt lies close to Rarotonga, we felt reasonably confident of having a fair wind to carry us on to Vava'u, the largest island in the northern part of the Tonga group; but in the event we had very little wind for the first few days of the 800-mile passage, after which it freshened.

One of the most exciting things about the Pacific, apart from its enormous size, is the large number of vigias shown on the charts, as well as reefs and islands about which information is scanty and sometimes conflicting. (A vigia is a reported shoal, the existence or exact locality of which is doubtful, and although many of these have been disproved by laborious search, sufficient remain to be a source of anxiety to the navigator.)

The chart of the south-west Pacific, which in that latitude has a scale of approximately ninety miles to one inch, showed two vigias near our route. The first was a three-and-a-half-fathom patch reported in 1916 and marked P.A. (position approximate)—the swell could break on that—and the other was 'Breakers reported 1945'. Some way beyond lay Beveridge Reef, and this intrigued us, for it appeared from volume II of *Pacific Islands Pilot*, that it might be possible for us to anchor there. When first reported in 1833, the sea was breaking upon it in many places. In 1840 the lagoon had an entrance on the north-west side, but in 1913 the entrance was said to be on the south-west side, carrying a depth of sixty feet (eighteen metres). In 1964, the entrance was reported to have a depth of twenty-three feet (seven metres) but with several coral heads in it, and the lagoon was four miles long by two miles wide. In 1967 the general depths within the lagoon ranged from twelve to forty-two feet (3·6 to 13 metres); fish were abundant, among them large numbers of sharks. It could be fun, we thought, to spend a night or two in such a remote reef, which would no doubt one day turn into a proper atoll with palms growing on it; but as there would today be nothing of it to be seen but breakers, good conditions for sun or star sights would be essential if we were to approach it with any degree of certainty or safety. It was, therefore, a great disappointment to us when the sky clouded over as we neared the vicinity of the reef, so that we could get no celestial observations, and we knew that for safety we must alter course and give the reef a wide berth, which we did, and passed to the north between it and the island of Niue. Later we learned that Tim and Pauline Carr in their engineless gaff cutter, *Curlew*, had also intended to stop at Beveridge Reef; they got a good star fix in the evening placing them twenty miles east of the reef, and there hove-to for the night; but another star fix at dawn showed that they had been swept past the reef, the west-setting current having been running at more than two knots. They, like ourselves, then gave it up and continued for Tonga.

After we had passed Beveridge Reef, the wind increased to twenty knots and was a little forward of the beam, and the swell from the same direction grew into a steep sea. One afternoon we passed through a band, perhaps a mile in width, and extending out of sight over the horizon to the north and south, of very steep and confused seas apparently near breaking point; in a gale, I imagine that area could be dangerous. There was no discoloration to suggest a shoal, and we were at a loss to explain the phenomenon until we realized we were on or near the edge of the Tonga Trench, which, with a depth of 5375 fathoms (about six miles) is one of the deepest known parts of any ocean, being approximately one mile deeper than Everest is high. Perhaps it was logical to suppose that in such an area there might be currents of unusual direction or velocity (such as we had suspected in similar conditions in the Indian Ocean), or an upwelling of water of a different density or temperature, to cause such a disturbance; on the other hand, it could just have been that we had discovered one more vigia to add to the long list of questionable Pacific dangers.

I had not often given much thought to the great depth of water beneath us as we sailed across the sunny surface of the oceans, but on this occasion I read what I could find about it on board, and it gave me an eerie feeling. Beneath our keel the filtered sunlight dimmed and faded so that there would be no plant life perhaps beyond the 100-fathom line; below that was impenetrable darkness, and down in the abyss of the trench deadening cold, the intolerable pressure of seven tons to the square inch (108 meganewtons per square metre), and utter silence. It seems that little is known of the strange creatures that exist down there, fighting for survival, preying on one another, or why nature should have chosen to people such an awful place with any form of life; but the few that had been brought to the surface displayed features which no other creature possesses, such as tiny lamps on stalks or articulated feelers, which are believed to attract or mislead their prey, though one may wonder why any of them are provided with eyes; for all we know there may be creatures of enormous size or terrible ferocity questing for food on the steep escarpments, and over the vast plains of ooze, which pave much of the floor of the abyss and have recently been found to have a depth of several thousand feet, yet it is believed 2500 years must pass for just one inch (2·54 centimetres) of sediment to accumulate there. My ignorant imagination took charge and, even if the opportunity had presented itself, I am sure I would not have cared to swim there above the unknown. In his customary simple and graphic manner Kipling expressed it so well when he wrote:

'There is no sound, no echo of sound, in the deserts of the deep
Or the great grey level plains of ooze where the shell-burned cables creep.'

I take it he was referring to the telegraph cables which snake their way down into the deeps and up over the shallows of the oceans of the world; but at least the cable companies did avoid the two great Pacific trenches by passing between them, for the cable runs from Vancouver Island to Fanning, Fiji, Norfolk and Brisbane, with an offshoot to New Zealand, thus leaving the Marianas Trench to the north-west and the Tonga Trench to the south-east.

On our eighth day out from Rarotonga we came into smooth water in the lee of Vava'u, rounded that island's north-west corner, and sailed in among the many remarkable little islands which, with deep water between them, guard the approach to the harbour of Neiafu, their waterlines so deeply cut in by the action of the sea that landing, except by birds, of which there were many, would be impossible. A glance at the chart might give the impression that Neiafu is one of the best harbours in the Pacific, for it is surrounded by land which nowhere exceeds 500 feet (150 metres), and its entrance is so well-sheltered that no sea or swell from outside could possibly enter. But a closer examination shows that over most of its area the depth is between twenty and twenty-five fathoms, and that wherever the nature of the bottom is given it is of coral. Merchant ships never anchored in it; either they lay at the little wharf or at anchor outside where they knew of a patch of sand in very deep water. Inside, we found ten yachts lying on a narrow shelf at the eastern side, and we brought up close outside them in five fathoms. We could see no gleam in the water to tell of sand, nothing but the brown and mauve of coral, and into that coral garden we reluctantly let our anchor go. Some of our neighbours were old friends with whom we had shared earlier Pacific anchorages, and the others we soon got to know, among them the Carkhuffs (Sy, Vicki and small son David) in their Hinckley-built forty-footer (twelve-metre), *Resolve*; their voyage had started in Maine, and not often had we seen a yacht that had come so far looking so immaculate, her brightwork gleaming, clean, crisp flags flying, and so perfect was the stow of her main and mizzen

---

15 *Top* The anchorage in the lee of Toopua in Bora Bora's quiet lagoon with the shallow water over the wide reef spreading away to leeward. *Bottom* We went by dinghy into the wild tangle of a mangrove swamp in the Exploring Isles.

裕漢貳拾貳號
NO. 22 YU HAN

that one might almost have thought there were no sails and that the wrinkle-free coats had been pumped full of air. (Later in New Zealand, Vicki took the fine photograph which makes the frontispiece for this book.) We were happy to learn the latest voyaging gossip, which in these days of ham radio has a wider net of smaller mesh than it used to have: officials in the Solomons were now charging each yacht 100 dollars 'light dues' on arrival; three wives were pregnant; a trimaran had been wrecked in the Tuamotu; the Woods in *La Mioche* had decided not to come on but to return to California; our buddy ship, *Grockle*, was reported in the Society Islands, and everyone warned us about the immigration officer at Whangarei, where we proposed to enter New Zealand.

Tonga keeps the rather peculiar time of thirteen hours fast on Greenwich mean time, and there are only two other parts of the world where that same time is kept: Wragnell Island (Alaska) and the easternmost part of the Soviet Union. So far as the clock is concerned, thirteen hours fast is, of course, the same as eleven hours slow, but the date is different. Some of the yacht navigators we met at Vava'u were confused about the date-line (I had been a bit confused myself in the past) and one was so muddled that he was taking the elements for working his sights out of the almanac for the wrong day.

As one sails round the world from east to west, the time of local noon gets later and later by four minutes for each degree of longitude crossed—one hour for every fifteen degrees. Therefore, by the time one has reached the antimeridian of 180 degrees (half way round from the meridian of Greenwich) local time is twelve hours slow on Greenwich. If one continued on to the west putting the clock back one hour for each fifteen degrees of longitude but did nothing else, one would arrive at the meridian of Greenwich twenty-four hours behind the date kept by the local inhabitants; if one circumnavigated the other way from west to east one would arrive at the Greenwich meridian a day early. To avoid the inconvenience of this the date-line was introduced, and it was agreed that when crossing that line (in approximately 180 degrees of longitude) from east to west a day should be skipped, making a six-day week, and when crossing from west to east a day should be counted twice, thus making an eight-day week.

---

16 *Top* Oriental fishermen at Suva. *Bottom* Porpoises at our forefoot.

However, the 180th meridian passes through the Fijis and the Gilbert and Ellice Islands, and so that those groups should not have the inconvenience of different days in different parts of them, the date-line was modified so that all the islands in any one group should be on one side or the other of it. Tonga, although geographically well to the east of the antimeridian, chose to have the date-line pass to the east of her so that she could share the same day with Fiji and New Zealand; but as Tonga lies in about 170 degrees west, the sun would rise and set there inconveniently early if the same time as in Fiji and New Zealand was used. Therefore, as I have already said, the kingdom keeps a time thirteen hours fast on Greenwich. This suited us well enough because, on arrival, we were keeping zone time plus eleven, that is, our clocks were eleven hours slow on Greenwich and so were in keeping with the clocks ashore; but we did have to remember to skip a day and so change the date.

While I was thinking about this matter of time, it crossed my mind that time in the twenty-four-hour notation is often expressed in an odd way. Surely 1500 is 'fifteen hours', not 'fifteen hundred hours' or (except perhaps by radio operators) 'one five zero zero hours'; 1510 is not 'fifteen ten hours' or 'one five one zero hours', it is correctly 'fifteen hours ten minutes', but most of us would be content to say 'see you at fifteen ten'. The BBC overseas service announcers, as one would expect, speak the time correctly: for each whole hour they use the word 'hours', but for all other times except 'midnight' (note, not 'zero hundred hours') they just say the figures, for example, 0450 is 'four fifty', 1510 is 'fifteen ten'. I believe the same rule should apply when writing or printing time in the twenty-four-hour notation, that is, use the word 'hours' on the hour, but not otherwise, and never use the word 'hundred'.

Although Tongatapu in the south, where the King had his palace, was wooing the tourist, and Russia was talking about upgrading the airport there to 'international' status, Vava'u remained almost unmolested and unspoiled. It did have a hotel with a staff of thirty-six, but when we looked in there we found that only two people were staying in it. The inhabitants of Vava'u were, therefore, not much touched by the outside world, and we found them to be quiet, courteous and helpful, and most had relaxed, happy faces and appeared content to busy themselves with the simpler things of life, and to spend much of the time just sitting in the shade talking. But yachts had been coming in such numbers that there was the understandable urge to try to make a little out of them, and we, like our neighbours, were bothered a bit by longshore boatmen seeking to sell fruit, baskets, shells and carvings, and we all soon found that if we bought from one we would have no peace at all. Not very much of the island was cultivated, nor were there many palms, yet to judge by the Saturday early morning market, which was held in the main road near the wharf, there was no lack of cheap food, though much of it was the starchy taro root. That was as well, for clearly the population was fast increasing, there were children in great numbers everywhere. A few small boats came in from outlying islands with a little produce, but we saw no serious effort made to catch fish.

One might suppose this area, with its reef-sheltered waters and many jolly little islands, to be a delightful cruising ground, but there were two things against it: almost everywhere the water was too deep for comfortable or convenient anchoring, and where it was shallow enough, the bottom was mostly of coral; the other drawback was that at the time of our visit, yachts were mistrusted and were not permitted to go for more than day sails, from which they must return each evening to Neiafu, unless they carried with them a Tongan official; I believe this restriction was lifted a few months later.

Although the harbour was so well sheltered, we did have one bad evening in it when for a few hours the wind blew at thirty knots. It was clear from the noisy complaints made by our anchor cable that it was foul of coral, and when we pitched a little it snubbed. We could not veer more cable because of our close neighbours, so with a rolling hitch we bent on a nylon spring which eased the shocks and reduced the noise. Heavy rain drove horizontally, but the scene was partly illuminated by one yacht which switched on her floodlights, and for two hours motored towards her anchor to try to ease the strain, but more likely increased it as the manoeuvre caused her to sheer wildly from side to side—next day her owner reported that the wind had blown at sixty knots.

Although a masthead anemometer registers a greater wind speed by about one third than does one at deck level, I fancy that those aboard many yachts had never been checked or calibrated, for often neighbours with such equipment had reported a gale when the rest of us had experienced no more than a fresh wind, and I suspect that much the same applies to speedometers, indeed I believe that some owners actually set theirs high to impress the crew. I recall the occasion when one yacht towed another which had a damaged rudder a distance of 400 miles; the owner told me it was just great and they were doing fourteen knots, but when I asked him how long the 400-mile tow had taken he said six days—that (an average speed of just under three knots) was very good going, something to be proud of, and called for no exaggeration. But some people will tell one almost anything. I do not so much mind them telling me such nonsense, but I do think it is unreasonable of them to expect to be believed. The setting of echo-sounders can also be misleading. I had thought that the adjusting screw should be turned so that the instrument records the depth of water from the surface; then the soundings, after allowance for the height of tide has been made, can be directly compared with those on the chart; but in some yachts no adjustment has been made and the instrument records the depth beneath the transducer; in others an adjustment has been made and the instrument records the depth beneath the keel.

* * *

As distances go in the wide Pacific it is not very far from Vava'u to the nearest of Fiji's Lau (or Eastern) Group, a mere 250 miles, but if we stopped in the Laus, where a few years before we had cruised enjoyably, we might have got into trouble for not first going to a port of entry, and there was no such port among the Laus; also it would have been unsocial because Vava'u was infested with the palm-killing rhinoceros beetle while the Lau Group was free of that pest. So one evening, having passed the uninhabited volcanic cone of Late, last outrider of Tonga, we steered to pass close south of the Lau Group, and would there alter course direct for the port of Suva.

With everything set to the warm beam wind, *Wanderer* slipped along at about five knots in silence except for the contented snore of her bow-wave. The night was fine and partly moonlit, the wake gleamed with phosphorescence, and we enjoyed the most delightful sail we had had in a long time; it was the kind of night that might have been specially made for people like Susan and me fulfilling the dream of sailing among the glamorous south sea islands. I did not expect such wonderful sailing to continue for

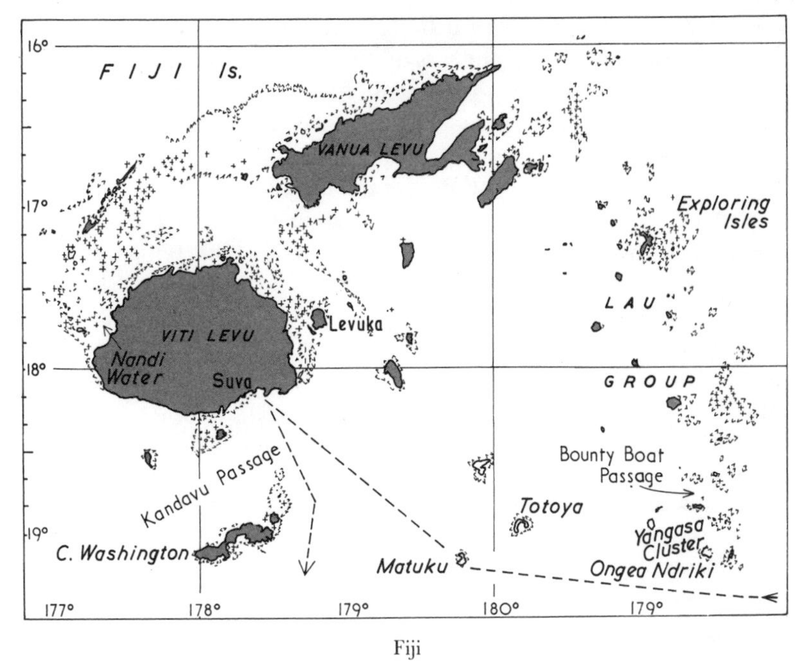

Fiji

long, however, for after our very poor passages in the rest of the Pacific, I had become gloomily pessimistic about that ocean; but it did continue all through the next blue and golden day, and through the following night, and not long after dawn we sighted Ongea Ndriki, the southernmost island of the Lau Group.

It was from that island three years before, having come from Suva, that we had started our cruise among the Laus, which we found had much to recommend them; at that time they were untouched by tourism, and very few yachts visited them because of the need first to go to a port of entry (Suva or Levuka) and then beat back against the trade. Between Ongea Ndriki and the Exploring Isles there are about forty reefs, all within the space of two degrees of latitude. Most of the lagoons enclosed by these reefs have islands of limestone or volcanic origin lying within them; some of the islands are inhabited, some are not, and a number of the limestone islands are so undercut by the sea that, like those near Vava'u, they are inaccessible. The majority of the lagoons, which may be anything between one and twelve miles along their east–west axes, have passes of deep or moderately deep water leading to them, and these usually lie in indentations on the lee (west or nor'west) sides. They are much of a pattern in that it is rare to be able to sail or motor straight through one, for the pass itself, or the lagoon immediately within it, is almost always partially blocked by coral patches, compelling a big change of course. At low water vast areas of the reefs are awash or dry, showing the brown or buff coral on the edge of which the swell breaks with unbelievable thundering fury; here and there may be a block of dead coral thrown up on the reef by the sea, and occasionally something on the reef, seen from a distance, proves on a closer view to be the wreck of an oriental fishing vessel perched up high and in silhouette against the sky. Anchorages within the lagoons enclosed by these reefs, though often deep, are safe in fine weather, and are reasonably comfortable if one can work up into the lee of one of the islands, but at high water [the tidal range is about five feet (1·5 metres)] sufficient sea may come in over the reef to set one rolling. This exciting area was our cruising ground on that occasion for several weeks.

At Ongea Ndriki on that earlier cruise we were weatherbound for several days with an unseasonable sou'west wind; caring little for the anchorage, we left it as soon as the weather became normal, and sailed out through the pass one brilliant morning which heralded a proper trade wind day, and headed nor'west for the Yangasa Cluster, a group of four uninhabited islands within their own reef. The pass into that lagoon is on the northern side, and to reach it we sailed to leeward of the reef which projects in a nor'-west direction for at least two miles from the nearest enclosed island—it is projecting reefs such as this that are so dangerous by night. Although the wind was in the south-east, a heavy swell was running from south-west, as it usually does, the lee sides of the reefs, therefore, being rougher than the windward sides; this, breaking on the Yangasa Reef, was one of the most beautiful and exciting things we had ever seen. From our position in the offing (about half a mile from the reef, as we did not care to go any closer for fear of the undertow or offlying coral heads) we could watch each swell grow steep and then steeper, the slope of its back a glorious vivid turquoise; a plume of foam then appeared on the crest and spread quickly along it, high-flung and startlingly white against the blue of the sky; then suddenly that swell burst into a giant breaker, a cataract of tumbling foam, its crest streamed out towards us. I thought of galloping horses' manes in the wind and of snow ridges on high mountains, but could find no good simile. The spectacle was unique, something that can be viewed properly only from the low deck of a small vessel in a place where a big ocean swell falls suddenly upon a reef rising almost vertically from a great depth. We did not hear the individual breakers crash, for the thunder of one overlapped the thunder of another, so that the air reverberated with one continuous deep roar, a stunning sound, and the last to be heard by many a seaman in those waters. The tide was low, and that long, wide, sun-heated reef, from which a powerful fishy smell came out to us, formed a magnificent break-water and, as soon as we had rounded its north-western point, we sailed into comparatively smooth water, located the pass by a bearing of one of the islands, and Susan climbed the ratlines to con us in.

For successful pilotage in coral waters, an eye aloft is essential, and the higher that eye is the better can it judge by the colour how deep the water is and where the dangers lie. But there are other requirements: the sun needs to be high and abaft the beam; the sea should be rippled by a breeze; the sky should not be overcast, and the wearing of polaroid spectacles is a great help. An advantage of cruising in that area is that as the passes are mostly in the west or north-west sides of the reefs, the sun is abaft the beam when one is leaving in the morning, and by afternoon, when one is approaching another lagoon, will be abaft the beam again.

Susan remained aloft to pilot us across the lagoon to a small bay on the north shore of the southernmost island. We were using one of the fine charts made by Captain H M (later Admiral Sir Henry) Denham when, with the ships *Herald* and *Torch*, he surveyed the Fijis in the 1850s; it was to the small scale of five miles to one inch, yet the detail in it was perfect, but some of it was so tiny that even Susan, whose sight is very good, needed the help of a strong magnifying glass to read it. On the chart, this little bay was only one-thirty-second of an inch (0·08 centimetre) wide, and in it were shown three tiny specks which, we discovered on arrival, denoted three small mushroom-shaped islets each in its proper position. We crept cautiously in and let go among them where there was not swinging room for us, but we knew that so long as the trade wind blew it would hold us clear.

I cannot now recall how many uninhabited islands we have visited—perhaps ten or fifteen. Often uninhabited islands are uninhabited simply because they have something the matter with them: there may be no fresh water, or they may be beset with dangers such as reefs, tide races or breakers; or they may be infested with mosquitoes, flies or land crabs; others have no landing places. When we could get ashore on one we found that the novelty had not worn thin, the thrill had not staled, and it was always new and filled with wonder—and we with gratitude that we could be two of the very few to have the delight of experiencing it. There we launched the dinghy and rowed across the shallows where, through the clear water, every detail on the bottom could be seen; we pulled the dinghy up a gently sloping beach where the only footprints in the sand were those that we made, and they would be erased by the next high tide; we walked into the bush to pick drinking nuts, and wondered who last had set foot there, when another would come, and from where. We gathered a few shells from the beach and the rocks, and then rowed back to our floating home which with raking masts and jaunty sheet looked so right in that bright but lonely setting.

But I am sure it would be tedious for you to read a day-by-day account of our progress on across Bounty Boat Passage, through which the remarkable Bligh entered Fijian waters, and through that maze of reefs, and our stops among them, engaging and exciting though it was for us. Nearly every reef presented some fresh problem: not always did the sun shine; not always did our position agree with the chart; not always was the anchorage a good one; and sometimes the sea was oily smooth so that we could not see the dangers beneath its mocking reflecting surface.

You may, however, wonder what sort of people we met on the inhabited islands. In the event we did not meet many because we preferred to anchor in an island's lee, rather than off its windward side where the village was usually situated to benefit from the breeze. We had brought with us a few things we hoped the islanders might like: canned milk and bullamacow (corned beef), sweets and magazines; our thought being that it would be a pleasure to offer gifts to the people on those remote islands, though we hoped not in a patronizing manner. Some of them, notably the women, did seem genuinely pleased with our little presents; but too often there were young men out in canoes to see what else they could get, and there were demands for cigarettes and sugar; of this last item there appeared to be a serious shortage, which was strange, as Fiji was a sugar-growing country; we did carry sugar, but naturally not in quantities big enough to be of much use in an island with a population of 1000.

In short trips from one reef to another we made our way slowly northward, but before reaching the Exploring Isles an overnight passage became desirable because we did not much fancy any of the anchorages offered by the intermediate islands. So we worked that trip out in advance in such a way that we could spend the long night (thirteen hours of darkness now that mid-winter was approaching) in an area free of isolated reefs, and bounded on all sides by high islands the reefs of which did not extend far seaward. Two of these bore names which had more of a Greek than a Fijian flavour, Thithia and Tuvutha, and we hoped to be able to keep a watch on them by moonlight. It all went very well, and so we came to the Exploring Isles, where we entered the big lagoon, coasted along the larger island's northern shore and, having passed round the little island which almost blocks the entrance, let the anchor go in Mbavatu, a harbour of a very different kind. It was ringed by densely bush-clad 500-foot (150-metre) hills, rising so steeply from the dark deep water as to be almost inaccessible, except in the area which lay just ahead of us and into which we took the dinghy. This was a mangrove swamp, a wild tangle of roots, branches and foliage (Plate 15 *bottom*), where even at noon the sun could only penetrate in narrow shafts; the hot, still air was filled with insects on which some birds appeared to be feeding, and the shallow water under the belly of the dinghy was alive with shoals of small fish being pursued by larger ones; several times a turtle raised its slow enquiring head above the surface, and once we saw the triangular dorsal fin of a cruising shark. A steamy smell of rotting vegetation pervaded the swamp, the squelchy earth where we landed was pock-marked with the holes dug by crabs, and that night the only sounds at the anchorage were the rustle of wind in the bush and the mournful barking of wild dogs.

It was a fascinating cruise, and we completed it by sailing right round the north side of Viti Levu, Fiji's biggest island, to Nandi Water, and then back to Suva. But now we had to bypass such attractions, and off Ongea Ndriki we altered course direct for Suva; just as though that was the signal for a change, the wind fell light, the sky hazed over, and a swell began to roll up from the south. Our course was laid to take us between the unlit high islands of Matuku and Totoya, and the early hours of the following morning were anxious ones, for we expected to be up with Totoya by or before dawn, and after the moon had set the overcast night was very dark, and no doubt the drizzle that had set in by then reduced the visibility; also, of course the current could be doing anything with us. We both remained on deck keeping a constant lookout, and as the grey dawn light spread over the scene we sighted an island off the starboard bow; this should have been Totoya, but we could tell by its shape that it was not, and, as the light improved, it turned out to be Matuku—so the current had in twelve hours set us as many miles to the south. The wind, after faltering a bit, then settled in the nor'west, an unusual direction for those waters, and for us a headwind if we continued for Suva; so in spite of our earlier resolution we decided to put in at Matuku and wait there for a change, and surely nobody could object to that if we did not land or have people on board.

The island looked angry as we closed with it; heavy cloud was piled upon its black mountains, mist or rain swirled in the valleys, and the swell broke heavily along its southern reef. But the pass is an easy one and if, as on that day, poor light from the wrong direction should make it impossible to see the reefs each side, one can go in on a bearing of Korolevu, a 1200-foot (365-metre) peak, which is clearly and accurately shown in the excellent sketch at the border of the chart; so without any difficulty we ran into the harbour, which is a good one, small and landlocked by thickly wooded hills.

It is sad that the fine set of British Admiralty charts of the Fijis, of which many, like that of Matuku, are on a large scale, is to be withdrawn and replaced with a new set of fewer sheets in the modern style and to a smaller scale, and that the dedicated care taken by the great hydrographer, Denham, is to be sacrificed in the name of progress or economy. We carried several hundred charts on board, the accumulation of many years, and would not willingly have parted with them in exchange for new ones because many of the latter lack much of the detailed information given on the old ones. There was no possibility of keeping them corrected, for most had been replaced by new editions. We carried up-to-date *List of Lights* and *Pilots*, however, and we looked through *Notices to Mariners* when we got a chance; I believed, therefore, that we were not likely to come to much harm by using old charts but, in areas where important changes were likely to have occurred, such as estuaries and commercial ports, we made a point of having the latest charts, or at least took a careful look at, or perhaps even a tracing from, those belonging to some other vessel. The cost of the charts needed for an extensive cruise is considerable, and some of the people we met had obtained all they needed by asking merchant ships for outdated or cancelled charts, and I never heard of anyone coming to grief on that account.

We soon had a party of islanders alongside begging for the usual things and wanting to come aboard, but we could not allow that. In the evening, however, we were boarded stealthily by two intelligent and well-spoken boys; they also were begging, but they had the grace to offer us a hand of bananas. We gave them some rope, chocolate and pencils; they also wanted a ballpoint pen but we had no spare, so one of them, we believed the elder who said he was going to be a policeman when he grew up, skilfully stole Susan's. We told them they must go, which they obediently did, but after we had turned in they came back again with a little friend and had to be shooed away.

As soon as the wind shifted we sailed on for Suva, an exciting trip because rain reduced visibility, as it so often does there, and we did not see the surf on the reef until we were close, while, of Viti Levu, there was no sign until we had entered the pass; at high water the swell sent such a surge into Suva's usually placid harbour that we refused to go alongside the main wharf, which the officials wanted us to do, for fear of getting damaged; instead, we anchored and then had to ferry off a customs officer by dinghy to carry out the distasteful imposition of a search—all yachts visiting Suva at that time were being treated with suspicion, all were searched, liquor and tobacco was sealed, and firearms were held by the police.

At first, we lay off the Royal Suva Yacht Club, which was handy for the town and was, rightly in my view, making a small charge for visitors using its facilities; but when, in a fresh puff of wind, some of our neighbours with poor ground tackle dragged, we shifted to a safer and less congested anchorage hard by Mosquito Island further up the harbour. Near it stood the Tradewinds Hotel, which welcomed yachting folk and seemed to like having them around, and at the anchorage we met many charming people and some characterful and interesting voyaging yachts. The Moeslys, who had efficiently circumnavigated the globe in their handsome thirty-eight-foot (11·6-metre) Atkin-designed ketch, *Rigadoon*, from California, were there and most hospitable. The Melhops of the trimaran, *Taurangi*, from New Zealand, with a ten-year circumnavigation to their credit, put their vessel ashore one day on the island's sandy beach; they dug a hole under the central hull and removed, straightened and replaced the keel which had been damaged on the slip at the Panama Canal Yacht Club. Shane Acton and his girlfriend, Iris, also beached their *Super Shrimp* from England for a bottom scrub; at eighteen feet (5·5 metres) she must have been one of the smallest vessels ever to have sailed so far; Iris told me she was *the* smallest, but I believe John Riving's *Sea Egg* was only twelve feet (3·6 metres) long, and he brought her out from England but was lost in the Tasman Sea. *Scud*, one of several replicas of Slocum's famous *Spray*, and built by her owners, George and Mary Maynard, sailed in and performed a seamanlike kedging operation to reach her berth, for, like the original, she had no engine. *Franda*, a steel ketch built at the same Dutch yard where *Wanderer IV* was born, was lying off the hotel but, when her owner heard that our bottom needed a scrub, he kindly brought her round and anchored near so that his sons with their new scuba gear could attend to our need.

At Suva, time went quickly by, as it always does in that busy, noisy, Indian- and Fijian-crowded, likeable place with its strong smell of copra; we watched the comings and goings of large cruise and cargo ships, colourful dilapidated oriental fishermen (Plate 16 *top*), and little interisland traders usually with topheavy-looking deckhouses. Rain fell so often and so heavily that from our awning we caught all we needed for extensive laundry operations and filling the tanks, and we took no water from the shore after leaving Rarotonga until we reached New Zealand, a period of twelve weeks.

* * *

Early in September we retrieved our shotgun from the police, got our clearance, and slipped away out of the harbour bound towards New Zealand on the final stage of our voyage. We left behind several yachts which would also be going our way but wished to wait until the equinox was past, for locally it was said that bad weather always accompanied that event. October is the most popular month for making the trip, because by then the equinox is over and the cyclone season should not yet have started, though a year or two before cyclone Bebe arrived in early October to stir things up at Suva. For the first few days of this trip one should have the benefit of the trade wind, when it is usual to leave Suva by way of Kandavu Passage and take one's departure from Cape Washington. But throughout most of our stay at Suva the trade had not been blowing, and there was still no sign of it the day we left, when what little wind there was came from south-west; so we left Kandavu and its neighbouring islands to starboard, which was a bad beginning.

On three earlier occasions when making this passage, we had found the wind to be strangely puffy, but never more so than this time. Again and again it dropped right away and the sails, particularly the poor old, hard-used mainsail, slammed so violently that we took them in to preserve them. We became quite good at taking in sail for calms, and could get everything stowed in twenty minutes, and in the first two weeks of the trip we took in and reset the sails eighteen times. The calm periods sometimes lasted for twenty-four hours but sometimes for less than half an hour. The strong puffs came without any noticeable difference in the sky to windward, and rarely persisted for more than an hour, but sometimes lasted for only a few minutes; through them we usually carried the whole main, the staysail, the small jib and the reefed mizzen, which was about right, for the puffs were strong. But to make proper use of the light patches called for more sail-shifting than we were prepared to undertake, and I often wished we had roller-furling/reefing gear for our largest headsail, so that by slacking off the sheet and hauling on the furling-line, we could quickly roll up as much of the sail as the strength of wind called for, and unroll it with equal ease afterwards. I had been opposed to such gears because of the difficulty or impossibility of getting the sail down should anything go wrong with it or its gear, but several firms now make the gears with an alloy tube to revolve on the stay, and the sail can be hoisted or lowered with its luff rope sliding in a groove in the tube. So the mechanical difficulties seem to have been solved, but there still remain some disadvantages: when the sail is partly rolled up it tends to become inefficiently baggy and, as the gap between it and the next sail aft (staysail or mainsail) increases as the sail is reduced in size, the slot effect is lost, and with the sail well-reefed, the sheet lead is not sufficiently far inboard; there is also the matter of damage to the sail by exposure to sunlight for, when it is rolled up, a narrow strip along foot and leach is exposed; but this can be overcome by sewing a strip of dark-coloured cloth along the exposed edges. Nevertheless, for cruising purposes with a small crew I believe the roller-gear has much to recommend it, and I intend to try it one day.

On this passage the wind remained stubbornly dead ahead and neither tack was the more favourable, so day after day, night after night with sheets hard in we plugged on, and our progress was pitifully slow, but nature did give us a few rewards: we saw one of the most brilliant and (perhaps because we chanced to be lifted up on the swell at the crucial moment) the longest-lasting green flash at sunset that we had ever seen. Also the stars, particularly the Southern Cross, stood as bright and clear in the night sky as we had ever seen them; this cheered me up a lot because until then I had thought my failing sight was the reason why on much of the voyage out from England the stars had looked so dim.

For the green flash to be seen calls for a sharp horizon, clear atmosphere, and an attentive observer, and by the last I mean a person who will keep his eye fixed unwinkingly on the upper limb of the sun just as it is about to sink below the horizon; often we had seen the flash clearly while people nearby had not. The explanation for the green flash is this: as light from the sun passes through the earth's atmosphere it is refracted, and the refraction is slightly different for each colour of the spectrum; therefore, separate images of the sun in different colours are formed. On the horizon, where refraction is at its maximum, the greatest refraction differences are between violet at one end of the spectrum and red at the other. The red image, being bent least by refraction, is the first to set, while the shorter wavelength blue and violet colours are scattered most by the atmosphere; so, as the sun sets, the green image may be the last of the colour images to drop out of sight. The flash may last from a half to two-and-a-half seconds, though we have never seen a flash as long as that. The green flash would also be seen at sunrise were it not for the impossibility of fixing one's eye on the exact spot where the sun will lift above the horizon. It is said that in favourable conditions a green flash may be observed at the setting of the planets Venus and Jupiter, but we have not seen it.

On a day when we lay becalmed on an oily swell, but with a wayward current that spun poor *Wanderer* round and round again, the shortwave radio told us that a huge swell was invading the south coast of Viti Levu, and that the sea raised by a great storm near New Zealand's Cook Strait was washing houses away. These events did not coincide with the equinox, which occurred on 22 September, a day when we again lay becalmed.

We were beginning now to see a little more wildlife. Birds were more plentiful, and we had a pair of albatross, or perhaps mollymawks (fulmars or petrels), with us for several days, their soaring flight being a source of great pleasure to us; porpoises also were more numerous. If anyone should ask what changes we had noticed on this our third circumnavigation, we would, of course, remark on the great increase in the number of yachts and the resulting congestion at ports and anchorages, also perhaps on the unfriendly manner in which some port officials treated us. But the biggest and saddest change that we had noticed was the lack of wildlife in the Atlantic and Pacific oceans. In some coastal areas, notably off western Europe, in the Gulf of Panama, near the Galápagos and New Zealand, birds and the fish on which they live appeared to be plentiful; but the wide spaces of the Atlantic and Pacific, though not so much those of the Indian Ocean, seemed to us to be almost empty. Away from the land we saw the occasional bosun bird and booby, but the hitherto ubiquitous storm petrel, of which in fair weather or foul there were on earlier voyages nearly always several in sight pattering on the surface of the sea, were on this voyage so rare that the appearance of one almost called for a mention in the logbook. Flying fish were seen and often came aboard, but rarely in sufficient numbers to make a meal, and not once did we see a pilot fish. As before, whales, sometimes in pairs, were only occasionally sighted, but in earlier years we used now and then to be surrounded by great gatherings of porpoises several hundred strong. On this voyage we still did see porpoises (Plate 16 *bottom*) and hear their whistling talk but, except in the Indian Ocean, they were in pathetically small parties of half a dozen or so, and the bodies of many of them were terribly scarred, apparently by steel or synthetic ropes leaving the marks of their strands to show that those warm-blooded and intelligent creatures, which have always been a source of comfort and delight to the mariner, had in some net or trawl had a near brush with death. Whether it was that we were just unlucky, or not sufficiently observant since we relied so much on vane gear steering, or whether it was pollution or the greed of man with his gigantic fishing enterprises that had denuded the oceans of their rightful inhabitants, I cannot say; but the latter assumption seems likely, for since the abominable 'porpoise technique' for catching tuna was put into operation, it was estimated that in a single year it may have accounted for the death of 130 000 porpoises. The United States then mercifully placed a partial ban on that form of tuna fishing, but other countries, such as Peru, continued to practice it.

It was not until we were nearing North Cape that at last the wind shifted to the west, allowing us for the first time in 1000 miles to head direct for our destination with sheets eased, and it very soon hardened into a forty-five-knot gale. Normally we would have stopped in such weather to wait for an improvement, but this direction of wind was just what we wanted, speeding us swiftly though roughly towards the land, so we made the most of it, though I cast many an anxious glance at the crosstrees I had patched up in Bora Bora's lagoon, and which were now being subjected to considerable strain. Unfortunately, however, the welcome change did not last long, and after a few hours the wind went round into the south again and we resumed beating; so when Karikari Bay appeared ahead in the afternoon of our nineteenth day at sea, we worked our way between its sheltering arms, anchored near the deserted beach, and turned in for a night of unbroken sleep.

The following day, conditions had not improved and, even with help from the engine for part of the way, we had a long, hard beat to get to Whangaroa; by the time we reached the entrance to that perfect, fiord-like harbour we were cold, wet and tired, and were very happy to get in and find a quiet anchorage among a party of gannets, replete, sleepy, and unafraid after their evening meal. From where we lay there was no building to be seen, and after nightfall the only lights were those of stars. This was the harbour from which we had set out two years and three months before to visit our friends in England and see a little of the world, and our return to it after a voyage of nearly 32 000 miles gave Susan and me great pleasure and satisfaction, and an increased affection and respect for the fine little ship which had done all that we had asked of her.

Appendix 1

BRIEF DETAILS OF *WANDERER IV**

Length on deck	49·5 feet (15·08 metres)
Length on waterline	39·9 feet (12·16 metres)
Beam	12·5 feet (3·81 metres)
Draught, loaded	7·0 feet (2·13 metres)
Displacement	22 tons
Rig	jib-headed ketch
Sail area	1045 square feet (97·1 square metres)
Designer	S M Van der Meer
Builder	J Jongert, Medemblik, Holland, 1968
Construction	welded steel
main deck	laid teak on steel
coachroof decks	plywood covered with GRP
Masts and booms	silver spruce, hollow
spinnaker boom	alloy
Standing rigging	1 × 19 stainless, swaged terminals
Running rigging	three-strand prestretched terylene
sheets	braided terylene
Sails	terylene by Cranfield
Engine	sixty-one horsepower, four-cylinder Ford diesel
Generating plant	single-cylinder Yanmar diesel, fifty-amp dynamo
Batteries	twenty-four-volt 400-amp lead/acid
Fresh water	200 gallons (910 litres)
Fuel	250 gallons (1137 litres)
Wind-vane steering gear	Aries
Main steering gear	Mathway
Electric autopilot	Pinta

*A full description of the yacht and her gear appears in *Sou'west in Wanderer IV* (Oxford).

Appendix 2

TABLE OF DATES, TIMES AND DISTANCES

	Time on passage in days and hours	*Distance in sea miles*
4 May 1974 to 12 May Whangaroa, New Zealand to Eromanga, New Hebrides	8d 4h	1040
13 May to 5 June Among the New Hebrides		295
6 June to 16 June Santo, New Hebrides to Port Moresby, Papua/New Guinea	10d 14h	1260
28 June to 30 June Port Moresby to Rennel Islet	2d 5h	258
1 July to 12 July In Torres Strait		91
13 July to 28 July Thursday Island to Darwin, with stops at Gove and Cape Hotham, Australia		871
3 August to 16 August Darwin to Christmas Island	13d 0h	1500
20 August to 23 August Christmas Island to Keeling Cocos	3d 4h	524
7 September to 24 September Cocos to Port Louis, Mauritius	17d 5h	2313
25 September Port Louis to Grand Bay		14
19 October to 1 November Grand Bay to Durban, South Africa	13d 13h	1593
6 December to 9 December Durban to Cape St Francis Bay	3d 9h	507

	Time on passage in days and hours	*Distance in sea miles*
29 January 1975 to 4 February Cape St Francis to Cape Town	5d 22h	460
27 February Cape Town to Salamander Bay		63
3 March to 17 March Salamander Bay to St Helena	14d 8h	1653
19 March to 25 March St Helena to Ascension	6d 0h	703
29 March to 24 April Ascension to Horta, Azores	25d 22h	3215
7 May to 23 May Horta to Falmouth	16d 4h	1216
24 May to 6 September On the south coast of England		310
7 September to 30 October Falmouth to Santa Cruz de la Palma, with stops in Spain and Canary Islands		1700
31 October to 4 December La Palma to English Harbour, Antigua	34d 1h	2764
5 December to 14 February 1976 Among the West Indies		270
15 February to 23 February Bequia to Cristobal, Panama Canal Zone	7d 21h	1144
29 February Transit of Panama Canal, and to Flamenco Island, Panama	10h	50
2 March to 9 April Flamenco to Fatu Hiva, Marquesas Islands	38d 7h	3897
10 April to 10 May Among the Marquesas		162
11 May to 17 May Nuku Hiva to Tahiti, Society Islands	5d 1h	760

	Time on passage in days and hours	*Distance in sea miles*
18 May to 5 July Among the Society Islands		227
6 July to 14 July Bora Bora to Rarotonga, Cook Islands	8d 4h	565
20 July to 28 July Rarotonga to Vava'u, Tonga	8d 4h	824
5 August to 12 August Vava'u to Suva, Fiji, with stop at Matuku		486
9 September to 28 September Suva to Karikari Bay, New Zealand	19d 5h	1132
29 September Karikari Bay to Whangaroa		28

Total distance made good	31 895 nautical miles
Best day's run	190 nautical miles
Duration of voyage	2 years, 21 weeks, 1 day
Nights spent at sea	292

INDEX